*Self-Construction
and the Formation
of Human Values*

Self-Construction and the Formation of Human Values

Truth, Language, and Desire

TEODROS KIROS

Westport, Connecticut
London

The Library of Congress has cataloged the hardcover edition as follows:

Kiros, Teodros
    Self-construction and the formation of human values : truth,
language, and desire / Teodros Kiros.
        p.   cm.—(Contributions in philosophy, ISSN 0084–926X ; no.
65)
    Includes bibliographical references and index.
    ISBN 0–313–30808–X (alk. paper)
    1. Power (Philosophy)   2. Self (Philosophy)   3. Values.
I. Title.   II. Series.
BD438.K57   1998
121′.8—dc21   98–15329

British Library Cataloguing in Publication Data is available.

A hardcover edition of *Self-Construction and the Formation of
Human Values* is available from Greenwood Press, an imprint of Greenwood
Publishing Group, Inc. (Contributions in Philosophy, Number 65;
ISBN 0–313–30808–X)

Library of Congress Catalog Card Number: 98–15329
ISBN: 0–275–97314–X (pbk.)

First published in 1998

Praeger Publishers, 88 Post Road West, Westport, CT 06881
An imprint of Greenwood Publishing Group, Inc.
www.praeger.com

Printed in the United States of America

The paper used in this book complies with the
Permanent Paper Standard issued by the National
Information Standards Organization (Z39.48–1984).

10 9 8 7 6 5 4 3 2 1

Contents

I dedicate this book to my wife, May Farhat,
and my daughters, Solonia and Ruwan.

Acknowledgments

This is a manuscript that I have labored over for many years during which time, at various stages of its writing, the following people extended their help. I would like to thank my wife, May Farhat, for undertaking research for the book and reading it over many times. George Katsiaficas has been a wonderful friend and an intellectual companion for the past few years. My sincerest appreciation goes to Anthony Appiah, Glenn Tinder, Lee Rouner, Doug Kellner, Steven Bronner, for reading the manuscript and offering many suggestions, which I have attempted to address. My editor, Elisabetta Linton, at Greenwood, has been an exceptionally competent and tactful editor. I am grateful to her for all her services.

Introduction

We forget too easily that a thinker is more essentially effective where he is opposed than where he finds agreement.
—Heidegger, *What Is Thinking*

Power and domination—contrary to the ancients' and the moderns' conceptions—are not the *same*. Rather than conceiving of power as domination, I have chosen to explore power as self-empowerment. Power as domination is destructive of the possibilities inherent in human power. Domination impoverishes one's self-confidence and destroys one's capacity to grow, change, and evolve. Power as self-empowerment, on the other hand, grounded upon the premise that humans are capable of self-construction and self-constitution, is creative, transformative, and enriching. The authentically self-empowered individual *who seeks to construct values* is critically aware that he/she is allured by power as domination, but he/she makes sincere efforts to struggle against the temptation and use the tool of self-control to purify himself/herself of the ever tempting "will to power" as domination. Self-construction, following Kant, requires self-generated principles of moral legislation. Of course, recent contributions in certain feminist theorizing have developed powerful ways of combining emotions and reason so that we can in the course of time nurture sensitive humans who will not shamelessly dominate others by succumbing to power as domination. I wish to join those feminist thinkers who have made a special place for compassion as a vehicle of profound thinking, by way of seeking to limit the excess of power, via placing principles as guides of morally sensitive political action. Principles alone cannot guide the self-constructing moral subject. As certain feminists have rightly stressed, principles must be blended with compassion and care.

Both modernity and postmodernity are critically lacking in a discourse that espouses certain virtues that could redeem the lost and fragmented self of modernity from the morass of bewildering cultural crises. The self is *existentially serious*, a seriousness that could fully flourish if it is given a conducive environment in which it could commitedly and doggedly struggle against thoughtlessness as the source of evil, an evil that tyrannically desires power *only* as domination, that is, as the distinctly conscious infliction of pain and anguish upon innocent and thoughtful others.

Guided by what I call the reflective *presence* and with the honest and self-chosen assertion of *self-control*, the self is quite capable of deferring evil that pushes it to experience life as imbued with the power that dominates. Such a self can be trusted to act upon values grounded upon truthful language, and expressive of deeply rooted desires. A collectivity forged out of morally engaged selves can then engage in critical revolutionary activity and can wake humankind from the slumbers of its deep sleep of detached indifference. Existentially serious selves are quite capable of controlling the will to power by dominating the will to will power as domination. *I call such potential self authentically free.* The impasses that Foucault has constructed as well as the highly attenuated conception of Western rationality of Habermas could both be transcended, through the redefinition of power.

What is needed, and what I hope to provide, is a vision of a self filled with a compassion that is a composite of reason and feeling. Such a composite self does not consciously manipulate language, truth, and desire to subordinate and dominate others. Language, truth, and desire are used by the compassionate self to construct values and norms that are themselves rich and capable of enriching others in a community of authentically free selves who think, consciously share their gifts with others, and devotedly control the will to a kind of power that inflicts pain and unwanted misery upon others, replacing it with a form of power that disseminates respect, recognition and comfort to all those who are extensions of humanity. I draw from the philosophy of language as evident in the works of the speech act theorists, and from the tradition of the novel, to advance the necessary arguments on the behalf of the existentially serious moral subject.

Modern moral and political theory/theories emerged as a result of the challenges to Descartes's subject-oriented philosophy, which centered all mental activity on humankind's capacity to think outside the circle of tradition and history. Humankind, for Descartes, is destined to rely on the power of his/her reasoning capacity if she/he is ever to found a firm ground for all his/her activities. It is in thinking that humankind will find his/her true being. Humankind exists only to the extent that he/she thinks, and it is only as a thinking being that humankind can assure himself/herself that he/she exists. Except for thinking, everything is subject to doubt. For Descartes, existence is anchored on thought. Thought itself is articulated by autonomous reason.

The centrality of reason is revisited in the nineteenth century by Kant, Hegel, Marx, and Nietzsche. These philosophers responded to the Cartesian challenge differently. Thus, Kant agreed with Descartes that the authority of reason is much more reliable than the authority of tradition and historical experience. Experience can be useful to man if it is governed by autonomous reason; empirical experience without the self-imposed direction of reason is almost meaningless. Kant, unlike Descartes, recognized the limitations of reason. For Kant, pure reason cannot know everything. In the moral sphere, in particular, reason is not the sole authority; there, reason can only think of freedom, God, and the human soul, which cannot be the objects of either doubt or absolute knowledge. Instead, such domains are the subjects of faith. The human arrogance of modernity—an arrogance that seeks to subject everything to the screening test of autonomous reason—is severely criticized by Kant in his three subsequent critiques: *The Critique of Pure Reason, The Critique of Practical Reason*, and *The Critique of Judgment*. These three critiques are essentially a defense of the limited use of autonomous reason and a critical recognition of the excesses of Descartes's claims on the behalf of reason. Kant ultimately defended reason's practical power—a type of power which effectively employs the Aristotelian categories in the order of things and in the order of language and thought.

Hegel was not convinced that Kant had said the last word on the limits and powers of thought. Hegel applauded Kant's efforts to empower humans as rational beings fully capable of following their own inner reason in the moral sphere of leading their lives. Hegel, however, radically disagreed with Kant's seeming relegation of history to non-importance. For Hegel, history is the teacher of reason. Correspondingly, every human thought, and reason itself, is the product of history. Man, for Hegel, as for both Descartes and Kant, is not merely a reflective thinker outside of time, space, and death; rather, man is a historical possibility who constructs his own historical world. As a historical entity, humankind progressively grows to become an effective historical consciousness—a consciousness that ripens in the tragic hands of periodic wars and violent deaths. Through struggle, suffering, and anxiety, humankind begins to see the necessity of death for the sake of peace. God reveals himself by using finite human beings as the vehicles of His hidden intentions. For Hegel, humankind is not immediately reflective. Humankind is potentially reflective; it is through experience and within the context of history that humankind grows and ultimately becomes rational.

In the sphere of knowledge, Hegel disagrees with Kant about the origin of the categories of thought. The categories, for Hegel, are not located only in the mind; they are also present in the world. It is the task of humankind to uncover these categories of thought that are in the world. The order of human thought reflects the order of the world itself. With this argument, Hegel puts to rest Descartes's conviction that there is no world, thus no order of things, only thinking. For Hegel, there is thought only because there is a world that grounds it. The world is already ordered by the highest intelligence, who is God. The human task is to appropriate an already ordered world, made significant and useful for man by the historic activity of mental and physical labor. The world becomes historically significant because men and women have added human activity to it. Although the world is ordered, it is also historically constructed by fully conscious human activity. Through these pointed arguments, Hegel managed to integrate thought and history, epistemology and social ontology, and mental and physical labor. In his hands, modernity becomes acutely sensitive to history and philosophical theology. The ideal of a rational world, guided by the rationality of humankind under the direction of a hidden God, is introduced as modern consciousness by Hegel, who has emerged as the preeminent philosopher of modernity.

It remained for Marx to attack Hegel for not being sufficiently historical. Marx argued against Hegel's view that the world of actual human beings is a rational world. Instead he believed this is a world that has alienated historical products of suffering human beings by unjustly separating human beings from the products of their own activity, the process of productive activity, other human beings, their own selves, and the world of universal beings. Human reason has become a commodity selling itself like a product. Reason itself has become a tool that is impervious to morality, insensitive to justice, and a calculating instrument in the hands of capital. The world of everyday living is irrational, egotistical, and centered on power. The potential rationality of human beings and the actual irrationality of the world are inevitably in contradiction. This irrational world cannot be changed by reason alone; it must be exploded by conscious and critical revolutionary activity.

The above themes are revisited by two contemporary thinkers, Jürgen Habermas and Michel Foucault, in their challenging confrontations to modernity's appropriations of power, truth, language, and desire. Habermas and Foucault locate the emancipatory promises and crippling effects of modernity on the level of the fundamentals of power. I agree with Habermas that language can be used communicatively. As a communicative and highly humanized tool, language can be used positively to found a nonalienated community of highly sensitive and inquiring beings. It is precisely this particular orientation that language still does not possess. Foucault rightly believed that in the modern age language is everything but communicative. The ancient ideal of the search for ground in the language of Forms, the Kantian move of the regulative ideal of autonomous reason, the Cartesian search of a neutral observer, has radically changed. Since Descartes, autonomous reason has increasingly succumbed to the subtle manipulations of the specific desires of the holders of power. Contrary to the claims of some of modernity's thinkers, humans are not freely encouraged to think for themselves, to construct values worthy of their intelligences and passions. The desires are stifled before they can take root. Basic desires are not given even minimal opportunity for mental and moral growth. At the formative process, all crucial thinking is done for individuals by self-proclaimed experts.

So I begin my exploration of power with an interpretation of the ideas of

Habermas and Foucault in their relentless struggles to face the challenges of modernity. For Habermas, modernity is a source of hope. He extracts from it a theory of communicative action. For the early Foucault, modernity is grounded upon a hidden will to power. Habermas and Foucault have both made compelling arguments against the instrumentalization of reason in modernity. Each attempted to link power to reason (thought), language, and desire. The early Foucault may have gone too far in the extremely tight connections he established between language, thought, and power. Where Habermas sought to topple the hegemony of instrumental reason in modernity, with transcendental and reconstructive arguments, the later Foucault does make some explicit moves in that reconstructive Habermasian direction, in his remarkable works on the history of sexuality. Foucault maintains a predilection for analytic and genealogical dissections of modernity, as well as an affection for the heterogeneous, the local, and fragments of the open styles of existence. However, in Foucault's later works—his powerful books on the history of sexuality—he seeks for a new ethics and aesthetics. His intellectual effluence is movingly informed by the mastery of Plato, Aristotle, Epictetus, among many others, from whom he draws an ethics for the care of the self. Foucault is moved by the way that these thinkers raised serious questions about the "care of the self," delving into a question of ethics. To think about the care of the self, I suggest, is to venture into the deep waters of reconstructing the fragmented, fractured, and alienated self of modernity, a promising project that Foucault did not live to complete.

Furthermore, I will argue that the early Foucault, in particular, paid limited attention to the subtle sense in which power and domination are not the same. He himself wrote, "I insisted too much on . . . techniques of domination."[1] I think that Plato, Aristotle, and, most particularly, Epictetus, do not confound power and domination in the way that moderns such as Hobbes, Freud, and Dostoyevsky do. Consequently, I am not ultimately satisfied with the efforts of Plato, Aristotle, and Epictetus not to conflate power and domination. In order to make a compelling argument for my thesis that power and domination are not the same, I need carefully to review what some of the great thinkers have said about power and domination in several chapters below. Among the numerous authors that I could have chosen, it is those who appear in this book who directly analyzed the concepts of power and domination. In his commendable attempts to develop a new meaning and practice of power, Foucault observed that, "The care for self was in the greco-roman world the manner in which individual liberty—and civic liberty, up to a certain point—considered itself as ethical. If you take a whole series of texts going from the first Platonic dialogue up to the major texts of the later Stoics—Epictetus, Marcus-Aurelius, etc.—you would see that the theme of care for the self has truly permeated all ethical thought."[2]

I so much agree with Foucault that I too will attempt to examine these texts and extract from them not only thoughts on sexuality, as Foucault brilliantly did, but also themes on power and domination, as they pertain to *self-construction and the formation of human values.*

Thus, this book seeks to participate in a reconstructive healing of the broken self that exists within the torn fabric of modernity. In order to accomplish my goal, it was necessary to struggle with the thoughts of some of the classical thinkers such as Plato, Aristotle, Epictetus, Aurelius, and Plutarch, as well as some modern thinkers, among them Hobbes, Kant, Freud, Dostoyevsky, Dewey, and James, with the interpolation of a literary thinker, such as Borges. In particular, I consider feminist analyses of power as most useful and challenging. I confront the ancients and moderns, liberals and Marxists, with the argument that they do not distinguish *power as domination* from other possible meanings of power.

The structure of the book is as follows:

In chapter 1, I summarize and critically analyze Habermas and Foucault, two prominent analysts of language, truth, and desire considered as the instruments of power in modernity. In chapter 2, responding to deficiencies in these analyses of language, truth, desire, and power, I introduce my own conception of *self-construction*, which I use as a grounding for the idea of *self-empowerment*. In chapter 3, to refine these concepts, I examine in detail the differences between power and domination. I contrast my conception of self-empowerment, which I free from the notion of domination, with the concept of power of Plato, Aristotle, Epictetus, Aurelius, and Plutarch (among the ancient philosophers of power as domination), and Dostoyevsky and Freud, among the moderns, and I end up locating allies among some feminist thinkers.

Finally, in chapter 4, I seek to construct a pragmatic conception of power as self-empowerment, a path (or condition) that existentially serious individuals may wish to choose as a way of life, in their capacity as language-speaking, truths-seeking, and desiring beings. I begin with William James's notion of a pragmatic conception of truth; I proceed to build on James by examining Dewey's Hegelian pragmatics which are at once respectful of individuals' autonomy freed from the dangers of subsumption under absolute reason and sharply aware of the dangers of crypto-relativism. Hobbes's forceful articulation of political life as the will to power is summarized and effectively combated by the will that can control the will to power itself. I distinguish between power and domination contra Hobbes, and I then begin my reconstructive attempts to build the foundations of the self-empowered existential individual by drawing from powerful sources in literature. I chose the works of some of socially sensitive twentieth-century novelists who are acutely aware of the agonies and possibilities of human beings. I examine the writings of Borges *on the fantastic*, Thomas Mann *on the formation of dangerous norms of racial superiority*, and Baudelaire *on images of paradise* juxtaposed with my own vision of a community of self-empowered and serious existential individuals seeking to construct human values.

NOTES

1. James Miller, *The Passion of Michel Foucault* (New York: Simon and Schuster, 1993), pp. 321–322.

2. Michel Foucault, ''The Ethic of Care for the Self,'' an interview with Michel Foucault (January 20, 1984), p. 115.

1

The Analysis of Power: Foucault and Habermas

FOUCAULT

Long before Foucault, it was Nietzsche who, with a disarming honesty and astonishing consistency, attributed the very origin of language—the language of human speech—to the ubiquitous concept of power. The concepts of "good and evil" or "good and bad" are not merely innocent words whose function is the facilitation of human thinking. In fact, these concepts are infused with the mystically designed power relations among and between human beings. Language itself is an expression of power as are the language-speaking human beings, through whom power makes its very presence felt by those upon whom power imposes itself. Power, whatever its precise nature, unmistakably *presents* itself insofar as its effects can be carefully analyzed in all human practices and activities, including ethics, religion, science, medicine, sexuality, and art. In all these practices and activities, power is deeply embedded; to understand what power *may be*, as opposed to definitively unravel what power *is*, we should seek to study the effects of power. These searches will lead us to sensitively study the values that have formed and deformed modern men and women. These *values*, which were not directly constructed, are moral and political in essence. Indeed, Nietzsche characterized the process of value formation as a distinctly political enterprise produced by the subtle yet diffuse, present yet hidden, play of power—power as domination. In a famous passage, Nietzsche wrote:

Now it is plain to me, first of all, that in this theory, the source of the concept "good" has been sought and established in the wrong place: the judgment "good" did not originate with those to whom "goodness" was shown! Rather, it was "the good" themselves; that is to say, the noble, powerful, high-stationed, and high-minded, who felt and established themselves and their actions as good, that is of the first rank, in contradiction to all the low, low-minded, common and plebeian. It was out of this pathos of distance that they first seized the right to create values and to coin names for values. . . . The pathos of nobility and distance, as aforesaid, the protracted and domineering fundamental total feeling on the part of a higher ruling order in relation to a lower order, to a "below"—that is, the origin of the antitheses "good" and "bad." (The lordly right of giving names extends so far that one should allow oneself to conceive the origin of language itself as an expression of power on the part of the rulers: they say "this is this," they seal everything and event with a sound and, as it were, take possession of it.)[1]

I submit that Foucault's *earlier* project on modernity—his unique understanding of the linguistic conventions of medicine, the law, the social sciences, and even his comprehension of our very private desires and passions—has been deeply penetrated by the meaning of power so forcefully characterized by Nietzsche. I will now provide various notions of power and Foucault's critical understanding. Sawicki[2] provides two elegantly distinct categories of Foucault's notion of power, "disciplinary power" and "juridical power." The passages below consist of both types. The first, third, and fourth modalities of power are disciplinary. The second is distinctly juridical. The fifth is a blend of both kinds of power. Kelly contends that a complete understanding of power requires the use of both forms.[3]

1. I would like to distinguish myself from para-Marxists like Marcuse who give the notion of repression an exaggerated role because power would be a fragile thing if its only functions were to repress, if it worked only through the mode of censorship, exclusion, blockage, and repression in the manner of a great superego, exercising itself only in a negative way. If, on the contrary, power is strong, this is because, as we are beginning to realize, it produces effects at the level of desire—and also at the level of knowledge. Far from preventing knowledge, power produces it.[4]

Or again,

2. This reduction of power to law has three main roles:

(a) It underwrites a scheme of power which is homogeneous for every level and domain—family or state, relation of education or production.

(b) It enables power never to be thought of in other than negative terms: refusal, limitation, obstruction, or censorship. Power is what says no. The challenging of power, as thus conceived, can appear only as transgression.

(c) It allows the fundamental operation of power to be thought of as that of a speech-act: enunciation of law, or discourse of prohibition. The manifestation of power takes on the pure form of "Thou Shalt Not."[5]

Again,

3. One doesn't have here a power that is wholly in the hands of one person who can exercise it alone and totally over the others. It is a machine in which

everyone is caught, those who exercise power just as much as those over whom it is exercised. This seems to me to be the characteristic of the societies installed in the nineteenth century. Power is no longer substantially identified with an individual who possesses or exercises it by right of birth; it becomes a machinery that no one owns. Certainly everyone does not occupy the same position; certain positions preponderate and permit an effect of supremacy to be produced.[6]

Finally,

4. The power of the norm appears through the disciplines. Is this the new law of modern society? Let us say rather that since the eighteenth century, it has joined other powers—the law, the word (*parole*) and the text, tradition— imposing new determinations upon them. The normal is established as a principle of coercion in teaching with the introduction of a standardized education and the establishment of the écoles normales (teachers' training colleges); it is established in the effort to organize a national medical profession.[7]

5. The individual is no doubt the fictitious atom of an "ideological" representation of society; but he is also a reality fabricated by this specific technology of power that I have called "discipline." We must cease once and for all to describe the effects of power in negative terms: it "excludes," it "represses," it "censors," it "abstracts," it "masks," it "conceals." In fact, power produces: it produces reality; it produces domains of objects and rituals of truth.[8]

From the above diverse passages we can draw the following propositions about the concept of power:

1. Foucault's chief Nietzschian feature (displayed in the first, third, fourth and partly in the fifth passages above as *disciplinary power*) is that human beings are fundamentally value-creating beings; in their capacity of producing values, they created a human language; the languages thusly created are names of human objects and human practices; the concepts of "good and bad" or "good and evil" are the prime examples of how human beings exercise their reasoning and judgmental faculties; these concepts and many others like them tend to permeate the various ways in which we as human beings are formed, that is to say, the way we develop our mental, moral, and physical selves—in one word, the *path* to construction of character and culture.

2. The possibility of understanding the formation and constitutions of the characters and cultures of modern individuals (individuals developed from the middle of the seventeenth century to the end of the nineteenth century) requires a subtle sensitivity to the power relations that are at work in the human and natural sciences via a study of the evaluative premises of the sciences, which modern individuals seem to have uncritically absorbed in the form of belief systems and habituses.

3. One of the most important effects of power is its astonishing production of highly "disciplined" individuals. The disciplined individual of modernity, however, did not consciously choose to discipline himself/herself. Rather, one of the silent forces of power is that it disciplines through the internalization of values, such as the law, the norm, or the normal, etc. Barry Smart is correct

when he astutely argues, "Power is not conceptualized as a property or possession which excludes, represses, masks or conceals, but as a complex strategical situation or relation which produces reality"[9] The disciplined individual is neither self-constructing nor self-empowered. He/she frequently experiences power only as domination. In a 1984 interview, Foucault argued, "I mean that in human relations, whatever they are—whether it be a question of communicating verbally, as we are doing right now or a question of a love relationship, power is always present . . . these relationships of power are changeable relations, i.e., they can modify themselves, they are not given once for all."[10] But even in his last ethical works, contra Habermas, Foucault continues to subscribe to the idea that power will always consist of domination. As he put it, "The problem is not of trying to dissolve them in the utopia of a perfectly transparent communication, but to give one's self the rules of law, the techniques of management, and also the ethics, the ethos, the practice of self, which would allow these games of power to be played with a *minimum of domination. . . . Power is not an evil. Power is strategic games. . . . To exercise power over another, in a sort of open strategic game, where things could be reversed, that is not evil. That is part of love, passion, of sexual pleasure.*[11] It is put even more strongly in another text, where Foucault writes, "*Domination is in fact a general structure of power whose ramifications and consequences can sometimes be found descending to the most recalcitrant fibers of society.*"[12]

4. The king, history, and the sovereign individual (exemplified in the second and fifth passages) are no longer useful in locating the origin of power; the king, the effective historical moment, and the genuinely sovereign individual are no longer the visible embodiments of power. Power has become truly invisible. Its effects, however, run through the soul and body of the modern individual. Power follows him/her up until his/her death, and its embodiments are all individuals— the individuals whose function is the disciplining of one another without the direct intervention of the king, the historical hero, or the sovereign ruler. Power governs indirectly, by producing truths that are reexperienced by individuals as if it is they who originated them.

5. Language in concert with the linguistic subject, namely the modern educator, the writer, the novelist, the public policy analyst, the priest, the psychoanalyst, the social worker, even the therapist—come to the aid of power in that they function as conscious and unconscious vehicles of hegemonic ideas: norms, beliefs, or standards, etc. To every domination induced by power, there is always a possibility of resistance. Therefore, the dominated modern subject is not hopelessly docile or permanently constituted by "totalizing structures," as Foucault had ambiguously hinted in his structuralist works.[13] In fact, Deleuze, and following him Rajchman, have correctly argued that for Foucault, subjects can be inspired to change intolerable situations not only by counter hegemonic ideas but, more fundamentally, by changing the way they see things and produce evidences. Visuality and the production of evidence are central components of effective practice.[14] Power can be subtly subverted by a visuality that counters

the established ways of seeing and doing things. For Foucault, sexuality is the realm where new spaces can be created for desire, since desire itself is a modality of practice, an exercise of care for the self, a potential source of resistance.

6. The analysis of power must be extended beyond the well-known "materialist" Marxist thesis that the state and its apparatuses control, structure, determine, or prohibit concepts of the good and evil, moral and immoral, in an explicitly repressive way. For the early Foucault, in order for the state to explicitly practice the above repressive measures, it must already have existing power relations; the state is not fundamentally structural but super-structural; it invests meaning in a whole set of relations such as the body, sexuality, the family, kinship, knowledge, and technology. To put it differently, the state, as a super-structural source of power, governs indirectly through the disciplining power of ideas with distinct material effects on the everyday practices of human beings. Power does not repress truths. It produces them. Foucault, argues Rorty correctly, "sees the desire for power as contrasting with the will-to-truth. He sees the whole Western project of philosophical reflection on the nature and prospects of human activity as part of a vast organization of repression and injustice."[15] For Habermas, on the other hand, power does not produce truth but can be effectively controlled by truth when truth itself is communicative, that is, capable of sincerely, rightly, expressively, and comprehensively orienting language toward a pragmatic goal of intersubjective interaction, as I will now seek to show.

HABERMAS

The concept of power does not seem to be at the center of Jürgen Habermas's research programs, although the power-seeking individual of the modern age is by no means beyond Habermas's political concerns. Indeed, Habermas's provocative thesis of the possibility of "legitimization crisis" within the normative or valuational spheres of contemporary capitalism is founded upon an acute awareness of the hidden or strategic workings of power, most particularly the intricate manipulations of the concept of reason as an instrument of the domination of man by man within the various services of political economy.[16] For Habermas though—and in this, he is fundamentally different from Foucault—the concept of power cannot be dissociated from powerful individuals and their ruling ideas. Power, for Habermas, is inextricably intertwined with ruling classes and ruling ideas. Communicatively speaking, power is a consequence of the distortion of language. Habermas, although a para-Marxist, shares with Foucault the belief that *power is diffuse and is ambiguously located at multitude centers of strategic relations.* Although power has its own capillaries and arteries, it is grounded upon the material and nonmaterial forces of capital, including capital's attempts to dominate the languages and possessions of the modern individual, which in the end tend to produce the modern alienated subject of modernity. Seyla Benhabib observes, "As money and power become increasingly autonomous principles of social life, individuals lose a sense of agency and efficacy. . . . Political alienation, cynicism and anomie are a result.''[17]

Habermas, like Foucault, argues that language, through which autonomous or emancipatory thinking is possible, has been deeply infected by the ills and abuses of instrumental or calculative thinking. To that extent, Habermas explicitly sympathizes with the lifelong worries of Foucault's analytics of power, the chief pillar of which is the growing contamination of language within the thought and methodological structures of the order of ideas and the order of things. From within this ever growing infection of language, however, Habermas attempts to salvage a core of rationality—the chief legacy of enlightenment— namely, the idealization of the possibility that the linguistic subject, in spite of his/her deep linguistic illness, is potentially capable of transforming language from an instrument of domination to an authentic beacon of critical or emancipatory thinking. Axel Honneth, one of Habermas's most able interpreters, has sympathetically argued, ''Social struggle, which Foucault had unconditionally introduced as a basic phenomena of social relationships and had made the conceptual basis of his theory of power, is thus perceived as a distorted form of intersubjective understanding.''[18]

Technology and power, for Habermas, are intimately interconnected. For him, technology has the same relationship to power that language has for Foucault. Habermas largely follows Lukacs's highly acclaimed characterization of the tendency of a highly developed industrial technological society not to treat human beings as active, thoughtful, and sensuous beings but as things—and things themselves as self-creating and self-renewing technological products. It was Lukacs who concocted the exhilarating concept of reification to capture the particularly new phenomenon of the reduction of reason, that potentially rational and moral human faculty, into a reified calculative tool, a tool that became prominent under the capitalist mode of production. For Habermas, as opposed to Adorno and Horkheimer, reification is peculiar to capitalism and may one day be overcome as a result of the potential force of an emancipatory speech act. The temporarily infected linguistic subject, if he/she becomes sufficiently critical and aware of the contamination of his/her human sensibilities, will therefore be capable of resisting total reification. Reification is thus nothing more than a highly dangerous historical phenomenon, which could be controlled by critical revolutionary activity, and an intricate process of collective will formation. Interpreting Habermas, Axel Honneth formulates, ''Thus, now it is no longer universal knowledge about the conditions of communication without domination but rather the concrete knowledge of suffered domination and experienced injustice that summons up the insight into the limitations of a social interaction.''[19] The reified and alienated individual of modernity then is not a biologically motivated seeker of power, a search that inherently pushes him/her to reduce his/her fellow human beings into things destined to be dominated, nor are those who thusly become dominated and disciplined incapable of counter-resisting. The sense in which individuals have become dominated and disciplined, which at best is a historically produced phenomenon but not a biologically constituted fact, is premised upon a dogmatic theory of power that inhibits analyses but also provides us with an historical conception of man as a power seeker. This thesis is an indirect attack on Foucault's early conception of power.

Habermas speaks for himself:

Lukacs used the concept of reification to describe that peculiar compulsion to assimilate interhuman relations and subjectivity, to the world of things, which comes about when social actions are no longer coordinated through values, norms, or linguistic understanding, but through the medium of exchange value. Horkheimer and Adorno detach the concept not only from the special historical context of the rise of capitalist economic system but from the dimension of interhuman relations altogether; and they generalize it temporally (over the entire history of the species) and substantively (the same logic of domination is imputed to both cognition in the service of self-preservation and the repression of instinctual nature).[20]

Clearly, Horkheimer's and Adorno's analytics of modernity, particularly their discerning of the logic of domination under the structures of power relations between humans and the objects of nature, seem to resonate more with Foucault's analytic of the power relation than they do with Lukacs's and Habermas's, as Axel Honneth[21] and Thomas McCarthy[22] have demonstrated separately. If we were to press Habermas to explicate where he stands in relation to Horkheimer/Adorno's and Foucault's stances, Habermas's response would be a programmatic promise that he would fully develop in the second volume of *The Theory of Communicative Action*. In the first volume of this treatise, Habermas concluded with a presentation of the dismissal of all rationality as inherently instrumental by critical theory's chief theorists, Horkheimer, Adorno, and Marcuse. Habermas disagreed with this position and attempted to salvage speech acts, the very vehicles of rational discourse, from the menace of instrumental rationality. Developing his ideas further, in volume 2, he rethinks the meaning of rationality by relocating it in the sociological theories of Mead, Durkheim, and Weber. For Habermas, it is Mead who paved the way for communicative action, so that acting and speaking subjects could be freed from interactions motivated by instrumental purposive rationality and adopt a guideline from the structure of language itself through the vehicles of gestures, significant symbols, and, most particularly, the internalization of the attitude of the other. Humans as gesture constructors and symbol originators and interpreters can cement intersubjective understanding of the objective (world of facts), social (world of norms, values), and subjective (world of private experiences) through Mead's manipulation of experiences ground on the "linguistification" of their world. Children, for example, can successfully be socialized into the world of the meanings of gestures and symbols in their quest for individuation that leads to the formation of identity and the constitution of behavior.

Gestures and symbols can always be linguistified as speech acts, and their validity claims put to communicative tests, free of domination and guided by critically rational dialogue. Thus any statement with a communicative intent uttered by person A in the illocutionary form of "that P" can either fail or succeed to generate an answer or response in the form of "yes"; either that is a fact or yes, that is right, or simply I feel that it is. In this way, humans can be taught linguistically the meanings and uses of gestures, sounds, and symbols in a communicative community.

Habermas contends further that although Mead usefully shows us the way speaking and acting subjects can make sense of their world, he does not demonstrate an understanding of the process of "the obligatory character of valid norms." For that, it is to Durkheim and his seminal notion of the sacred that Habermas turns. The sacred essentially displaces "the mediation of symbols," as in Mead, where the collective goal is the socialization of individuals in order that moral values can function as imperatives. Even children, through the work of parents, can systematically be introduced to the domain of the sacred. The sacred is a socializing agent and aims at the cultivation of collective consciousness, enabling individuals, as acting and speaking subjects, to ground the possibilities of intersubjective agreement. Rousseau's notion of the general interest is one such rational form of the sacred. To this extent, the sacred can be expressed in language going a step beyond Mead. Unlike Mead, however, Durkheim lacks a notion of individuality that is not coerced by the collective consciousness of the sacred community. It is Mead, Habermas argues, who, by developing the notion of the "I," that is, an authentic expression of a person's subjective needs, distinguished it from the "me," the deceptive discloser of the intimate world of the "I," an expression of individuality. Using these concepts, the coercive tendencies of social solidarities can be controlled by the liberating idea of individuation which Mead worked out meticulously by way of complementing Durkheim's communitarian liberalism.

The mediational uses of gestures, symbols, and the sacred are not enough to explicate the rich structures of human experiences as lived both in archaic and modern times. Habermas develops the concept of the lifeworld, which originated in Husserl, to fill the lacuna of the communication community (which has thus far been filled with gestures, symbols, and the sacred as tools of communication).

The concept of the lifeworld can be said to house gestures, symbols, and the notion of the sacred to a greater degree than does the idea of the instrumentality of purposive rationality. The lifeworld is also a world governed by the implicit presences of gestures, symbols, and sacred rituals from which humans draw to make sense of their experiences. In the lifeworld, everything is taken for granted, and individuals intuitively interpret the meanings of gestures, symbols, rituals, and role plays. Archaic and modern societies foster binding traditions, customs, and ethos that make sense to the citizens in their attempt at nurturing loyalties to their state through an intersubjective understanding of citizenship, duties, and responsibilities in a self-perpetuating way and without unnecessary tutelage under priests, kings, and sovereigns of all kinds. In the able hands of Parsons, Habermas notes, the lifeworld is reexamined through the tools of Weber's sociology of action, and most particularly the idea of the vocation or the "calling" which Weber had effectively treated as an attribute of the early periods of capitalism in Western Europe since the seventeenth century. For Weber, and following him Parsons, Habermas notes, the idea of the calling had penetrated the lifeworld and rationalized it. This rationalization eventually created an advanced form of a modernized capitalism that went through three revolutions: the industrial revolution in England, the French revolution of 1789, and the educational revolution in the Western world.

Through systems individuals develop a loyalty to society by way of the institutionalization of the value or norm of individuality. In this way individuals are socialized and integrated. Therefore, social integration and socialization become marks of modernity. These societal institutions enable individuals to form identities, following Mead's notion of identity formation via the internalization of the values of the other. Similarly, the idea of secularization serves the same purpose as Weber's conception of the calling. The difference between the two thinkers is that for Weber, the calling was a specific attribute of early modernity. Advanced industrial modernity, Weber contended, lost it, and with it individuals were denuded of meaning, ethically and existentially. Parsons disagreed when he argued that the idea of the calling is not lost to advanced modernity's children. Rather, they have secularized it, and secularization coupled with individuality are the glues of modern society. Habermas agrees with Parsons and opposes Weber by citing the contributions of de-ontological, therefore consciously secular, moral thinkers such as Rawls who prove Parson's contention that advanced modernity is not lacking in the possession of meaning. In fact, individuals now draw meaning from moral/practical resources as communicative subjects, who live in a communicative community, through various acts of political constructivism, as Rawls has recently argued in *Political Liberalism.*

I will now return to Foucault, this time in order to explicate the precise process of the interaction of language with power and the intricate way in which propositions, speech acts, and discourses are produced by *power relations* since Foucault (contra Habermas) had argued that power does not repress truth but rather *produces* it. The process of the production of truth may be formulated in the following way.

For Foucault, the question or, if you prefer, the problem of language revolves around at least two central questions which I wish to formulate as follows:

1. How are the components of language (words, sentences, propositions, and statements) formed and what is the nature of the formations?
2. Who determines what is and is not to be accepted as language?

HOW ARE THE COMPONENTS OF LANGUAGE FORMED?

For Foucault, the formation of language made up of words, sentences, propositions, and statements is always examined within the horizons of the intriguing questions of truth and power. The horizon of the truth and power questions envelops or frames the formation of the design of language or, if you prefer, the order of language; that is to say, the fundamental process by which letters are formed into words. Words are further formed into sentences, out of which propositions emerge, and thoughts are expressed in the form of statements. It is the mechanics of human speech that are Foucault's foci when he raises the question: what is it that we human beings do to the various components of language when we utter a word, construct a sentence, craft a proposition, or express thought, feeling, or intention? His question is never simply about what we do with language, but rather how language frames our thoughts and feelings by producing certain forms of truth. The speaker of the language, or the author, is not as important as the underlying structure, the so-called, *unconscious* of language.[23] As Frank Kermode has lucidly argued, "Language is at the root of the argument. In the preclassical system language was considered simply as a significant part of the creation, part of the interlocking system of universal resemblance of the analogy."[24]

One of the chief functions of words is the power they attain as they seek to represent thoughts. In this exceedingly difficult representational task, words really seek literally to represent thoughts, just as thought attempts to represent itself, which was the dread of Descartes, embodying the dominant *episteme* of the time. The ideal of authentic representation is the approximation of the most precise thinking done by the most adequate words. Formally put, we can say:

Word A is a *representation* of thought B such that A(B) is the *most adequate representation* of thought B relative to the ideal of a precise representation A=B.

As Foucault puts it, "From the classical age, language is deployed within representation and in that duplication of itself hollows itself out."[25] Richard Rorty has lucidly contended, "Whereas Descartes and Locke and Kant and the positivists and the phenomenologists have assumed that the job was to represent pre-existent reality (even if only phenomenal reality, constituted by consciousness), I will show you a new way to look at what people say."[26] However, the quest for a fresh start by Foucault does not make Foucault an epistemologist as Ian Hacking contended in his insightful article "Michel Foucault's immature science," Rorty has observed.[27]

Prior to the classical age, the signifying function of words, as well as the rhetorical use of words, mattered significantly. Indeed, it is the sign function of words that commanded the attention of the linguist in his/her quest of the origin of human language, particularly the origin of the phonetic act—for example, the noise "Brr. . . ." With the subsequent emphasis on the representational function of words arises the discussion of general grammar, that is, the notion that words should be combined into a grammatical formation that will eventually constitute a linguistic convention, which language-speaking beings must necessarily master if what they say or what they write is to be accepted as language that makes sense.

Words, of course, as Plato[28] and Hobbes recognized, were initially defined arbitrarily such that a noise such as "Brr . . ." was not accepted as a sensible word, whereas a phatic utterance such as "The cat is on the mat" was accepted as a sensible combination of words. In the end, Hobbes, in particular, emphasized that words are nothing more than an arbitrarily founded system of notations that were imposed upon language-speaking human beings by covenant and violence.[29] The apparent order that one sees in language is imposed from outside; the order was not founded by intersubjective agreement among human beings; rather, it was imposed upon us by violence. The so-called universal language is ultimately a language founded upon domination and not upon the free-spirited dimension of intersubjective agreement. A modern universal language, such as English, is the final by-product of a long historical evolution of the oldest "mother language."

Furthermore, in addition to the above evolutionary growth, languages evolved in accordance with the effects and impacts of migrations, victories and defeats, fashions and commerce; that is to say that the smooth evolution of the original language of the eternal is deeply affected by the political dimension of power relations between the victors and vanquished, the exploiters and the exploited, the commercial invaders and the invaded. The continuous flow of the words of the eternal are interrupted by the historical acts of the passions and the desires of the powerful, the arbitrary imposers of a system of notations that rigidly defined the representational function of words once and for all, or so it seems. Edward Said has accurately noted, "Discourse, says Foucault, is things that are said (*les choses dites*)—profoundly, *chatter*—whose rarity (purification and elevation) is the form of judgment (on what is being excluded and on whomever does the exclusion), exteriority, and knowledge."[30]

Words are often nothing more than human noises, human cries, human attempts to say something. When words are somehow combined so as to produce the propositions of modernity, then one can say that language definitely began, according to the classical age's one-sided view of language. For the classical age, language is a tool of communication made possible by the systematic ordering of words, the immediate consequence of which is the proposition. Thus, a word, in and for itself, is simply a human cry or a noise until after it joins another word or other words to form the discourse. Humans, like animals, can utter an expression A, but it is when humans, unlike animals, utter the proposition B that language becomes C—that is, discourse.

A proposition is founded upon the logics of general grammar, which is minimally composed of verb, subject, and object, out of which a proposition is designed—for instance, the proposition "This is John." The verb, in particular, is considered to be an indispensable part of language; the indispensability of the verb constitutes the ideology of this linguistic philosophy of the classical age. Foucault is determined to penetrate this ideology so as to unmask the undercurrent of power relations upon which it is based.

Put the following question to Foucault: What is the function of the verb in language? Foucault replies: "The verb affirms."[31] Consider the function of the verb in the proposition, "This is John." The verb "is" here judges by affirming the links between the words "this" and "John." It thus says that "this" is "John," but not that "this" is "Paul." By affirming certain links, it excludes others; thus "This is X" cannot mean "This is Y"; "This is John" cannot mean "This is not John." The entire essence of language is concentrated upon that undisputed and wholly internalized affirmative power of the verb.[32] As Foucault puts it: "Without it [the verb], everything would have remained silent, and though men, like certain animals, would have been able to make use of their voices well enough, yet not one of those cries hurled through the jungle would ever have proved to be the first link in the great chain of language."[33]

The verb may be an indispensable part of language, but it is only one of its parts. The "whole" is language in its totality, which was founded upon the relationship of the word as "sign" to what it represents. The classical age abolishes the importance of the sign, elevates the importance of representation,[34] and dogmatizes the affirmative power of the verb "to be." In the course of time, the verb, which is only a very important part of language, comes to dominate the structure of language. The part becomes the whole; the verb becomes language as such. But, asks Foucault, "From where does this power derive?"[35] Foucault answers: "Comparing language to a picture, one late-eighteenth-century grammarian defines nouns as forms, adjectives as colors, and the verb as the canvas itself, upon which the colors are visible."[36]

Words are articulations of language. By combining similars and separating dissimilars, ideas are structured as the continuum of horizontal and vertical dimensions. Further, words also classify the things of external nature. Thus "things," such as Earth or Sun, are called substantive nouns whereas those that signify human manners, such as good, just, or round, are designated by the name, adjectival nouns. The substantial, as opposed to the adjectival, noun connotes "subsistence" or permanence of things that can subsist by themselves; the adjectivals are marked by their "perishability" and "accidentality" in marked contrast to substantivals. Thus, substances are designated by substantivals whereas accidents are designated by adjectivals. By these modes of designations, words began to become articulated discourse; they became devices under the service of the speaking subject. Through the power of the new articulative function allotted to them, words (which originally were nothing more than unpenetrable human cries) became breakable and controllable. The "endless murmurs," the inexhaustible values with which words were impregnated, gradually gave way to the classical period's dream of reducing words to propositions, and thus "each word, down to the least of its molecules, had to be a meticulous form of nomination.''[37] *Eventually, the propositional form of language becomes the object of a science.*

The power of words to name is a fundamental function of language, as Plato long ago argued in *The Cratylus*.[38] Human beings, as speakers of language, emit inarticulate cries very much as animals do. That first inarticulate cry was the beginning of language; it was an expression of a feeling. That inarticulate cry, that gesture, was meaningful; it said something, it stood for something, and it was an attempt to name something. It was this something that Plato attempted to characterize in *The Cratylus*; since then, the naming function of language has become a prominent feature of the origins of language. The naming function of language in the wake of the classical period developed into the theory of designation.

Designation, as opposed to simple naming, implies the possibility of ordering human cries into words and sounds that can generalize similar feelings, as gestures under one totalizing category, under a dominant meta-discourse. Under the science of designation, ''It is no longer a particular oak that is called tree, but anything that includes at least a trunk and branches. The name also became attached to a conspicuous circumstance: night came to designate not the end of this particular day, but the period of darkness separating all sunsets from all dawns. Finally, it attached itself to analogies: everything was called a leaf that was as thin and flexible as the leaf of a tree.''[39]

Foucault concludes his complex reflections on the origin of language with a striking passage that reads: ''From the theory of the proposition to that of derivation, all classical reflection upon language—all that was called 'general grammar'—is merely a detailed commentary upon the simple phrase: 'language analyzes.' It was upon this point, in the seventeenth century, that the whole Western experience of language was founded—the experience that had always led men to believe, until then, that language spoke.''[40]

For the classical age, the name—that ideal of impeccable precision, that brightness which is beyond all confusion—is the end of discourse. As George Steiner has perceptively argued, ''The *episteme* of the 17th–18th is radically different. . . . The old kinship between knowledge and divination, the mirroring reciprocities of language and fact, break off. Now, instead of similitude, the crucial instrumentality is *representation*. Foucault seems to mean by this that words are entirely transparent and arbitrary counters.''[41]

WHO DETERMINES WHAT IS AND WHAT IS NOT ACCEPTED AS LANGUAGE?

According to Foucault's thesis, it is those who speak, and speak in specific ways, under definite circumstances, assuming certain authorities and strategies, who determine what is and is not accepted as language. In a passage in which Nietzsche's name is directly mentioned, Foucault writes: ''For Nietzsche, it was not a matter of knowing what good and evil were in themselves, but of who was being designated, or rather who was speaking when one said Agathos to designate oneself and Deilos to designate others. For it is there, in the holder of the discourse and, more profoundly still, in the possessor of the word that language is gathered together in its entirety."[42]

By using the concepts such as discontinuity, rupture, threshold, limit, series, transformation, tradition, influence, author, development, evolution, etc., we take the risk of truly disturbing the tranquillity of the unities and thus are confronted with genuine theoretical problems. These concepts are inherently shaky unities and questionable hypotheses. These concepts must be dissolved, disturbed, and deconstructed if they are to be usefully appropriated. These points were powerfully enforced by Michel de Certeau, when he wrote, "He (Foucault) is therefore led to uncover, beneath the continuity of history, a discontinuity more radical still than the evident heteronomy that lies beneath the fictional homogeneity of our time. . . . The heterogeneous is for each culture the sign of its own fragility, as well as of its specific mode of coherence."[43]

Statements, like concepts, are also very questionable unities that ought to be subjected to deconstruction. Statements, as components of language, are not adequate for the understanding of the constitution of language. From the standpoint of authority, it is the speaking subject, with definite intentions, and with a strategic mastery of the rhetorical dimension of language, who states: "X is Y." What makes this particular statement acceptable, among other things, is the authority that Person A assumes when A uses the affirmative word "is" to assert the statement "X is Y." Furthermore, Person A, as a speaking subject, articulates his/her thoughts, intentions, or feelings by making statements, which actually hide certain invisible murmurs. The apparent statement then is covered by the hidden sublanguage, or subtext; a statement is thus less of a complete assertion than it is an event, an inexhaustible human cry, the meaning of which is never completely understood. Consequently, one easily speaks without fully disclosing what one means and, due to a lack of the speaker's critical awareness and the nature of the finite human speaker, constrains the meaning of one's statements. The speaker often assumes that his or her statements are true, incorrigible, unlimited by finitude, and thus acceptable statements. The statements of the law, medicine, psychology, biology, economics, or political science—the human sciences as such—are profoundly affected by their uncritical acceptance of concepts or statements as unproblematic. It is this arrogance of the finite speaking subject, who uses human discourse—such as concepts, statements, propositions, or speech acts—without an awareness of his/her finitude and historicality that disturbs Foucault and leads him to make some excoriating remarks about modernity and a will to power, the power that dominates.[44]

Statements are not units, are not coherently developed, and do not possess crystal meanings; instead, they are divisions, incoherent, with inexhaustible meanings.[45] As B. Brown and M. Cousins put it, "As such the statement is not a thing or a unit but a function, what Foucault calls the enunciative function, a function which bears upon signs."[46] But the authors fail to note that the statements of the human sciences are filled with specific languages of experts and that it is a community of experts who use statements as discursive formations. It is always the doctor (representing medicine), the psychologist, or the judge (representing the law) who is speaking. Those who speak are conferred with the authority to speak; they speak within a linguistic community that is itself penetrated by power, for whom the conferring of the authority to speak is a definite convention. It is the holders of discourse or the users of words who determine the nature of arbitrary statements and scientifically verifiable propositions, according to Foucault.

We must now ask Foucault: What then is a statement? For Deleuze, Foucault's sympathetic interpreter, "Foucault's statements are like these dreams: each one has its own special object or world." So "The golden mountain is in California" is indeed a statement. It has no referent, but one cannot simply invoke an empty intentionality where anything goes (fiction in general). The statement "The golden mountain . . ." does have a discursive object, namely the specific imaginary world that "does or does not authorize such a geological or geographical fantasy."[47] I agree with Deleuze. However, we must further ask: Is a statement a proposition, or a sentence, or a speech act? Foucault's response may be summarized as follows. A statement is not a proposition. Consider the statements (a) "No one heard" and (b) "It is true that no one heard." These two statements are indistinguishable from a logical point of view. Both statements seek to report that something did not get heard by someone. Statement (a) does it in such a way that it is not properly structured since it lacks the verb "is," whereas statement (b) is propositionally well formed and has a different enunciative function—it begins with "it is true that," whereby a report is being asserted as true. Clearly, statements are like propositions in that they have the well-formedness of a typical proposition, but they are unlike proposition in that both have distinct enunciative functions. If a propositional structuration is a necessary and sufficient condition for a statement to be a proposition, then strictly speaking (a) is not a proposition whereas (b) is. Foucault argues that this criterion is determined by power and is not objectively convincing.

Is a statement a sentence? Consider the following statement: "That man." "That man" is a statement, but is it a sentence? Strictly speaking, according to grammarians, the statement is not a sentence in that it lacks verb, subject, and predicate. The subject-predicate validity talk of the grammarians is really a dogma; that is, it is impervious to thought and discussion. But a dogma, by definition, precludes the possibility of critical validation and, in that sense, cannot be justifiably used as a valid criterion that is to be used to distinguish a sentence from a mere statement. Foucault's reasons for the rejection of the above criterion is tied up with his attempt to analyze the question: Is a statement a speech act?

A statement, when used by those who speak, defies a strict definition, but it does have an enunciative function that is determined by the rules of use—rules that are founded by power, or human desires in general. A statement such as

"The golden mountain is in California" is not accepted as a meaningful statement because it has a defective (unhappy) structure in that the possible referent cannot be verified and that verification is an accepted criterion by which statements are designated as true and false. Consider the sentence: "Colorless green ideas sleep furiously." Clearly, given the accepted rules of usage, the sentence is meaningless. Consider, however, that the sentence may be a description of a dream, part of a poetic text, a coded message, or the language of a drug addict or a mad person. If it is any of the above circumstances, could the sentence be meaningful? Certainly, you might say, particularly if the rules of usage included another rule which stipulates: "Any proposition is a statement if a part of the proposition refers to something which is not necessarily a visibly existing thing, but a referential possibility." According to this rule, the sentence can become an acceptable statement if the rules of usage are left open to generate new meanings with new references.

Statements are not brute facts but "laws of possibility,"[48] which defy the facticity of things. Statements are not authored by unidentifiable human speakers of language. They are parts of a network of other statements but are never "independent statements," "events" that occurred in a particular time and place; nor "ideals" that are one day going to be completely understood without traces of any dark region that is not fully known.[49] For Foucault, "The enunciative function reveals the statement as a specific and paradoxical object, but also as one of those objects that men produce, manipulate, use, transform, exchange, combine, decompose and recompose, and possibly destroy. . . . Thus the statement circulates, is used, disappears, allows or prevents the realization of a desire, serves or resists various interests, participates in challenge and struggle, and becomes a theme of appropriation or rivalry."[50]

This powerfully articulated statement seems to be a direct descendant of Nietzsche's forceful statement: "For it is there, in the holder of the discourse and, more profoundly still, in the possessor of the word that language is gathered together in its entirety." Foucault has inventively appropriated the Nietzschian insight of the origin of language, the word, the statement, or language in its totality.

The statement, for Foucault, cannot be defined in terms other than the languages of power: challenge, struggle, manipulation, composition, or destruction. However, we can describe a statement. A statement, we might say, is a systematic ordering of words with the following characteristics:

(a) it belongs to a person's speech in a text,

(b) it has neither hidden nor visible definite meanings, but only an infinite possibility of meanings;

(c) it is a product of history that is practiced by men and is therefore historically analyzable;

(d) it has an enunciative function revealed by flashes of meanings in sentences, affirmations, and series of propositions articulated by a finite human user of words; and

(e) it makes possible our understanding of what is involved in speaking a human language or engaging in a discourse.

A discourse, for Foucault, has a technical meaning: "We shall call discourse a group of statements insofar as they belong to the same discursive formation; it does not form a rhetorical or formal unity, endlessly repeatable, whose appearance or use in history might be indicated (and, if necessary, explained); it is made up of a limited number of statements for which a group of conditions of existence can be defined. Discourse in this sense is not an ideal, timeless form that also possesses a history; the problem is not therefore to ask oneself how and why it was able to emerge . . . it is from beginning to end, historical."[51]

With these bold words, Foucault seeks to understand language not as a speech act, not even an ideal speech act, but simply a historicized discourse. This conception of language is really the area where Foucault and Habermas are seemingly irreconcilable; it is also the area that I will attempt to mediate through a constructive synthesis of two extreme positions of the promise and limitations of language, before I proceed to formulate my own reconstructive theory that distinguishes power from domination as defined by Habermas and Foucault.

I asked earlier: Who determines what is and is not to be accepted as language? I am now in a position to directly answer the question based on the ideas I detailed. Foucault is well known for his denial of one of the Marxist dogmatics—the existence of an empirically identifiable "ruling class" that determines the contents of the thoughts, feelings, and intentions of the modern human subject. For him, the ruling class, a highly self-disciplined class itself, is much too diffusely spread to be in a position of determining how the individuals who are structurally outside of its circle ought to think, feel, and intend. Thus, it is not the ruling class who systematically determine what is and is not to be accepted as language. Rather, it is those whose speech is deemed authoritative: the medical experts, the high priests, the judges, the acclaimed university professors, the psychologists, the anthropologists, the sociologists, the political scientists, or the economists—the acknowledged experts—who diffuse certain vocabulary, disseminate certain "normal" ideas, establish certain models, popularize effective notions of the good, the noble, and the beautiful, and then systematically intervene in the private and public spheres to educate the human subject of modernity.[52] Those who speak do, of course, frequently speak as members of a class; to that extent, the concept of class does illuminate the social positions, the fields, or the class spaces of those who are speaking. The discourses of the experts, however, are relatively autonomous from the direct determination and linear guidance of the ruling class. The discourses are themselves normalized and disciplined by hegemonic ideas[53] with a material basis—ideas that give language its component words, sentences, propositions, and statements—which are in turn systematically ordered as acceptable modes of discourse with conventionally internalized rules of the formation of objects, concepts, effective strategies of manipulation, rules of appropriation, inclusion, exclusion, and accumulation.

Barry Smart puts the point well when he writes, "Foucault's work has opened up the question of hegemony with analyses of the operation and effects of techniques of power and the associated rationales or regimes of truth through which forms of social cohesion are constituted."[54] Speech acts, like discourses, are also penetrated by power. Foucault, unlike Habermas, does not idealize speech acts as potentially emancipatory; rather, speech acts are contaminated by power.

Relative to his intricate reflections on statements, Foucault does not discuss speech acts in a sufficiently extensive way.

Let us now see where Habermas agrees and disagrees with Foucault.

For the early Foucault:

(a) Given that modern speaking subjects are power hungry, the resentful and spiteful powerless majority, if they ever come to power, might themselves become just as cruel, insensitive, and manipulative as the power holders.

(b) Those who actually possess power would do anything to maintain that power; they distrust the powerless to ever genuinely wish to share power with them by founding a community.

(c) Language is not a redeemer nor a human tool of communication with emancipatory potential; it is an object of rivalry, challenge, competition, and mystification.

Habermas may in principle disagree with the claims of (a); he agrees with the spirit, if not the letter, of (b); but he fundamentally disagrees with (c).

To begin with, Habermas believes the speaking subjects of modernity are not ontologically power hungry, resentful, spiteful, insensitive, and manipulative. Although they have indeed become what Foucault thinks they fundamentally are, Habermas would say that the speaking subjects have become intensely alienated from themselves—the effects of alienated labor—from those "others" whom they perceive as threats to their commodious living, from external nature, and finally from the human species. To say that the modern subject is intensely alienated, though, is not to simultaneously assume that the intense alienation cannot be overcome; an awareness of the alienation may lead to engaging in a "critical revolutionary activity," the end of which is fundamental change of all those wretched conditions under which human beings find themselves. Lukacs, in particular, was hopeful of precisely such a possibility, and the possibility was of course historically shattered by the advent of the Nazis whose chief virtue was the manipulation of the wavering, unstable, and disordered desires of the German people. The German phenomenon caused Horkheimer and Adorno to seriously question the adequacy of the alienation or reification thesis of Lukacs; for them, alienation was not a historical phenomenon that was bound to pass. Rather, it was deeply rooted, as Foucault was to explicitly argue after them, on the power-centered psychological makeup of human beings.

The role of the individual (in modernity, as I have attempted to show above in my readings of Foucault and Habermas) in determining the content of the way of life is severely restricted by the arrogant and paternalistic guidelines of the experts of knowledge. Lyotard is instructively right when he exhorts us that metadiscourses of any kind—the World Spirit, the proletariat, science, religion, etc.—are all devious ways that hopelessly keep the self from struggling to fathom the mysteries of life and from formulating infinitely "contestable" and confutable opinions. In particular, he protests against the ideal of Habermas's model of consensus toward the "forceless force" of the better argument, by arguing that consensus has become suspect and outmoded.[55] For Lyotard, all totalities are inherently oppressive.

The self of the modern condition, I argue, is intellectually and emotionally poor. There is a responsible way, however, contrary to the dominant opinion of some totalitarian thinkers, by which the self can be redeemed from self-imposed poverty. I will attempt to show in the next section that one such way is to view and encourage the self to be capable of responsibly constructing values, norms, and interests with existential seriousness and self-chosen legislative guidance, by what I call the "reflective presence."

The theses that I wish to defend in this section may be formulated as follows.

1. Any human being who wishes to live a life in a humanely acceptable manner does so by constructing values—values that in turn provide that human being with principles, standards, and qualities he/she considers truly worthwhile, useful, and intrinsically, as well as extrinsically, gratifying. Authentic principles, standards, and qualities then become norms (standards, models, and patterns) for other human beings. Note that constructing, valuing, and norming are crucial for the formation of a human being who wants to live his/her life in a morally acceptable way. Such a human being I wish to call the moral subject.

2. The construction of values, which is a necessary condition for the emergence of norms, is fundamentally affected by human desires; desires are themselves expressed in the words, sentences, and propositions of language. Language itself is conditioned by desires since desires arise prior to language, as we learned from Foucault and Habermas.

3. Not all human desires are, however, equally expressed, accepted, and legitimized by the human community as equally valuable, thus worthy of becoming respectable norms. Since desires are not classified equally, can we hypothesize that some desires are expressing themselves in language as the fundamentals of power, because power is inherently disposed toward repressing human desires of the powerless?

4. It is at that critical juncture where desire and language are opposed that power deeply penetrates the delicate process by which construction values are constructed for the sake of the founding of norms, a point that was effectively demonstrated by Foucault.

5. The penetration of desires, truth, and language by power is vividly displayed in the formation of the absent moral subject in modernity.

6. Modernity is thus a rather fascinating but also frightening period of our human history, where we see an involved interpenetration of desires, language,

truth, and power. I wish to next systematically reflect on those three concepts that are crucial to my theses: *Self-construction and the intricate process of the formation of human values, through the vehicles of truth, language and desire, as was masterfully assessed by the later Foucault.* Finally, I wish to show how the self—when given an opportunity—can actually engage in the construction of values, norms, and interests that are inherently empowering. The noble gift of self-construction, I argue, has been systematically preserved only by the self-proclaimed ''rational'' and aristocratic minds that Burke self-consciously defended. Instead, I argue that all human beings are very capable of the self-construction of values and norms if they are authentically educated and sensitively and severely nurtured. Modernity's teachers have not extended the privilege of self-construction to all persons.

HABERMAS AGAIN: HIS CRITIQUE OF FOUCAULT

In lectures entitled, *The Philosophical Discourses of Modernity*, Habermas has two remarkable lectures on Foucault, where he seeks to distinguish his own conception of reason as communicative action from Foucault's Nietzchian and Bataillian conception of reason as the will to power and knowledge. In these lectures, he begins with modernity's consciousness of time and proceeds to establish Hegel as the philosopher of modernity who simultaneously revitalized the Aristotelian conception of the polis as an ethical substance (a position that Hegel relocates in the nonpositivist, nonauthoritarian practices of Christianity) and in later years developed the concept of reason that replaced false particulars with the genuine concrete universal of absolute reason.

Over and against Hegel, Habermas introduces first Nietzsche and then Bataille as the precursors of a total critique of all reason as instrumental and oppressive. In its stead, the Nietzsche/Bataille tradition defends the ''other'' of reason: the will to power, the sovereign, the mystical, the beyond language, the heterogeneous.[56] It is within this latter tradition that Habermas locates Foucault's project as a whole.

In the first lecture on Foucault, ''The Critique of Reason as an unmasking of the Human Sciences,'' Habermas rather impressively presents Foucault's major attempt of unmasking the scientific treatment of madness as displayed in Foucault's *Madness and Civilization* (1961). Throughout the lecture, Habermas makes great strides to assimilate Foucault's Nietzchian critique of ideology into that of the Frankfurt School of Critical Theory.[57] As Habermas puts it, ''In Foucault's hands, the history of science is enlarged into a history of reason because it studies the constituting of madness. . . . He classifies insanity among those limiting experiences in which Western logos sees itself with extreme ambivalence, faced with something heterogeneous.''[58]

Habermas contends that Foucault, like Bataille before him, treats madness as the ''other'' of reason, as the excluded manifestation of an unaccepted sovereign.

After the lecture's humble beginning, Habermas slowly draws his dagger against Foucault, whom he accuses of failing to make a successful link between practices and scientific discourses of practices as a whole. "There is some unclarity, to begin with, regarding the problem of how discourses—scientific and non-scientific—are related to practices: whether their relationship is to be conceived as that of base to superstructure, or on the model of a circular causality, or as an interplay of structure and event."[59]

To me, the connection between practices and discourses of practices is rather clear. If I understand Foucault correctly, the practice of madness and discourses about it are established by a theoretical language that judges norms and values hierarchically. Madness then is intrinsically judged as outside of rational, normal, acceptable human practices as are those multifarious discourses concerning madness. The way that madness is abnormalized is itself a function of a theoretical discourse that has permanently scarred the mad as outsiders, outcasts, marginalized, nonmembers of the rational world. Those called mad are, very like the racialized and sexed subjects of modernity who have been effectively removed from history, that powerhouse of the normal, and replaced by the well adjusted, who possessed right "race" and "gender." Foucault is not so much defending madness as normal as showing the ways by which scientifically motivated values are made concerning its abnormality. Foucault is less interested in claiming that madness itself can make a truth claim than he is in descriptively, perhaps positivistically, establishing the way its abnormality is structured. To understand the structures that order, regulate, and design a practice such as madness, Foucault uses archaeological and, at the same time, genealogical methods, so that he could simultaneously examine the constitution of madness and the way it came into being.[60] Foucault uses both methods to analyze practices and discourses, and yet Habermas remains irritated and unconvinced. Habermas writes, "Under the stoic gaze of the archaeologist, history hardens into an iceberg covered with the crystalline forms of arbitrary formations of discourses. . . . Under the cynical gaze of the genealogist, the iceberg begins to move: discourse formations are displaced and regrouped, they undulate back and forth. The genealogist explains this to-and-fro movement with the help of countless events and a single hypothesis—the only thing that lasts is power."[61]

Here Habermas is essentially right. Michael Kelly defends Foucault effectively when he argues, "Habermas's interpretation of Foucault unquestionably has some basis in *Discipline and Punish*, but it plays off an ambiguity in the text. Is Foucault primarily investigating the French prison in the late eighteenth and early nineteenth centuries. . . . Or is he primarily analyzing modern society as a whole."[62] The only thing that remains is power. This is of course true only of the Foucault of the first volume of his monumental work on sexuality. The last two volumes change the direction of power from power as domination to power as something regulated by a self-constructed limiting norm that is inherently present in all norms, in the form of an ethical practice, the care for the self—a new concept that Foucault integrated after a fresh confrontation of classical Athenian texts. But Steven Best was quite right when he wrote, "Through his lifelong refusal to specify the normative underpinnings of ethics and politics, and to employ any positive moral language, Foucault eschews the forms of pleasure which should be satisfied and which should not."[63]

The conclusions of this first lecture of Habermas are quite harmless. Nothing fundamentally damaging is said against Foucault. By the time that the two lectures are given, the debate with Foucault is restarted. The chief text that Habermas tackles in the second lecture is Foucault's epistemological text, *The Order of Things*, which Habermas thinks is Foucault's structuralist contribution. It is in that text that Foucault uses the archaeological method of digging up the "monument"-like structures that underlie the human activities of the body: work and labor, guided by the relentless unmasking of the sciences of biology, language, and economics. The rules, signs, and categories that were created to regulate life at every instance hide the will to power in the apparently harmless form of the will to knowledge. As a result, scientifically motivated discourses by therapists, public opinion experts, and social technologists came into being. In *The Order of Things*, Foucault develops a new theory of power that is directly linked with the constitution of knowledge itself, power/knowledge. I would go further than Habermas and add that Foucault grounds the will to power in the very fundamental structure of language first as speech (*parole*) and then as writing (as a system of signs). In order to argue thusly, Habermas writes, "Foucault postulates a will; constitutive of truth for all times and all societies."[64] I agree with Habermas here, and I, too, have quoted the appropriate Nietzchian passage above, which the *early* Foucault appropriates. I will quote part of that passage one more time. "The lordly right of giving names extends so far that one should allow oneself to conceive the origin of language itself as an expression of power on the part of the rulers."[65] David Hoy has put the matter bluntly, "Foucault stresses discourse to show that discourse can be a form of coercion . . . Whereas for Habermas discourse and power must be kept separate, for Foucault discourse is a form of power."[66]

This passage enables Foucault, as I suggested above and as Habermas correctly points out, to affirm that all wills to knowledge are hidden wills to power under the innocent veils of the will to truth. Foucault himself has argued that power (*macht*) affects not just the body in the coercive form of force (*gewalt*) but, more insidiously and permanently, the human desires and passions, including the desire for knowledge. Power produces knowledge and is not merely affected by it.

Habermas, however, is not entirely satisfied by the way Foucault simultaneously views power as a tool with which to critique modern forms of knowledge (that is, ideology) and treats power itself, in my language as domination (following the tradition of Plato in the *Republic*, and the views of Thrasymachus; Hobbes in *Leviathan*, and, finally, Nietzsche in the *Genealogy*). Again, Habermas's discomfort is quite right, for Foucault indeed equivocates, at least in both *The Order of Things* and the *Archeology of Knowledge*. In these texts, as Habermas points out, the early Foucault conceives of power as a kind of permanent value that cannot be transcended and is in need of a response. I am attempting here to provide this response by providing an existentially grounded conception of power, not as domination, but as self-empowerment capable of limiting the human tendency to use power as domination.

However, despite of the "ambiguities" of power, its form as domination has enabled Foucault to write one of the masterpieces of the twentieth century, *Discipline and Punish* (1976), where Foucault demonstrates with remarkable success how the social sciences domesticate and docilize our bodies by effectively using the ruses of sciences to exclude forms of knowledge and practices. This view, among other texts by Foucault, produced Edward Said's *Orientalism*, where the subject is the gaze of the orientalist as he looked at the Arab "other" as fundamentally different, thereby needing the Western master to humanize him/her. Similarly, as I will show later, feminists have used Foucault's notion of power to understand themselves as sexed subjects, the objects of the masculine gaze.

Habermas remains unconvinced by the one-sidedness of this thesis. Contra Foucault, he asserts,

In the 1970's objectifying approaches no longer dominated the field in the human sciences; they were competing instead with hermeneutical and critical approaches that were tailored in their forms of knowledge to possibilities of application other than manipulation of self and other. . . . This tangible positivizing of the will to truth and to knowledge becomes clear in a self-critique presented by Foucault in Berkeley in 1980. There Foucault said,

"If one wants to analyze the genealogy of the subject in Western societies, one has to take into account not only the techniques of domination but also techniques of the self. Let's say one has to take into account the interaction between those two types of techniques, the point where the technologies of domination of individuals over one another have recourses to processes by which individual acts upon himself."[67]

This particular conception of power reminds Habermas rather forcefully of Weber for whom power is "the possibility of forcing one's own will on the behavior of others."[68]

So for Foucault, Habermas writes, "Power is that by which the subject has an effect on objects in successful actions."[69] But, Habermas would contend, even this critical conception of power as domination is itself the product of yet another subject, another human being, by the name of Foucault. In the end, like the scientific discourses that Foucault is genealogically analyzing, his, too, is a yet another self-referring philosophy of the subject.[70] His methods are themselves trapped by the frames of the human sciences, rather than existing outside of them. The pretended objectivism of archaeology is a hidden manifestation of subjectivism. In the strongest language imaginable, Habermas attacks Foucault by saying, "To the extent that it retreats into the reflectionless objectivity of a non-participatory, ascetic description of kaleidoscopically changing practices of power, genealogical historiography emerges from its cocoon as precisely the presentistic, relativistic, cryptonormative illusory science that it does not want to be.''[71]

Again, I am not convinced that these criticisms damage completely Foucault's accomplishments in assessing the pitfalls of modernity's surrender to scientific discourses. Had Foucault lived, he would have, through his customary modesty, defended himself against Habermas's intelligent critique. I agree with Michael Kelly's argument that, if Foucault's and Habermas's characterization of modernity are conjoined, the result is that ''the permanent activation of a critical attitude'' inaugurates modernity's task of ''creating its own normativity.''[72] Before I attempt to defend Foucault, I need to first travel a bit further with Habermas. The rest of his criticisms of Foucault may be summarized as follows.

First, Foucault's historiographical genealogy, or critical history, ignores (a) the roles of meaning, (b) validity claims, and (c) evaluations in its analysis of practices, by relegating (a) merely to explanations, (b) to effects of power, and (c) to descriptions.[73]

Second, a historical example, such as the prohibition of gladiatorial fights in late Rome by humanistic Christianity, is reduced to a new power formation displacing an older one.[74]

Third, the ''genealogy of knowledge'' makes a specific place for the new presence of ''subjugated knowledges'' although this is not a new argument. The early Lukacs has already established the appropriate arguments. Fourth, Foucault's methods do not allow for the play of ''counter power,'' of which his method is simply a counter power to another. Fifth, Foucault falls short of the objectivity that he so much desires. Sixth, he does not allow any possibility of judging certain formations as better than others. Seventh, there are no answers to questions such as why domination should be resisted. Eighth, ultimately, Foucault's ''bio power''—unlike Bataille's normativity of ''sovereignty,'' or Nietzche's ''aesthetic modernity,'' Heidegger's ''being,'' or Derrida's ''difference''—is a call for a new science, a ''science'' that he borrowed from the empiricists he so much disliked. Ninth, in his sweeping judgments that all power is a disciplining of docile bodies, he ignores relaxed ''penal laws'' that have safeguarded the civil rights of the oppressed. Even the welfare state for him is a sort of panopticon.[75] Finally for Foucault, Habermas concludes, ''Socialized individuals can only be perceived as exemplars, as standardized products of some discourse formation—as individual copies that are mechanically punched out. Gehlen, who thought from opposite political motives, but also from a similar theoretical perspective, made no secret of this, a personality that is an institution is a single instance.''[76]

HABERMAS ON POWER

Habermas's conception of power as communicative action is beautifully stated in his article entitled ''Hannah Arendt's Concept of Power.'' There he begins building his concept of power by locating it close to Arendt's definition and in contradistinction to Max Weber's. For Weber, power is "the possibility of forcing one's own will on the behavior of others," whereas for Arendt it is "the ability to agree upon a common course of action in unconstrained communication."[77]

It is the ideal of reaching agreements via unconstrained communication that is common to Habermas and Arendt. Both of them aim at generating truths by guaranteeing to the communicative or speaking subjects that if they genuinely try, speaking subjects can in fact, in contrast to Weber, cease treating each other as instruments of manipulation (for example, by lying to others) and instead collectively or in concert galvanize events that would eventually lead to a common understanding. Such communal action would cause them to be collectively empowered. For Habermas and Arendt, in contrast to the early Foucault and later Weber, truth can be experienced as something that human beings produce in concert. Truth/s can be disclosed only in an intersubjectively oriented human interaction. When truths are thus disclosed, humans collectively bring about power, power as value, that is the property of humans as opposed to the property of a single individual. As Hannah Arendt put the matter, "Power corresponds to the human ability not just to act but to act in concert. Power is never the property of an individual; it belongs to a group and remains in existence only so long as the group keeps together. When we say of somebody that he is 'in power' we actually refer to his being empowered by a certain number of people to act in their name."[78]

For Weber's "teleological model of action," power (*macht*) and force (*gewalt*) are one and the same. According to Habermas's interpretation of Arendt on the other hand, power can filter down itself to force, or, if you like, force can engulf power. Once power loses its sovereignty, it is invaded by force. Thus power, that sovereign property of the group in concert, loses its legitimacy. It is no longer power, the kind of power that empowers a group by legitimating their right to participate in the affairs of the city freely and honestly without hiding their intentions or expressing their desires. When power—power as a political quality, the quality of communicative subjects, guided by Habermas's concern with truth, sincerity, expressivity, and a comprehensive quest for the right thing to do—is engulfed by force, it dissolves as if in water. At that moment, power gives way to force, and the people's sovereignty surrenders to tyrannical leaders or pseudo experts in the form of technicians of knowledge.

Once power is instrumentalized by force, language suffers tremendously. Using the language of speech acts, Habermas notes that speech is employed "perlocutionarily," that is rhetorically, or as Weber would say, to coerce others to do another's will. In the ideal communicative situation, language is used "illocutionarily," that is, free of rhetorical communication.

For Arendt, according to Habermas, power is embodied in institutions that secure political liberty, protect the destruction of political liberty by force, and nurture revolutionary actions and opinions that produce novel ideals as expressions of liberty.[79] For Arendt, power, that is, people's power, is ontologically grounded upon the fact that humans are destined by the fact of their plurality and natality to permanently originate novel ideals and ideas, which power protects and encourages. In Habermas's formulations, "In communication, individuals appear actively as unique beings and reveal themselves in their subjectivity. At the same time, they must recognize one another as equally responsible beings, that is as beings capable of intersubjective agreement. The rationality claim immanent in speech grounds a radical equality."[80] I will comment later on this passage, which I will use to distinguish my existentially grounded conception of power as a constructive/creative self-empowerment from this Habermas/Arendt communicative concept of power.

When judged by this specific concept of power, Hitlerian Germany, as well as many deformed forms of modernity's political democracies, fall far short of amounting to anything remotely resembling the most thinned out forms of democracy. For Arendt, any institution that does not attempt to both secure liberty and allow the expressive possibilities of human natality and plurality is not worthy of its name. Institutions derive their names from their actual performances and not from their idealized utterances.

All democracies that obliterate power with the most well-intended force quickly degenerate into embodying powerlessness, and thus human anguish or alienation. These institutions devolve into an abyss, preserving the most depoliticized and dangerously uninformed masses of people who lack any sense of community, belonging, or orientation.

This particular definition of power enables Arendt to partake in the great theatrical emancipatory debates of critical theory, including those of Habermas. It is, in fact, because of this view of power that Habermas feels very drawn to Arendt as opposed to Weber and Foucault. Indeed, he accuses Foucault of lacking a transcendental, reasonable sense of community, particularly the common will, generated by ideology and lacking a sense of common destiny, and the common need for collective emancipation from the will to power, expressed as the yearning for violence, chaos, or destruction. David Hoy vehemently disagrees: "Genealogy (Foucault's Method) is a form of developmental theory and proceeds reconstructively, but unlike Habermas's projected model, genealogy is reconstruction without the assumption of progress."[81]

There is a dimension of Arendt's classical conception of power that is partly inspired by Aristotle's conception of man as a political/social being, which because of his/her finitude is pressured to seek others in community. This dimension of Arendt's concept of power disturbs Habermas. He states it thus,

I want only to indicate the curious perspective that Hannah Arendt adopts: a state which is relieved of the administrative processing of social problems; a politics which is cleansed of socio-economic issues; an institutionalization of public liberty which is independent of the organization of public wealth; a radical democracy which inhibits its liberating efficacy just at the boundaries where political oppression ceases and social repression begins—this path is unimaginable for any modern society.[82]

He is also dissatisfied with her rejection of force as apolitical. For Habermas, modernity cannot be understood without the acknowledgment of the pivotal role of force as violence. For him, it is equally unacceptable to not consider modern institutions responsible for production of the structurally caused phenomena of global poverty. Laboring and working, as opposed to action, are pushed out of the sphere of the political for Arendt; and this Habermas thinks is a major flaw in Arendt's communicative conception of power, and thus, of political life.

A comprehensive view of power must inevitably face issues of violence that cannot simply be expunged from the strategic spheres of everyday life. These strategic spheres are administered by the technicians of power, precisely those whom Weber had in mind when he conceptualized power as power holder A imposing his/her will on the powerless B. As Habermas put it, "Politics cannot, as with Arendt, be identified with the praxis of those who talk together in order to act in common."[83]

He defends Arendt's conception of power on the grounds of her thesis, which speaks persuasively to the fundamental question of legitimacy—that any political system would ultimately be dissolved by the governed if it takes their natural property away from them, and that property, as Arendt taught us, is power. It is the presence of power that binds people to their institutions because without that natural property, they cannot express their yearning for liberty. In this sense, power is a collective good and an intersubjectively shared value. If and when power is engulfed by force, institutions in which it was previously embodied lose their legitimacy.[84] Arendt's thesis speaks against her, however, when she uproots "structural violence" from politics by arguing that it is merely force. In fact, unlike force, which is visible, structural violence as an expression of force, operates invisibly. It presences itself by hiding behind the facade of speech (as rhetoric) or behind disciplinary institutions: clinics, discourse of sexuality, prisons, and schools. This remarkable sensitivity to power as structured violence brings Habermas much closer to the early Foucault.

In order to complete the picture of communicative action, I will now add some useful insights that Habermas provides in one of his lectures in *Philosophical Discourses of Modernity*, as I pointed out in the introduction. A subject-centered reason, as in Descartes, Kant, and Hegel, is ultimately self-referential. For it is the subject that is producing the categories of thinking and then appropriating them solitarily to understand the world. In this subjectivist model, truth is not disclosed objectively, but rather, persons understand each other only because they share self-constructed categories of knowledge.

Communicative action, on the other hand, assumes the categories of thought and appeals to individuals' implicit capacities of "mutual understanding." This understanding empowers them to venture into intersubjective relationships, not as solitary possessors of novel categories (as in Kant's moral philosophy expressed in *The Critique of Pure Reason* and *The Critique of Practical Reason*) but as social beings who are systematically socialized to communicate effectively by being morally right, sincere, truthful, and aesthetically harmonious. As

Habermas puts it, ''Only then does the critique of the domineering thought of a subject-centered reason emerge in a determinate form—namely as a critique of Western 'logocentrism' which is diagnosed not as excess but as a deficit of rationality.''[85]

Communicative subjects are language speaking in that in their interactive mode (a) they advance propositions when they are describing a state of affairs, (b) they speak illocutionarily, motivated by the search for truth, and (c) they speak in such a way that there is a rough correspondence between their intentions and what is expressed.[86] All the above have serious implications for the theory of meaning, the ontological presuppositions of the theory of communication, and the concept of rationality itself.

By rationality, in this lecture, Habermas refers in the first instance to the disposition of speaking and acting subjects to acquire and use fallible knowledge . . . rationality is assessed by how the isolated subject orients himself to representational and propositional contents. . . . as soon as we conceive of knowledge as communicatively mediated, rationality is assessed in terms of the capacity of responsible participants in interaction to orient themselves in relation to validity claims geared to intersubjective recognition. Communicative reason finds its criteria in the argumentative procedure for directly or indirectly redeeming claims to propositional truth, normative rightness, subjective truthfulness, and aesthetic harmony.[87]

Habermas suggests that a pragmatic, as opposed to a reason-centered, concept of rationality can be worked out on the behalf of communicative action. The pragmatic model would concentrate on building possibilities of a noncoercive consensus in which participants learn how to overcome their subjectively oriented disagreements through the intersubjective possibilities of rationally motivated agreements.[88]

Unlike subject-centered reason which fosters divisions or usurpations, the communicative model aims at nurturing pragmatically compelling agreements and harmonies. It is only under capitalist modernization that the communicative potential of reason has been distorted. Reason as such is not inherently uncommunicative. Communicative reason can in fact vigorously renew Hegel's early assurance that the ethical life would be accompanied by the constructive recourses of the lifeworld, the world of ''traditions, social practices, and body-centered complexes of experience that coalesce into particular totalities. These particular forms of life, which only emerge in the plural, are certainly not connected with each other only through a web of family resemblances; they exhibit structures common to lifeworlds in general.''[89]

I would now like to propose that there is another unexplored avenue by which humans can be drawn to participate in choosing from varied of styles of existence. I call this path an existentially motivated self-construction of values that genuinely empower. Habermas's pragmatically motivated communicative subject and the early Foucault's power-motivated actor do not in the end allow humans radically to be themselves. In both modes of being, the self is not allowed to take its existence seriously and self-construction is not treated as a serious way of leading one own life. Habermas in particular is seriously worried—absent the concept of control by comprehensive reason—about the dangers of what he feared in Foucault's critique of reason that it will inevitably produce relativity and cryptonormativity. However, according to Annemiek Richters, "The blind spot of the European Enlightenment is its inability to recognize heterogeneity, otherness, and difference. 'Reason' and 'rationality,' like 'humanity' and 'human nature' have functioned as highly pretentious moral imperialism.''[90] Along the same lines, some esteemed theorists, Seyla Benhabib,[91] Nancy Fraser,[92] and David Rasmussen,[93] have as well contended that Habermas's project of finishing the enlightenment entails "the biases of a middle-class, male European" conceptions of rationality and reasonableness.

Indeed, Habermas is right that any attempts at self-construction, including this author's modality, unless regulated by a transcendental force, is vulnerable to dangerous anarchistic adventures. Luckily for me, insofar as selves can take stock of their precious existence, they will know how to establish boundaries of actions they can undertake but should not, values they should construct and deconstruct. It sounds a bit too easy perhaps to make such sweeping generalizations and abstractions, but short of possessing a God-like power to study human behavior, I can only suggest that taking one's existence seriously is not as impossible as nervous experts think. If nothing else, almost all human beings, although they may not know very much else, are quite aware that life is short, that learning how to live it cautiously quite difficult, and that risking one's life for the sake of a morally bankrupt and intellectually incompetent value such as racism or sexism is ultimately not worthy of the passions and intelligence of human beings. Although modern individuals have unsuccessfully separated morality and rationality, and some contend that values such as racism and sexism might be immoral without being irrational, I am of the opinion that a self that would consciously construct racism as a value worth fighting for is, in fact, not only choosing immorally but is also doing so irrationally.

When one chooses irrationally, one is not only jeopardizing one's own existence but also that of all those others who are indirectly but fundamentally affected by his/her own actions. An existentially motivated self-construction protects itself and others from avoidable lapses of choice. Furthermore, the agonal conception of power, presented by Arendt and Habermas after her, does not leave much space for solitary subjects who cannot enter into intersubjective dialogues aimed at reaching truth. Indeed, there will always be selves with highly localized and regionalized ways of thinking and living who may never smoothly fit into any community. Such selves will be outside the circles of rationality and moralities, though always conscious of their existence and their own heterogeneous styles of regulating them. This would not, however, inevitably lead to either cryptonormativity or relativity. Power as self-empowerment seeks to speak directly to Habermas's rightful fears by carefully articulating the self-founded tools of control that the constructive/creative subject develops to defend himself/herself from the vulnerabilities of imbibing values or norms, such as racisms and sexisms, that would destroy the privilege of existence and via it the honor of moral/cultural civilization.

Foucault is right when he modestly refrains from imposing any norms by which styles of existence are to be judged as right, sincere, or harmlessly expressive, unlike Habermas, who imposes such norms in his otherwise broadly gagged conceptualization of reason as a definite "good" without which we cannot live. Miller has insightfully argued:

For Foucault, the "substance" at stake in taking care of himself was neither his desires nor his thoughts, but, as he remarked to Dreyfus and Rabinow, one's bios—life in its chaotic, prepersonal flux. This substance he has glimpsed firsthand, at the limits of experience, by exploring without inhibition "bodies and pleasures." . . . That he felt moved to exercise care at all was due neither to a divine law, nor a natural law, nor a rational rule, but rather to a passion for beauty, which led him to try to give to his existence, as he explained to Dreyfus and Rabinow, "the most beautiful form possible."[94]

An existentially motivated defense of the constructive subject does not require any explicit authority here. The only authority, should there be one, is the unavoidable fact that we exist and that there are both pitiful and more fulfilling ways of living life. Existentially serious individuals know this as a root fact of their struggle to determine their destinies within the context of what is sayable, what is doable, and what can be roughly anticipated with the help of moral luck, and self-imposed legislation of moral principles. With these preparatory remarks, I now proceed to show several modes of construction from among which I choose and then attempt to theoretically defend self-construction, as opposed to construction by modelling oneself after others or by simply following rules, as the best condition for human beings, or in Foucault's language, the best practice of liberty. The idea of self-construction is not new. A long line of thinkers, beginning with Plato and culminating in the works of Foucault's concern with *self-Fashioning* and Habermas's notion of the *communicative community*, have taken the idea of self-construction very seriously. My attempts at a working out the intricate demands of constructing human values and norms that empower moral subjects who take their existence seriously tallies with the tradition established by Kant in his moral philosophy. Indeed, I borrow the idea of self-legislation, without which serious construction is impossible, from Kant's powerful articulations in his seminal essay, "What Is Enlightenment?" I think however, that the idea of self-construction, which I am attempting to develop, and Foucault's notion of self-fashioning, are guided by two different visions of human possibilities. Consider Foucault's own vision below, "in reference to the dandy, an exemplary model of Self-Fashioning. The dandy 'makes of his body, his behavior, his feelings and passions, his very existence, a work of art.' "[95] For me, the possibility of constructing human values that empower seeks to confront the will to dominate as a perennial dimension of human constitution. The possibility of overcoming the will to dominate is a permanent moral project for some human beings, as Dostoyevsky and Plato emphasize. The self-imposed task of constructing values is a privilege that must be earned. Part of earning it necessitates that humans come to terms with the nature of power, power as domination and power as the will to overcome the will to dominate, or power as embodied in Habermas's "ideal speech situation"[96] but vigilant to the distorting effects of human irrationality powerfully expressed in Dostoyevsky's presentation of evil. In the chapters that follow, I will trace the history of power in the works of some of the most serious voices in the tradition of moral philosophy, political theory, and literary writing. Among the numerous thinkers which I have chosen, I will concentrate on those who seemed to consider power and domination as perennial dimensions of the human condition. Before I move on to an analysis of power and domination, the tempting objects of the desiring subject, I will first articulate the notion of self-construction.

NOTES

1. Fredrich Nietzsche, *On the Genealogy of Morals and Ecce Homo*, ed. Walter Kaufmann (New York: Vintage Books, 1969), pp. 25–26.

2. Michael Kelly, ed., *Critique and Power* (Cambridge: MIT Press, 1994), p. 374. Kelly correctly instructs that by power, Foucault claims to mean "relationships of power," n 2, p. 391.

3. Ibid., p. 378.

4. Michel Foucault, *Power/Knowledge* (New York: Pantheon Books, 1980), p. 57.

5. Ibid., pp. 139–140.

6. Ibid., p. 156.

7. Michel Foucault, *Discipline and Punish* (New York: Vintage Books, 1979), p. 184.

8. Ibid., p. 194.

9. Barry Smart, ed., *Michel Foucault: Critical Assessments* (London and New York: Routledge, 1994), "Introductory Essay," p. 5.

10. Foucault, interview, pp. 122–123. See also Miller, *Passion of Michel Foucault*, p. 327. Miller persuasively argues that Foucault's extraordinary seriousness with living life as art inevitably led to experiment with S/M to discover "new forms of life."

11. Foucault, interview, p. 129. Emphasis mine.

12. Michel Foucault, "The Subject and Power," in *Michel Foucault: Beyond Structuralism and Hermeneutics*, ed. Hubert L. Dreyfus and Paul Rabinow (Chicago: University of Chicago Press, 1982), p. 226. In this remarkable text, the authors argue that Foucault's notion of power is "not one of the areas he has most fully developed," pp. viii–ix.

13. These subtle points are usefully analyzed by Barry Smart, ed., *Michel Foucault (1): Critical Assessments*, p. 4. They are also equally carefully examined by Roger Garaudy, "Structuralisme et 'Mort de l' homme,' " in the same work.

14. Ibid., John Rajchman, "Foucault's Art of Seeing," in *Michel Foucault*, ed. Smart, pp. 224–236.

15. Richard Rorty, "Foucault and Epistemology," in *Michel Foucault*, vol. 1., ed. Smart, p. 263.

16. One of the best treatments of Habermas's entire work is still Thomas McCarthy's classic, *The Critical Theory of Jürgen Habermas* (Cambridge: Massachusetts Institute of Technology Press, 1978).

17. Seyla Benhabib, *Situating the Self* (New York: Routledge, 1992), p. 80.

18. Axel Honneth, *The Critique of Power: Reflective Stages in a Critical Social Theory*, trans. Kenneth Baynes (Cambridge: Massachusetts Institute of Technology Press, 1991), p. 271.

19. Ibid.

20. Jürgen Habermas, *The Theory of Communicative Action*, vol. 1 (Boston: Beacon Press, 1985), p. 379.

21. Honneth, *The Critique of Power*, pp. 176–203.

22. Thomas McCarthy, "The Critique of Impure Reason," in *Critique and Power* (Cambridge: Massachusetts Institute of Technology Press, 1994), pp. 243–283.

23. Foucault's implicit structuralist hypothesis here is a notorious subject of heated debates. For a careful documentation of the themes, see Barry Smart, ed., *Michel Foucault: Critical Assessments*, vol. 2 (London, New York: Routledge, 1994). Section 2 is devoted to the question of Foucault's structuralism.

24. Frank Kermode, "Crisis Critic," in *Michel Foucault*, ed. Smart, vol. 1, p. 11.

25. Michel Foucault, *The Order of Things* (New York: Vintage Books, 1973), p. 79.

26. Richard Rorty, "Foucault and Epistemology," in *Michel Foucault*, ed. Smart, vol. 1, p. 259.

27. Ibid., p. 260. For Rorty, Foucault, much like Wittgenstein, is an intellectual historian interested in the description of discursive practices. Again, much like Wittgenstein, his attack on the sovereignty of the signifier resembles the attack on the concept of language as a picture. See pp. 262–263 in the same article.

28. Plato, *Cratylus*, in *The Collected Dialogues of Plato*, ed. Edith Hamilton (New Jersey: Princeton University Press, 1973), p. 423.

29. Foucault, *The Order of Things*, p. 82.

30. Edward Said, "An Ethics of Language," in *Michel Foucault*, ed. Smart, vol. 2, p. 84.

31. Foucault, *The Order of Things*, p. 94.

32. Ibid.

33. Ibid.

34. See Richard Rorty's remarkable situating of Foucault in the history of philosophy in "Michel Foucault and Epistemology," in *Michel Foucault*, ed. Smart, vol. 2, pp. 259–265.

35. Michel Foucault, *The Order of Things*, p. 95.

36. Ibid., p. 95.

37. Ibid., p. 103.

38. Plato, *Cratylus. The Collected Dialogues of Plato*, ed. Edith Hamilton (New Jersey: Princeton University Press, 1973).

39. Foucault, *The Order of Things*, p. 113.

40. Ibid., p. 115.

41. George Stiener, "Archeology: Discourse, Language, Literature," in *Michel Fou-

cault, ed. Smart, pp. 400–401. See also Richard Rorty's seminal essay in the same text. p. 259.

42. Foucault, *The Order of Things*, p. 305.

43. Michel de Certeau, "The Black Sun of Language," in *Michel Foucault*, ed. Smart, p. 250. For Foucault, argues de Certeau, the history of reason is a history of discontinuities, the history of order is the history of shaky unities of language. The same point is nicely enforced by Richard Rorty in "Michel Foucault and Epistemology" in the same work, p. 264. See also Stanley Aronowitz's "History as Disruption: On Benjamin and Foucault," ibid., pp. 344–362.

44. For an insightful reinforcement of these themes see Martin Jay, "Limit and Transgression in Contemporary European Thought" *Constellations* 2, no. 2 (1995): p. 168.

45. Michel Foucault, *The Archeology of Knowledge* (New York: Pantheon Books, 1972), pp. 1–71.

46. "The Linguistic Fault. The Case of Foucault's Archaeology," in *Michel Foucault*, ed. Smart, p. 93.

47. Gilles Deleuze, "A New Archivist," in *Michel Foucault*, ed. Smart, p. 386. Deleuze perceptively observes that structures are propositional forms guided by homogeneous axioms whereas statements seek to remain open-ended multiplicities, p. 390. Given this characterization of statements, Foucault's works themselves are statements that resemble poetic forms rather than structured propositions, concludes Deleuze, p. 392.

48. Foucault, *The Archaeology of Knowledge*, p. 91.

49. Ibid., p. 105.

50. Ibid., p. 105.

51. Ibid., p. 117.

52. For a carefully crafted argument of how the humanities institutionalize the facets of speech and action, see Paul Bove, "The End of Humanism: Michel Foucault and the Power of Disciplines," in *Michel Foucault*, ed. Smart, pp. 312–326.

53. Bove also makes a direct reference to Gramsci's notion of hegemony and compares it to Foucault's notion of episteme and how some epistemes become dominant. See his essay "The End of Humanism," in Smart, p. 323. See also Smart's own essay "The Politics of Truth and the Problem of Hegemony," in *Michel Foucault*, vol. 3, pp. 208–219.

54. Smart, "The Politics of Truth and the Problem of Hegemony," p. 218.

55. Jean-François Lyotard, *The Postmodern Condition: A Report on Knowledge* (Minneapolis: University of Minnesota Press, 1979), pp. 60–66.

56. Jürgen Habermas, *The Philosophical Discourses of Modernity* (Cambridge: Massachusetts Institute of Technology Press, 1987), p. 236.

57. The similarities between the early critical theory of the Frankfurt School of Max Horkheimer and his colleagues and Foucault's genealogy of power knowledge as displayed in Foucault's *Discipline and Punish* is masterfully analyzed by Thomas McCarthy, "The Critique of Impure Reason: Foucault and the Frankfurt School," in Michael Kelly, ed.

58. Habermas, *Philosophical Discourses*, p. 240.

59. Ibid., p. 243.

60. This point is perceptively developed by Paul Bove in "The End of Humanism: Michel Foucault and the Power of Disciplines," in *Michel Foucault*, ed. Smart, p. 318. The point is reinforced by Michael Kelly in *Critique and Power*, pp. 367–372.

61. Ibid., p. 252.

62. Michael Kelly, ed., ''Foucault, Habermas, and the Self-Referentiality of Critique,'' in *Critique and Power*, p. 367.

63. Steven Best, *The Politics of Historical Vision: Marx, Foucault, Habermas* (London: The Guilford Press, 1997), p. 128.

64. Ibid., p. 220.

65. Nietzche, *The Genealogy of Morals*, pp. 25–26.

66. David Couzens Hoy, ''Two Conflicting Conceptions of How to Naturalize Philosophy: Foucault versus Habermas,'' in *Michel Foucault*, ed. Smart, vol. 3, p. 93.

67. Habermas, *Philosophical Discourses of Modernity* (Cambridge: MIT Press, 1987). p. 273.

68. Habermas, ''Hannah Arendt's Communication Concept of Power,'' p. 3.

69. Habermas, *Philosophical Discourses*, p. 274.

70. Ibid., p. 274.

71. Ibid., p. 276.

72. Michael Kelly, *Critique and Power*, p. 384. Nor does Habermas's ''presentism'' imply ''relativism'' and if I may add, ''nihilism,'' p. 384.

73. Habermas, *Philosophical Discourses*, p. 277.

74. Ibid., p. 277.

75. Ibid., pp. 276–293.

76. Ibid., p. 293.

77. Habermas, ''Hannah Arendt's Concept of Power,'' p. 3.

78. From Hannah Arendt, *On Violence*, p. 44. Quoted in Habermas, ''Hannah Arendt's Concept of Power,'' p. 4.

79. Ibid., p. 7.

80. Ibid., p. 8.

81. Hoy, ''Two Conflicting Conceptions,'' in *Michel Foucault*, ed. Smart, p. 89.

82. Habermas, ''Hannah Arendt's Concept of Power,'' p. 15.

83. Ibid., p. 21.

84. Ibid.

85. Habermas, *Philosophical Discourses*, p. 310.

86. Ibid., p. 312.

87. Ibid., p. 314. Critics such as David Hoy charge that Habermas's pragmatics of language does not take the need of fulfilling truth conditions, as Davidson does, and consequently, its reliance on intention and meaning is inadequate for understanding the language model of understanding human action. See Hoy, ''Two Conflicting Conceptions,'' in *Michel Foucault*, ed. Smart, p. 92.

88. Habermas, *Philosophical Discourses*, p. 315.

89. Ibid., p. 326.

90. Annemiek Richters, ''Modernity-Postmodernity Controversies: Habermas and Foucault,'' in *Michel Foucault*, ed. Smart, vol. 1, p. 303.

91. Seyla Benhabib, *Situating The Self*, 148–78.

92. Nancy Fraser, (1985) ''What is Critical About Critical Theory? The Case of Habermas and Gender,'' *New German Critique*, p. 35.

93. D. M. Rasmussen, (1985) ''Communicative Action and Fate of Modernity,'' *Theory, Culture and Society*'' 2 (3).

94. Miller, *The Passion of Michel Foucault*, p. 347.

95. Michel Foucault, *The Foucault Reader*, ed. Paul Rabinow (New York: Pantheon

Books, 1984), pp. 42–43. James Schmidt and Thomas E. Wartenberg seek to provide a complicated summary of Foucault's life-long interest in Kant's essay "What is Enlightenment?" to provide a grounding for Foucault's efforts at developing a vision of self that is autonomous, critically aware of the present, and finally self-fashioning in an ontologically inventive way. See James Schmidt and Thomas E. Wartenberg, "Foucault's Enlightenment," in *Critique and Power*.

96. In *Autonomy and Solidarity*, "ideal speech situation" is retheorized and its ideality is de-emphasized. Habermas writes, "But at no time have I 'hypostatized the unlimited community of communication, transforming it from a necessary presupposition into an ideal to be realized,' as Schluchter, drawing on Wellner, assumes." p. 260. As we recall, Wellner had sought to disclose the utopian moments of communicative rationality guided by the "ideal speech situation." See, Albrecht Wellner's essay in *Habermas and Modernity*.

2

Self-Construction and the Formation of Values that Empower

THE MEANING OF CONSTRUCTION

To construct[1] anything at all requires tools, parts, raw materials of nature out of which something can be formed by the human being as an intelligent tool-maker. As we saw above, the ordinary dictionary comprises this meaning. The ordinary meaning of the word construction also correctly stresses the role of activity in the act of constructing. Thus, constructing something is an activity in which (1) things are made from the assembling of other things and (2) things are made, assembled, and formed creatively. True, one cannot construct anything without readily accessible parts of nature. This first requirement is particularly true of works of art. An artist can construct something only by the creative forming or reforming of the parts of external nature. Hence, Michelangelo constructed his sculptures out of nature's marble and stone by the force of his imagination and spiritual power. He, of course, did not thoughtlessly assemble parts or mindlessly cut stones. Rather, he originated the manners, thereby fulfilled the difficult demands of the second requirement above. The assembling and the originating dimensions of the art and science of construction, I wish to argue, are also in a less than clear way, applicable to the construction of values from which norms inevitably arise.

Constructing something involves assembling, making, and originating. On first blush, it appears that assembling, making, and originating are so technical, so demanding, and so specialized that they demand the powers of a genius. The silent premise is that constructing cannot be undertaken by just anybody. There are some individuals who are specially called to construct great works of art and great scientific discoveries, and others who are inherently incapable.

Assembling and making are more rigorously requirements of painting and sculpting than they are of literary and philosophic writings, the subjects that concern me in this book. Creativity and originality, on the other hand, are definite requirements of literature or writing in general. However, the requirement for creativity, one can argue, often infiltrates the arts of painting and sculpting, particularly if the painter is either a writer, a student of literature, or a thinker/philosopher. The painter who is also a writer and thinker brings thinking to bear on his/her painting, or lets his/her painting be penetrated by the highly creative activity of originary thinking. My point is simply that the writer/thinker is less constrained by the first requirement in that he/she may have nothing out of which to assemble or make things in the strict sense that the sculptor/thinker does. For the writer/thinker constructing often means to originate something out of virtually nothing, except in cases where he obtains available social practices, customs, values, norms, conventions, implicit opinions, moral sentiments, systematic philosophies, religious beliefs, symbols, signs, or representations, which are reworked, re-presented, reinterpreted, or corrected in an originary way. The writer/thinker, in such instances, uses the gifts of history by assembling them in an originary way.

The sculptor/thinker assembles, makes, and originates. The painter also assembles, makes, and originates. The writer/thinker can also assemble, make, and originate whenever assembling and making are possible. For the most part, though, the writer/thinker is primarily an originator. The question is: How does the writer/thinker originate? Or rather, out of what does the writer/thinker originate, particularly when he/she rejects what I called above the gifts of history? I am concerned here with the phenomenon of how the human self constructs values.

We now understand that construction as such implies assembling and making, and creating or originating. It is of course human beings who construct things and ideas. As we yet do not know—and we may never know—how and from what ''materials'' they construct. But we do know they construct. They construct various things. They do so by either

(a) watching others construct and reproduce a thing,

(b) modeling themselves after things, ideas, or persons that are right at hand, and that are already done, finished, and crystallized into tradition, or

(c) doing the construction themselves. Each of the above modes of construction is different, and I wish to discuss them separately.

Self-Construction and Reproduction

The most typical way of learning to do something is by imitation. When a learner wishes to master the process of doing something, he/she directs attention to the way that somebody else, who is reputed to know, does the thing. The potential learner seeks to do exactly what the one who knows does; he or she seems to be less concerned with the logic and reasoning of what he or she wishes to learn than he/she is with the simple task of reproducing something. Note that imitation does not require too much activity; in fact, it seems that the imitator's mental life in the act of imitation is not active at all. Exaggerating a bit, I wish to say that imitation is proximally and primarily the absence of mental activity. Passivity or complete absorption in what an accomplished actor is doing is indeed the central feature of imitation.

Imitation is grounded upon observation, and observation as such is, loosely speaking, a passive activity. The imitator is a passive observer. When the imitator observes, it is not readily apparent to others that the imitator observes; nor is it clear that the imitator has really mastered the logic and reasons behind what he/she is observing and which he or she could reproduce without giving a logos of the action. Passive observation then could easily become a thoughtless activity, an activity that does not challenge the imitator to go beyond reproducing something. Consider the following example. In one of the many regular walks that person A took, he one day encountered a beggar on the street. He approached the beggar and helped her out with some money. When this was taking place, and without A's knowledge, person B who had witnessed the moral event was stunned by A's silent action. At an appropriate moment, B approached A and they talked about the event, and B was given some moral lessons that he hoped would sharpen his moral powers. Thus, B proceeded to practice the lessons he had been given.

As every child knows, one does not become moral by simply wishing to be, and so B, who was a mature adult, did not immediately wish to be like A and help out the objectively needy when he was confronted with them on the streets. But, B did wish—at the appropriate moment, and when guided by genuine moral powers—to reproduce the moral event that he witnessed. Thus, he began to struggle.

B retains the image of the force of A's moral action and that—given the appropriate moment—B wishes to reproduce A's action. To do so, B can only recall what A did mechanically. It is quite easy for any person to thoughtlessly imitate A's action when confronted with a similar event. All that one has to possess is some money and the willingness to give that money to beggars on the street. So B does just that. Has B thus become moral just because he has mechanically reproduced A's moral action? Is imitation of an action, no matter how skillfully done, sufficient to enable us to know the inner principles that produce the great moral action? Do repeated imitations of an action cultivate a person who knows what he is doing? These are very involved questions that must somehow be dealt with. It cannot be denied that the road toward mastering an action can begin with imitation, and that the inclination to imitate something that is deemed worthy is itself admirable. However, it is the marked absence of mental activity in imitation that reveals the intrinsic limitations of imitation per se. B's ability to reproduce A's moral action does not tell us anything about the character of B as a person. All that we know about him is that he can carefully and skillfully reproduce the great moral actions of others. We only know that he is an impressive imitator. We don't know, by merely observing his imitative actions, that he/she is genuinely convinced by the rightness and worthiness of A's moral actions, which he has made his own; nor do we know that he is joyously and sincerely practicing virtuous actions. In short, we know nothing about his desires—the desires that may reveal who he really is.

Imitation is thus inherently limited in telling us about the rightness and worthiness of actions. There may be a way of overcoming some of the inherent limits of imitation as a model of construction. One such way, described below, is the quest for locating exemplary models in things, ideas, persons, and traditions. Thus, mere imitation is an inadequate model of constructing values, norms, and interests that are self-empowering.

Modeling Oneself After Ideas, Persons and Tradition

I wish to retain, as an example, A's and B's moral actions to elucidate the idea of modeling. Models of course are patterns of ideas. Ideas in turn are often expressed visibly in the language of beauty. Beauty itself is embodied in a beautiful form, a beautiful idea, a beautiful action, and a beautiful person. Persons wishing to penetrate the idea of the beautiful pattern often orient their lives toward a model idea, a person, or form.[2] Thus B seeks to perform A's moral action not merely by imitation, but most importantly by modeling himself after A—A's beautiful ideas, authentic ways of life, or desires. In short, A has become a model for B. Now that B has chosen A as his model, the rest is a matter of learning the ways of A—those very ways that thrilled B's moral senses. B has now resolved to dig deeply into the thoughts and desires of A instead of his own thoughts and desires.

It is easy to say that I want to be like the person whom I admire the most; it is quite difficult to be like that other person. It is precisely the challenging tension between wanting to be and actually becoming that B experiences when he models himself after A. Unlike learning by imitation, learning by modeling demands much effort. A's exemplary moral action was accomplished through years of effort, training, painful habituation, triumph and failure, joy and sorrow, exceptionally attentive parental as well as teacher's guidance, privileged home environment, early and sustained exposure to the world of disciplined thinking, wide reading in literature, and above all a measure of blessedness. When B modeled himself after A, it is not immediately apparent that he knew what he was modeling himself after. It is equally important to note that models are human beings and that they can make mistakes. We should not revere models only because others admire them; we should not follow models just because tradition extols them. But disciples by definition admire models nonindependently, and this is not a virtue.

It is admirable that B wills himself to model his life after A. Indeed, by many other people's judgment, A is a worthy model and B is an impressive devotee. However, there are limits to blind devotion. B's subjectivity is worthy of our deep respect. B's subjective desire to be like A, however, confronts the powerful resistance of objective conditions: lack of conducive home and school environment, his own unique early training and habituation, lack of early experience in thinking, unfamiliarity with "noble humane values" of good literature, and an absence of friends. The lack of all these profoundly complicates B's desire to be like A. A and B have two totally different life histories that cannot be overcome by a mere individual struggle. Modeling, unlike imitation, is grounded upon the interpenetration of wanting and becoming, subjectivity and objectivity, creative impulse and resistant empirical history, and desire and truth.

Modeling, unlike imitation, is not passive. On some considerable level, modeling engages the mind. It draws person B to the world of thinking, the world of changing habit and entrenched attitudes. If person B has become socialized contrary to the historic formation of A's personality, and if B—as B clearly does—wants to be like A, a symbol of moral/rational excellence, then B knows that he must change. Change is one of the central features of becoming through modeling.

Furthermore, A's exemplary moral action requires of B, whose personality is fundamentally different from A's, that he/she change in order that he/she may become a changed, therefore, a new person. As in the mode of construction through imitation, in the mode of construction through modeling there is the danger that modeling, like imitation, does not allow the individual to truly know what he/she is doing. Thus B does not fully and originally understand why helping others is intrinsically good; B does not or has not fully reflected on what his/her obligations, duties, and responsibilities are to the objectively needy. Thus, B is rightly fascinated and even deeply impressed by A as a moral agent. But, whereas A knows what he is doing, there is the possibility that B does not. B is simply following A as a model without understanding the reasons behind the moral actions that A practices.

It is also possible that B, who is consciously attempting to be like A and who strenuously exercises all the necessary efforts to change himself so as to be like A, tragically fails. B begins to realize that one—however honestly and valiantly he/she tries to fundamentally change—might not succeed at all. Such a tragic view of life has grave consequences for the idea of modeling. Consider one such consequence. Human beings are actually different, although their differences may be minimal. The minuteness of the differences notwithstanding, they do crucially affect the idea and practice of modeling. If human beings are minimally different, but some human beings attempt to model themselves after those who profoundly dazzle them, and if some human beings succeed in the venture and others do not, the case of those who wish to succeed but objectively can not exposes rather starkly the intrinsic deficiencies of the idea of modeling.

Recognition of the excellence of the model ideas embodied in model human beings gives pain to those who desire to internalize a model's norms but tragically cannot. Are model ideas all equal to one another? Why are some human beings chosen to be models and others their devoted followers? What are the criteria of choice? Are the choices those of the power holders? What are the relationships among power, truth, and model ideas and model persons? I will reflect on these questions a bit later.

To summarize, modeling ourselves after persons and ideas that we do not fully understand—intellectually and emotionally—is not an adequate way of empowering ourselves.

Self-Construction

My reflections here are preliminary since I will pursue these important themes in the context of the discussion of values, norms, and the idea of self-construction in the next section.

It is a commonplace observation to assert that whatever one directly makes and assembles, one cannot generally fail to understand the process of its making. In the last two sections, as I analyzed the modes of constructing via imitation and modeling, I repeatedly stressed that the acts of making, assembling, and creating, which are the pillars of construction, are external to the self. In the case of the imitator, it is the original person who performs a moral action who may conceivably know the basis and reasons behind his/her action; similarly, in the case of the model person, it is he/she, and not those who wish to model their ways of life after him/her, who understands the rationale behind his/her admired actions. Thus, the privileges of the original moral actor and the model person are not necessarily the privileges of the disciples. The originating powers of the model person in particular are exclusively his/hers. Originating power is not communicable. It originates in the primary moral agent and it remains deeply connected to that particular person. Creativity, in particular, cannot be taught in the way that assembling and making sometimes can be. A's moral action and the seriousness and devotion of the person that created it cannot possibly be persuasively earned either by imitation or modeling. Constructing anything thus requires the direct participation of the moral actor. Construction, both in the strict sense of creativity and in the derivative sense of assembling and making, is self-directed. If an action is to really endure and be valuable, it must be self-constructed. The merits of self-construction are the following.

1. Whenever someone is constructing something himself/herself we can safely hypothesize that the person's mind and heart is directly involved in the activity if it is in a self-directed activity; even the derivative qualities of assembling and making cannot be performed thoughtlessly; therefore,

2. The self-construction of moral actions requires the active engagement of the mind and the body;[3] as a consequence,

3. The product of a self-directed moral action is bound to be good or is potentially good because pride, dignity, self-respect, and even humanity are implicated in the activity itself. The person thus is profoundly motivated to do his/

her best and slowly march toward the attainment of distinction and even moral excellence,

4. The attainment of moral excellence, I wish to argue, is also a product of mental and physical struggle.

5. It would be simple-minded to assert that just because an individual struggles to attain moral excellence through a relentless, tenacious, and consistent mental and physical struggle, he/she will become an excellent, perfect, and saintly human being. Rather, the moral/rational excellence-oriented self-construction of ideals is simply a duty, obligation, and responsibility that is available to human beings. For those who wish to attain excellence, the struggle toward it—without even getting there—becomes a way of life.

6. It is during this relentless struggle that the self learns the nature of truth, happiness, and freedom in the hard way. Unlike learning by imitation and modeling, where one seeks to reproduce thoughtlessly what others deem as a model, believed to be a symbol of excellence—although it may not be—in self-construction, the road toward excellence is sometimes characterized by failures, sorrows, or tragic events. However, the self knows that excellence is a sublime prize; failure must necessarily precede it. The self knows further that in this world nothing truly great is achieved without struggle. It is only after repeated trials that excellence may be achieved and that self-empowerment begins to be empirically attainable.

7. Self-construction aims at achieving excellence in the realm of action and not in the realm of truth. The norms that guide the person to meaningfully and coherently lead a particular way of life are not grounded upon a single Truth. Rather, ways of life and styles of existence are grounded upon individual truths—truths that reflect the plurality of human nature. Truths may be discoverable by devoted and serious individuals after years of self-training, discipline, honest curiosity, and mental and physical struggle.

8. Self-construction is characterized by the conviction that human beings are diverse. Diversity itself is unconsciously grounded upon the deep and genuine respect of human desires, and the desires are truly multifarious. The norms that human beings develop are conditioned by the diversity of their desires; and the truth they aim at leads to the realization of the plurality as opposed to the singularity of truth. When a person engages in the construction of a way of life, a pattern of existence, a style of everyday living, or an ethics of life, he or she is invariably guided by the vision that one's cultivated norms are only good for oneself; and that they should not be imposed on others gently or forcefully. It is worth repeating that the person, through self-construction, originates something that is humanly meaningful, significant, and ultimately the source of enduring norms, that is, an ethical orientation for that particular human being.[4]

Values, Norms, Self-Construction, and Self-Empowerment

Values are principles and standards that are considered worthwhile and intrinsically desirable. This dictionary meaning of values is sufficiently precise to serve us as a guide in our reflection on the philosophical significance of the concept of value.

Human beings are value-creating beings. Many human beings live and die for the sake of principles and standards they really think and feel are worthwhile. Very often, not all independently created values are necessarily right and truly worth dying for; for those persons who originated the values, the rightness or wrongness of their principles is never important. What is important to their eyes and hearts is the existence of the values they originated. The inevitable question is why are values so important for us?

It may initially appear that values are important to us because we created them. Indeed, one may reason, we cannot possibly dislike what we ourselves brought into being just as we cannot dislike our own child, at least up to a point. The issue here seems to be original possession—the power of bringing forth something ourselves and the sense of spontaneous love that follows. Originating anything more often than not produces love—self-love. A critical assessment of values we ourselves brought into human existence is not part of the first stage of the formation of values. For some persons, a critical distance from one's own creation is part of that mature phase of growth; for others, critical distance from self-created values is part of no phase at all; still for some others, growth toward abandoning aspects of one's values is a possibility. The point is that growing out of self-love, when reason demands it, is a possibility but not an inevitability; nor can growth be forced upon those who are not ready for it. It must naturally evolve. I will explain this last point later.

Humans are value-creating beings, and what they create, by way of developing principles and standards, is so fundamental to them that one could say that self-constructed values are constitutive parts of the structure of being. To say that we are value-creating beings does not necessarily mean that we always do create values, or that we are obligated to do so. Rather, we potentially can create values since doing so is an integral part of our constitution, or part of the ontology of being. Potentiality, however, is not actuality. But potentiality does make it possible for us to freely create values as possibilities. Possibility is an expression of freedom.

Human beings then are value-creating possibilities, and there are various kinds of values just as there are various kinds of human beings. As distinct possibilities, we can create many kinds of values under the direction of an active mind and the cooperation of the human body. As possibilities, humans can create values that reflect their authentic desires, desires that empower a self that is tenaciously and courageously seeking freedom as self-realization.[5] Values that are self-constructed are also the ones that are genuinely self-empowering.

I have already asserted that human beings are diverse and embody active possibilities of freedom insofar as they are creators of values. The kind of values that they bring forth into existence are ultimately reflective of the diversity of human nature. Thus, there is not a singular value that all human beings can create and, upon creating, immediately conform to. There is a plurality of values.

In ordinary life, not only do individuals create values but individuals value different ideas and things of this world and the ''afterworld'' world. Some value life and its blessings—health, clothing, shelter, moral and intellectual excellence, or the happiness and well-being of others; some value intelligence and the power of thinking, accompanied by limited wealth; still others value pain and suffering and strive to inflict it on others.

Valuing wealth is not necessarily compatible with valuing thinking, just as a wealthy business man is not necessarily the same as a thoughtful person. The two values exemplify the existence of two different characters. There is no law that says that a wealthy person cannot become a thoughtful one as well if he/ she wishes. By the same token, nothing would prevent a thinker from becoming wealthy, unless the way he became wealthy compelled him to abandon thinking in favor of a merciless exploitation to gain wealth at the expense of others.

Wealth is one value, and thinking is another; the pursuit of wealth is one vocation, and the pursuit of thinking is another; the end of wealth is the accumulation of capital; the end of thinking is the possibility of the opening up to the disclosure of truth. Clearly, these two values have antithetical forms, vocations, and ends. The very difficult question that awaits us is this: How can any individual, given the open-endedness of the activity of self-construction, construct values that truly fulfill him/her as a moral/rational being?

Strictly speaking, self-construction is one of human beings' intrinsic properties. Any individual, as a possibility, constructs values as he/she deems fit. The rightness and wrongness of values does not enter into the initial phase of the self-construction of values. The ordering of values, as I argued earlier, may enter into the self-construction of values at the latter phase of the activity of construction. Initially, to emphasize again, judgment should not accompany construction. Construction must be as free as possible from the notion of judgment so that, through creativity, human beings can reveal ontologically the possibility of freedom.

When asked, individuals can provide several reasons for choosing either wealth or thinking as a value. Consider the following possible reasons that individuals may give for having different values.

1. Wealth is an end in itself. Wealth is an avenue toward heaven. Working hard—which may often require us to step on others—and saving money is a noble activity in the eyes of the creator. There is nothing wrong with privately amassing wealth—even God will reward such an activity. The wealthy will inherit not just this world but the next world as well. One may, of course, argue that the above reasoning is a distortion of God's ways. In spite of this objection,

however, adherents refuse to listen to arguments. These individuals are essentially convinced that God is on their side and that they should not yield to arguments. Such individuals indeed construct values, but their self-construction is grounded upon a one-sided argument.

2. Other individuals, who choose thinking as a value, may reason thus: Thinking, like wealth, is a definite activity. It too has an end. Wealth enriches the body, and thinking enriches the soul. In fact, it is critical thinking that could also enrich and fulfill the comfortable body of the wealthy—if the wealthy were willing. For the one who values thinking, the body requires the basic human necessities—food, shelter, and adequate money but not wealth. Wealth is an unnecessary luxury. The adequate necessities of life are crucial for the human soul to be put in the condition to be able to develop its capacity for thinking. If the soul is overwhelmed by the desire for wealth, it would be prevented from cultivating the desire for thinking. The desire for thinking does not require wealth for it to be cultivated. It only requires the adequate necessities that make life worth living. Besides, thinking may provide its practitioners a wealth of another kind. I wish to call it spiritual wealth, a form of wealth that silently teaches human beings their obligations to themselves, to unknown others, and to the world in which they live.

3. There are individuals who are motivated by the restless quest for status as well. For these individuals, man is a status-seeking being. Man seeks and obtains wealth by any conceivable means, since the end of wealth is the attainment of status as the main point of life. The perpetual seeking of status often leads to a hostile confrontation with the activity of thinking. A thoughtful person may come to the conclusion that insofar as one is guided by the restless quest for status, he/she is not really living right, he/she must fundamentally change his/her nature. The devoted thinker sometimes denounces the unexamined life as not worth living, feeling that this miserable world must change and that he/she must participate in changing it.

The quest for status, one may argue, is nothing more than a particular expression of what human needs have become under a determinate form of human society, contrived by specific human beings, with money, wealth, and power as ends. For the adherents of the concept of man as a status-seeking being, the quest for status is an integral part of the structure of being. Recalling the structure of the human soul that I diagrammatically portrayed earlier, status is a part of the irrational aspect of the soul—the aspect that consciously refuses to be guided by reason or by reflective and meditative thinking. Therefore, the adherents conclude, humankind's quest for status is not merely a relative, particular expression of human nature, but also a constant and ontological expression of his/her nature.

4. The quest for power is a definite value for a considerable number of individuals. Indeed, power has served as a definite value for human beings all the way from the classical period in Greece to the modern age. Why does power continue to serve as a regulative ideal in modernity?

To think of power as itself a definite value with a specific end brings us to reflect directly on several central questions.

When various individuals construct different values—such as wealth, thinking, status, and power—as ends, how do they decide on the merits of these different values? Who judges and how is one value judged as either superior or inferior to another?

No matter what individuals are told not to do—even at the risk of death—they choose at their own discretion. They may appear to listen—to the injunctions of positive law, the admonitions of informed medical advisors, the prophetic warnings of priests, even the sustained advice of all their loved ones. When individuals construct ends, their ends are guided less by others who claim to know the good than by their own restless and capricious desires. This is, of course, a working generalization.

The non-reflective construction of ends (a) occurs without the individual contrasting ends, and makes a person (b) incapable of weighing different ends failing to choose the end that maximizes not merely the most immediate happiness but also a condition that stabilizes the person's mood. I now wish to elaborate on (a) and (b).

Choosing a Value Non-Reflectively

I will use wealth and thinking as two such ends and examine what individuals do. When individuals construct ends, they do so, although they may not be conscious of the ends of their actions, in order to cultivate themselves as moral subjects. A given individual works very hard and lives in a world that rewards hard work with money. The money that individuals acquire is not intended only to keep them alive. The harder they work, the more the reward; the more the reward the greater the desire to accumulate money. In this way, a simple and humanly legitimate desire to remain alive becomes transformed into the desire to accumulate money, in order to create new and self-perpetuating wants. These wants or needs become the objects of desire. Wealth becomes a want, a need. Individuals' desire for life and its plenitude is reduced to the desire for wealth. Wealth, we may say, becomes the particular end of life and becomes the means through which immediate happiness is acquired for such individuals.

The cultivation of any end requires devotion, commitment, and hard work in order to develop the appropriate material skills that correspond to the activity of ends. It would be unfair to think that the wealthy are nothing more than voracious, power-hungry, and ruthless individuals who arbitrarily accumulate wealth. Wealth as an activity obviously requires a corresponding skill. Let us call that an ''entrepreneurial'' skill guided by business acumen, a knack for profit making, appropriate timing, relevant human contacts, intelligent risk taking, etc. There is thus a distinct form of calculative, business-oriented thinking to which individuals devote themselves for the sake of the particular goal of becoming wealthy.

In the course of acquiring wealth, it is possible that the wealthy are compelled to take advantage of the poor who serve them as their employees. The need to maximize profit might force a businessman to pay his/her employees less than they deserve, and this without the knowledge of the employees; or the businessman may pay minimum wages, provide inhumane working conditions, and force the unnecessary infliction of psychological torture on some rebellious workers. The businessman could do all these deliberately and not feel an iota of pain or a sense of moral shame. He does it because the end that he decided to choose unfortunately imposes these abominable behaviors on him.

Wealth as an end requires a particular means. Calculative thinking is the appropriate means. The businessman as a human being, however, is also a potentially rational/moral being and thus he/she is expected to restrain himself/ herself from irrational desires. The ancient moral philosophers introduced the notions of self-control and self-restraint in order to make it possible for individuals to become less ruthless and more caring for others. Thus, the businessman, who could ruthlessly take advantage of his/her employees, confronts the powerful tension between what he uncaringly does and what he could caringly and rationally do. Calculative thinking, we might say, confronts rational/moral thinking. For the ancients, it is those who (a) are aware of the tension between amoral desires and moral desires, (b) decide to deliberately struggle against their capricious desires, and (c) can thus cultivate less resentful enemies against their greed that are capable of becoming moral subjects.

Such individuals, I wish to argue, by interpreting the ancient moral philosophers, are capable of contrasting ends—such as wealth as an end versus moral/ critical thinking as an end—given that individuals are interminably confronted by the dictates of their rational and irrational desires.

Weighing Different Ends and the Failures

Choosing a value nonreflectively leads to the incapacity to weigh different ends and the failure to choose the end that both maximizes immediate happiness and stabilizes mood. I noted above that the businessman who is motivated by wealth, when confronted with an ambiguous moral situation in which he himself has to restrain the desire to seek wealth, is thereby compelled to contrast ends. This proper contrasting of ends requires the engagement of our capacity for prudent judgment. Given that the two ends of wealth and moral/rational thinking are profoundly different, we need the capacity to judge prudentially when we want to weigh ends and choose the one that suits us the best as rational/moral human beings.

The need to weigh ends is not an inevitable consequence of all ends per se. If there exist self-sufficient, complete, and conflict-free ends, then my argument that we need a yardstick with which to measure the most suitable need for us as potentially rational/moral beings does not apply, and my argument becomes useless. However, if I am right in that most ends do come into conflict, and that human beings are then compelled to contrast ends, weigh the ends that they are contrasting and choose accordingly, then we need to think very seriously—as the ancients have done—about the possibility of founding some truly inspiring pluralistic norms.

The notion of norm gave the ancients a most difficult puzzle to solve, and we the moderns are as much in the dark as they were. The ideal of all the great thinkers was and continues to be the identification of a norm or norms that could provide the absolutely correct path on the long road toward the land of truth, justice, beauty, and happiness. The ideal, which is a self-imposed duty for some serious minds, is the isolation of a pattern, a model(s) that could judiciously guide and orient human beings. For some individuals, desires are only the source of judgment, but not an end per se. The desire for wealth, for example, is one way by which we orient ourselves to the world; the desire for a reflective rational/moral life is another. On the other hand, when an individual consistently and tenaciously habituates himself/herself to the singular end of wealth, the perpetual seeking of wealth becomes a style of existence, a way of life, a normal form of behavior, or an ethical standard. The individual becomes incapable of critically judging when the end introduces a dreadful and disturbing interruption into an otherwise carefree everyday life. Plato and Aristotle considered such a human being thoughtless but not ruthless, slavish but not ''evil,'' ignorant but not uneducable. It is for the sake of educating such individuals from the tutelage to dogmatic, unparadoxical, tensionless, and tyrannical desires that thinking or, if you prefer, philosophy emerged. Thinking was a form of therapy, a form of self-made medicine. Sick souls—the souls who defy inquiry—are incapable of nondogmatic communication, unable to sense the hidden deficiencies of a way of life, custom, or tradition and are all advised to seek the ultimate cure not from the philosopher (who is also a finite human being) but from the way of philosophy, the way of thinking.

One potent source of norms, the ancients reasoned, voicing a belief I fundamentally concur with (a belief I affirm in contrast to the dominant, mainstream, traditional interpretation of Greek moral philosophy) is not real philosophers—however wise, normal, and self-controlled they claim to be—but thinking or philosophy itself. It is thinking as an end that may rescue our unhealthy human soul. *It is not the philosopher—as a norm, as a model—who will redeem us. By thinking, we may be able to redeem ourselves.*[6]

Thinking, I wish to argue, as opposed to being wealthy, is a potentially conscious universal activity. Wealth is an unconscious particular activity. What I mean by a universal activity can be elucidated by the following example. Let A be an honest, God-loving, hardworking, consistent, formally educated owner of a business enterprise. The only world he knows, in addition to schools and universities, is the business world. By the accidents of history, he was born into a very wealthy family—a family that primordially blessed him with material wealth from his very first day. He did not choose to inherit his family's wealth; you may say, the family vicariously imposed wealth on him. His sole responsibility to his family was the silent promise that by honest devotion to God and science, hard work, consistency and a sustained study of wealth—that is, through the study of political economy—he will perpetuate the family tradition, the family's honor, status, power, and name. It is precisely to this end that he devotes his entire life, his material and spiritual being.

Now, let B be the slaves, workers, thieves, beggars, or criminals who inhabit our earth. A is destined to perpetuate wealth and B is destined—by his/her labor and consistency—to provide his/her body and intelligence as a necessary means for the end of the activity, which is wealth. For A, wealth is the end of life; for B, his/her body is the necessary means to achieve wealth. Wealth realizes itself in the wealth the slave creates for the master; thus, slavery becomes the necessary consequence of the natural activity of the production of wealth. Both A and B truly believe that life as activity is composed of accumulating wealth and enslaving others to do it. A believes that he is a "blessed" possessor of other human beings, and B is compelled to accept the natural fact of being a thing, an article, born to be possessed by the "blessed."

The ancients were right in their insistence that slavish are those who cannot control their desires. If that is the case, then one must also argue that slavish also are the masters, who cannot control the desires that force them to use other human beings as a means to developing the institution of self-proclaimed paragons of virtue. The regulative ideal of loving the philosophically fulfilling life, or a way of life guided by thinking, can in no way—to the extent that one is a rational/moral human being—justify the ruthless use of other human beings on the unjustified ground that those who were born to the condition of slavery, produced by convention, are also slaves by nature.[7]

One could, of course, use power to prevent oneself from asking certain questions. Those questions that touch the deep bottom of the foundation of norms and that delve to the ocean floor of truth may not even be given a forum. The holders of power must necessarily cling to the foundation of the seat of power. The hidden agenda in ancient moral discourse is the use of truth to justify a possible untruth.

It is in fact the slave (the other) that makes the existence of the master (the master of language and thought) possible. A owes his material life to B. It is B's endurance, patient labor, and spiritual nobility that made A's serene, secluded, philosophic life a definite actuality. A, as a self-proclaimed master, however, refuses to recognize B—his own other—as his genuine fulfillment, the true realization of A's spiritual and material well-being. Rather, A attempts to unjustly and irrationally designate B as the true other—the other who does not and cannot possibly belong to the same world to which A belongs. A refuses to use reason thoughtfully and meditatively. A uses reason rather calculatingly. For A, B is only a means, a thing, an article, by the body of whom wealth is created. The fact that B is born into the condition of slavery and A is born into the condition of mastery convinces A that B is indeed an inferior, a lesser human being who must be controlled, dominated, and enslaved. For A, B is incapable of self-mastery and self-control. Therefore, he must be controlled by those who are the supposed exemplars of moderation. This is how the holders of power justified slavery. They used the unreasoned argument and gave it the appearance of reason. They intellectually and politically used language to close the door on thinking. In all fairness though, Plato and Aristotle did not fail to recognize that true freedom is reached in the unconditional realization of human needs—such as the need for food, sex, friendship—and that these needs emanate from our desires, our passions. Thus, it was not only the so-called slaves who desired without the mitigation of thinking. I am in fact arguing that the desire for wealth or for power is just as pernicious to the structure of the soul as is the desire for forms of Aphrodisia. The ancients were right in their denunciation of excesses. They are disappointingly wrong in thinking that excesses were the exclusive vices of the slavish members of humankind. What is even more disappointing is that the thinkers of modernity also inherited the prejudices of the ancients and that unthought-out, ideologically motivated premises have gradually contaminated the current analyses of the role of values, norms, language, and thinking itself, or so I will argue below.

POWER, MORALS, AND THE PROCESS OF NORMING IN MODERNITY

Modernity and Morals

Those who sacrifice and save are the ones who are destined to materially rule those conspicuous consumers who are driven by impulses and governed by their emotions. Those who dominate their desires, govern their emotions, and are capable of postponing the immediate gratification of their desires must necessarily and inevitably discipline those who cannot. The accumulation of money, as a consequence of the total internalization of the ideal of self-control, is a representation of power. When self-control descends to the level of civil society, when it melts into everyday social practices and becomes life, at that time the self-controlled hero of modernity's political economy emerges. Self-control as a moral and social practice and the self-controlled modern individual are fundamentals of power in modernity.

In what follows, I wish to argue for the thesis that the norming process in modernity has truly construed the meaning of self-control. Modernity has borrowed the ideal of self-control from the Greeks and used it as a way of grounding power. Political economy in particular gives self-control a reductionistic economic meaning that serves the purpose of differentiating those who should hold power from those who must be disciplined by power; those who are wealthy and therefore must rule from those who are poor and are therefore necessarily fit to be ruled.

It is in the activity of a self-controlled human being—a human being who has mastered the potential chaos of the desires by suppressing some, for example, the desire for perpetual sex, and by releasing others, such as the desire for meditation—that the nature of power is starkly revealed. Power has penetrated the ideal of self-control by infecting the content and the lifestyle of the self-controlled modern subject. The values that modern subjects have internalized—wealth, status, sexual partners, and friends—in most cases are not values that they have thought through and then resolved to adopt.[8] In most cases, values are assimilated through imitation, either unconsciously or dogmatically, or inculcated by fear of the power of disciplining modern societies. This power pushes modern disciplined individuals to conform, agree, obey, follow, flatter, and believe but never, never to question authority—and, most particularly, not to think independently as self-empowered subjects. But true values, I modestly contend, can be nurtured only by independent and honest thinking. The power of those whom we have to imitate, the silent glances of the models that we wish to be like, and the subtle but mendacious power of society all obstruct the initiative to create, innovate, imagine, fantasize, dream, and originate. The modern subject does think as a conformist but not as an originator of values that empower.

The capacity to think can easily atrophy if it is not practiced continuously and consistently. Any thing we imagine, anything we judge as immoral, or any action we undertake as exemplary can form an authentic imagination—moral or immoral, right or wrong—if and only if it is guided by a self-constructed mode of thinking, a self-construction that may yield self-empowered beings.

It is true that thinking cannot be defined. I myself, if pressed to define thinking, would not be able to provide a definitive definition. On the other hand, I can safely reflect about what we should not, cannot, and even must not do when we are genuinely thinking. When we are genuinely thinking, I contend, we should not accept norms per se as definitive, given, or sacred so that we can be exonerated from thinking. There is a norming process, however, that reason cannot ignore. The acceptance of norms must be preceded by the mastery of the inner design hidden by the process of norming. That inner design ought to be revealed by thinking. One of the fundamental parts of the inner design of norms is the subtle role of the desires in their relationship to power.

The desires themselves are both the sources and the victims of power. The desires are the sources of power when one imagines, judges, and acts at one's own discretion; the desires are the victims of power when what one imagines, judges, and acts originates elsewhere—such as from a great teacher, a revered priest, a well-reputed book, etc. It is when what one desires originates outside of one's innermost soul structure that the desires of others function as instructing, forcefully guiding, threatening, and intimidating him/her to imagine, judge, and act in the most insincere way. It is that resultant insincerity that compels one to assert that the invisible ever present desires of others are the concrete proofs of the presence of power and that power is invisibly infused with desires. The imaginations, moralities, and activities of others may be very good, indeed even superior to those who are following them. But that is not the point. The point is simply who is originating what, who is following whose norms, and how well one understands the way a given set of norms is designed. Of course,

Seyla Benhabib is right when she has brilliantly engaged Rawls and Habermas with the argument that the self cannot be hidden behind the "veils of ignorance," or, engage in disembodied "speech act situation." The self, and the norms it develops, are situated.[9] Nor is the self-constructing moral subject an isolated and atomistic being. Rather, this "unique" and "self-creating" being, following Amy Gutman "is not to be confused with a picture of 'atomistic' individuals creating their identities independently of each other. . . . Human identity is created, as Taylor puts it, *dialogically*, in response to our relations, including our actual dialogue, with others."[10]

Insincerity is the manifestation of the fear of the powerful other—the other who is guiding one's desires. The powerful presence of any external desire kills the burning fire of inner desire and, along with it, independent thinking. Authentic thinking must at all times struggle against the possible death of inner desire. Power need not kill directly by aiming at the body; power kills indirectly by aiming at the soul and its deep inner desire. The death of inner desire, which is the affliction of the soul and the body, is also the death of the capacity and willingness to think. Power afflicts us deeply when it discourages us from truly thinking by ourselves, for ourselves, and for those others among whom we live in solitude. The process of norming is then always penetrated by the power of the other, who would never let us be, in order that we may know who we were, who we are, and who we may become.

What is everyday life after all if it is not guided by the endless task of serious thinking—the type of thinking that dreams of possibilities, imagines utopias, improves fragile and inconsistent human characters, and converts our very existence into the struggle to live well? Life without the will and human curiosity to know for oneself, to discover the good, imagine the just, or self-construct happiness is utterly meaningless. It is precisely the meaninglessness of a life guided by the minds and hearts of others—the great exemplars—that self-construction of norms led by the vigor and boldness of independent thinking seeks to overcome. Imitation and modeling, as I have stressed above, are powerless in the face of self-constructed norms. Norms that are self-constructed have the capacity to give us truly stable, self-controlling, responsible, and original human beings, for whom everyday life is integrated with self-constructed principles that are self-empowering.

Power, Norms, and Values

Power, norms, and values are different concepts; in spite of their difference, however, they do work in concert. Power has something to do with the will to dominate, think, desire, and imagine for others; norms are standards, patterns, exemplary models of the correct, acceptable, decent, and normal ways of life; values are principles and desirable qualities by which individuals are discreetly educated so that they can structure their lives according to certain norms. Power, norms, and values work in concert in the cultivation of the moral subject.

Power, as the will to dominate, can frequently operate by using brute force in its drive to impose certain values in the particular form of norms. The process of norming, or more directly, the process of distinguishing "normal" ideas from "abnormal" ones can be accomplished by the brutal use of weapons. The force-oriented process of norming requires no subtlety; it suppresses rebellion and resistance by instilling fear of the echo of its violence. Discourse, principled reasoning, and dialogue have no place. Force is terroristic; it does not respect or fear anyone[11]; it has a very limited use for the subtle power of ideas.

Values are created and then formed into norms; the norms thus formed are actualized directly as social practices through the imposition of systems of violence. Values and norms are backed by pistols; language and rhetoric are used offensively and not communicatively. Norms and values are not actualized gradually and discreetly. Rather, they are actualized immediately. The firm digestion of values and norms as the contents of fully thought-out mental and moral cultures are not the fundaments of the force-oriented process of norming, whereas they would be a base for the ideas-oriented process of norming.

Power, values, and norms work in concert through the gradual and ideas-oriented process of norming as well. Under modernity, the ideas-oriented process of norming is the most dominant, although the force-oriented process of norming is available for immediate use when recalled or when the ideas-oriented process of norming has not taken root in the minds and hearts of modern subjects. The ideas-oriented process of norming is most vivid in the ways beliefs become states of mind or ideas become hegemonic. Consider the case of religious sentiments and the ways in which they function in our everyday lives as values, norms, and expressions of power.

I choose to speak about religious sentiments, that is, the capacity to believe in a God—as opposed to speaking about religion. The great religions of the world cannot be talked about in one great sweep, whereas it is reasonable to focus on religious sentiments or the capacity for belief via religion. The object and subject of religious sentiments is the possibility of believing in a God. This God need not necessarily be the Judeo-Christian one; He/She could also be another God of another culture. God, as the subject and object of rational belief, does not have a set of specifiable qualities. He or she is above and beyond color, race, sex, and culture. The language of God is always universal—it is the language of universal compassion, love, sisterhood and brotherhood, harmony and genuine communication.

It is by creating values—such as God is One, God is a Judeo-Christian, God is the author of the Ten Commandments, God is the creator of all values that we must uncritically follow—that we impute qualities, quantities, relations, and modalities to God. By so doing, some believers tend to reductionistically reduce the capacity to believe. The universal God thus becomes the particular God of a particular segment of humankind; particularity, which is otherwise alien to the most intelligent Being, becomes one of God's properties.

In this instance, we use the hidden desires that compelled us to believe in the Judeo-Christian God to deny the possibility of becoming a believer without necessarily embracing the Judeo-Christian God. Those who do not believe in the God of our choice are subtly pushed out of the otherwise open circle that houses religious sentiments. It is not enough sometimes to possess the capacity for religion; that capacity must be unconditionally premised by the dogma that God is Judeo-Christian. This dogma is anchored upon power, upon one of its fundaments—the will to dominate via values, which in the form of norms are used to coerce others to believe in what the powerful believe. In this particular way, often without conscious intentions, beliefs are invested with a power that secludes, excludes, classifies, and judges; religious sentiments do not thereby fraternize and harmonize but rather divide, persecute, and produce warring sentiments.

It is desires that stir the heart, and it is thinking—a rather calm, cool, judicious and extraordinarily gentle activity—that in turn calms, cools, and gently guides the human heart. When religious sentiments are stirred by desires, it is the fiery, prejudiced, partial, and rough edge of desires that causes us to magnify our particularity at the expense of our universality, our differences at the expense of our measured similarities. When we are solely guided by our passions, we experience God as a particular God, one who abnegates His/Her universal love and respect for humankind. We thus become disrespectful of all those human beings who think, experience, and feel God in ways we cannot and do not; this feeling begins to serve the perilous goal of power—the will to dominate the different, the truly independent, the nonconformists.[12]

Desires do not always stir the heart only toward the will to dominate. Under different conditions, desires can stir the heart toward the will to cooperate, think, feel, and imagine not *for* others or *against* others, but *with others*. I call this self-empowerment. I wish to develop this point a bit later. For now, I simply want to share with you my awareness of its deeply buried presence somewhere in the human soul.[13] It is a presence that can be retrieved, but not without major difficulties. This possibility is at least a source of hope.

It is tempting to assume that when A dominates B, A is thus free of domination by any other force. A, as a dominator, seems definitely uncontrolled by any human or nonhuman force; A seems in total control of his/her life. The assumed fact that A thinks so does not validate the assumption. The fact that A is unaware or not fully conscious of the ways in which the machinery of domination works does not liberate A from the burden of thinking nor from the realization that his/her desires might be under the domination of the inner forces, such as resentment, spite, alienation, prejudice, ignorance, irrational faith, arrogance, and pride. Thus, the religious person who ignorantly, arrogantly, and, in the name of his/her own freedom, excludes and even kills those who do not share his/her particular God, particular idol, and particular ideals is also a victim of domination. Person A is a victim of the domination of his/her desires— wrongly and thoughtlessly directed desires. Person B is dominated by the desires of person A, whereas person A is dominated by the inner desires of the unreasoned which are manifested in prejudicial beliefs and behaviors.

Human beings have the potential to maintain a vision of God as a universal being—the God of humankind. Their desires often are expressive of this vision; but it is a vision that modernity does not actively encourage. This potential vision of God as a sublime intelligence that commands the depth and loyalty of faith, as well as the conviction and persuasion of reason, is precisely what has not as yet become disentangled from the avarice, one-sidedness, and rancor of power. Power, when negatively used, divides, produces spite, and cultivates resentment. When power leads the desires toward the ideals of the "beautiful and sublime," it can nurture the bonds of love, brotherhood and sisterhood, unity and diversity, particularity and universality, rational freedom, liberty and conformity, and tradition and innovation.

Power, norms, and values always work in concert. I have above attempted to use religious sentiments as an example of how power, norms, and values can become stuck. In the case of religious sentiments, I have argued, power uses the desires both negatively and positively. Power uses the desires negatively when it selects values and norms—such as the value that God is a Judeo-Christian being—to exclude human beings whose vision of God is different. Power could also use religious sentiments to redefine and innovate a vision of God that is authentically universal, nondivisive, and comprehensively and deeply reasonable. The modern attitude, I have argued, has not discovered the universal God and has used power negatively. The God of true intelligence does not yet exist in our time, but the possibility of thinking about such a God is a comforting source of hope. Modernity has yet to retrieve such a God, a God who would empower the self as a plenitude, a convergence of dissimilarities.

Power, Taste, and Value

The relationship among power, taste, and value may be formulated as follows. Person A exercises power over person B when A, under the guise of rational persuasion, attempts to effect A's taste for a value onto B, a value B knows is contrary to B's own original taste. The various and often paradoxical styles of existence as well as the ethics of living, in a relative and absolute sense, have something to do with the unique and subjective phenomenon of human taste. Tastes are themselves forms of value. They may be considered values that express a state of mind; an orientation toward the human world; the state of the desires themselves; a relentless and painful struggle to live rightly; a quest for the appreciation, understanding, and recognition by others of one's way of life, and an attempt not only to tolerate the diverse styles of existence but to truly recognize them as respectable ways of life. Human tastes—however repulsive, shocking, paradoxical, or even irrational they may be—cannot be cultivated without the creative dimension of self-construction. Human tastes cannot blossom if they are continuously restricted by rules that are assembled by others.

Rules tell us very little about the rightness or wrongness of tastes as such. The taste for styles of existence is a very private value. A's taste cannot be absolutely judged as inadequate or useless from objective standard Z; if a need arises, A's taste, relative to B's taste, can be reasonably compared. When Z, an objective standard, becomes an absolute, it surreptitiously becomes a source of power. In this way, power can penetrate the formative process of the cultivation of tastes.

It is conceivable that a certain style of existence, such as married life, is intrinsically superior to another—say, a single person's life—or that heterosexuality is better than homosexuality, etc. However, those who are married, or those who love only the opposite danger should in no way coerce those who think and believe otherwise. Married life, heterosexuality, and religiosity are profoundly values, and as such deserve our deep respect and unconditional recognition; as values, they cannot be the objects of arbitrary judgments that condemn, persecute, classify, or normalize. These tastes for ways of life and styles of existence bring to their practitioners a sense of self-hood, a measure of happiness, a modicum of pride, and a feeling of control and self-reliance. They are values that are self-constructed; they are values that give a sense of deep satisfaction that language cannot fully articulate. As self-constructed values, they resist any conquest by the tastes and values of the power holders. If power is present at all in the construction of values, it is not the *external power* that is exercised by empirically identifiable individuals; rather, it is *internal power* that is the power of our deep passions, our desires. It is this internal power that I call self-empowerment.

True, person A's taste for a particular style of existence—an existence that is characterized by drunkenness, gambling, or sexual lust may not be good for him/her. He/she, however, may not immediately see the harm; he/she may be immediately interested in simply creatively constructing a taste for a particular way of life, although this may be a way of life that he/she may one day be ashamed to remember. But growth toward a well-thought-out and artfully designed way of life is not easy. Harder still for us human beings is the challenge of doing good to our selves and all those we live with.

Warning someone of the potential danger of one style of existence in contrast to another, however, cannot be imposed by force or intimated by calculated indifference, nor can a lifestyle be discouraged by the withdrawal of recognition. It certainly cannot be contained by physical or psychological torture. A change from one style of existence to another may be made possible by the extension of encouragement combined with deep and respectful love.

Styles of existence are nourished by taste. Taste is a value and values are resistant to other values just as one style of existence resists the advances of another. Authentic dialogue between the holders of many different tastes is possible if it is grounded upon the absolute respect of all tastes, therefore all values. This respect of values does not preclude the possibility of resisting values that are disrespectful of the dignity, freedom, and liberty of some human beings. The freedom to create values per se does not mean that all values are equally great, just, and good. Some values—independent of the imperative of self-construction that dignifies creativity—are inherently "evil," bad. If a value's worthiness to human beings is questionable, then it is truly irresponsible not to criticize it or, if necessary, even to resist it with violence. One such value is slavery. Values that are proven to be disrespectful and abusive of human intelligence must not be taught at public institutions; if they have to be taught at all, the teaching must be done with a critical bent.

The process of growing into a human being, capable of fully respecting himself/herself and capable also of creating values, during which a person cultivates the humanly appropriate tastes for reasonable styles of existence, does not analytically entail an indiscriminate craving for all values. All values are neither equally good nor worthy of the same respect. There are fundamental differences among values as there are among the human beings who uphold them. The values of human beings are essentially deep reflections of different histories and biographies. Some tastes or values become significant only after a sustained and turbulent path of mental and moral growth is traveled. While traveling that growing path, some values may be constructed and immediately appreciated by all of us, while others may never become certain good values for us, or they may take longer than others for us to recognize as intrinsically good for us; still others may never be developed into sensible judgments. The path of moral and mental growth is long and frustrating as well as tragic. It is marked by starry nights and dark days. As human beings, we have a capacity for good and bad tastes. We are also historical beings, which means that we create values, and sometimes we are born to values we then struggle to appropriate in a historically meaningful way—a way that directly speaks to us and that is attentive to the language of our desires, which are those powerful multiplicities and differences.

Truth, Language, and Desire

Since time immemorial, truth, like language and desire, has been used as the fundamental of power. Modernity, like the historical periods which preceded it—antiquity, the Middle Ages, and the Renaissance—has used truth, language, and desire in the establishment of powerful values.

The inextricable connection of truth, language, and desire is really not peculiar to modernity. Since our appearance on Earth, we human beings have always been struck by the absolute infinity of truth; we have always used and struggled with speech; we have used and abused language; and the most fundamental fact about our human constitution is that we are overcome by our desires—the desires that impel us to hope for ideals. We, of course, are often deeply disappointed when we realize the ultimate unattainability of certain ideals; this disappointment is a source of a tragic sense of life.

When we honestly reflect, we cannot help recognizing the tragic fact that we are fundamentally desiring beings. The desires that we may strongly affirm are dimensions of the very structure of our being, our soul. The serious ancient thinkers, Plato and Aristotle, knew the importance of human desires. For them, the desires had a dual nature, as the sources of potential disaster and potential joy. Eros could easily show us the way to truth if it is rightly used just as Aphrodisia could prevent us from ever contemplating truth when we are over-determined by the needs of the body.

Eros and Aphrodisia constitute a major part of our everyday life. Hence, in the ethics of the ancients, a meditative attention was given to the care of the self. Indeed, one could affirmatively say that life without the desires or the subjects and objects of desire is almost meaningless. Desires cement us to earthly life and give us the will to live. Desires provide us with the stimulus to live in concert with our reflective power.

Human beings, as desiring beings, have a passion for truth—the duty to know the nature of God, the structure of the universe, the meaning of human existence, and the purpose of living—expressed in language. It is language that is the most mystical expression of human thought. Language, the house of human beings, theoretically should be the most intimate, the nearest, and the warmest, whereas in reality it is often the least known, the most aloof, the most distant, and even the coldest. It is the "nature" of language, as well as thinking, to disclose itself as paradoxical and contradictory.

The exceedingly difficult nature of thinking is, in the end, a reflection of the impenetrability of the desiring being's articulation of his/her presence in the signs, symbols, words, and representations of language. Signs, symbols, words, and representations of "things" we desire stand for something. This "something" of tastes, which are values, is gradually frozen, through the presence of power, into tradition, custom, habit, ways of life, styles of existence, or ethics of "correct living."

In what follows, I wish to share with you a series of questions that must be reflected upon if we are to seriously study the roles of power, truth, language, and desire in our relentless quest to become moral subjects who are authentically self-constructing and self-empowered.

1. What is the nature of the language by which we attempt to fully communicate our desires and often uncritically assume we have succeeded?

2. How do we know that the things we desire are really generated by us as opposed to merely being the products of subtle processes of socialization or the effect of hegemonic ideas?

3. When and how would we know, even in the act of self-construction, that we are constructing values as historical beings who can freely and imaginatively create varied possibilities for leading our lives?

4. Who orders things by developing schemas and categories of classification and representation?

5. If it is the power holders who do the ordering of things and who consequently make it possible for us to say certain things and not others, why should we give them this ultimate power—the power to order the world?

6. Is the order of the world an exact representation of the order of the primordial desires?

7. Is the birth of science and the representational power of language that made science possible an acceptable dogma?

8. Could language—given its ultimate mysticalness—ever be capable of fully disclosing the hidden longings of the desires?

9. Did desires arise prior to language? If they did, how can desires be represented by language, of which desires are the foundation?

10. If the foundation is not fully known and, furthermore, if the expression of the foundation—namely, language itself—is unknown, how can language be used as a tool?

11. What is representation itself? Can person A ever fully represent person B's desires?

12. Can person A's self-chosen style of existence, when imitated, be reproduced or even modeled after by person B, thus become fully represented?

13. Can the road toward leading one's life—as a moral project—ever be represented by those who know the correct way of living?

14. Should the path toward constructing a "reasonable" and pragmatically useful style of existence not be grounded upon a participative engagement of the moral subject?

15. Is it possible for the desires to more adequately express themselves in engaged communicative participation than in representation?

16. Is participative disclosure of the desires in language potentially nihilistic?

17. If human beings are possibilities and if possibility is freedom, does it follow that anything will be allowed insofar as human beings express their freedom?

18. What are the merits of self-construction as an affirmation of possibility, therefore as an expression of freedom?

19. What has modernity done to truth, language, and desire that other historical periods did not do?

20. Are power and domination the same?

I will continue my attempt to answer these questions. I specifically wish to share with you my meditations on questions 18 and 19. I think that these questions are directly relevant to the concerns of this book, particularly questions of the fundamentals of modernity. (I will deal with the last question in chapters 3 and 4 below.)

In question 18, I asked: What are the merits of self-construction as an affirmation of possibility, therefore as an expression of freedom? I have stressed that it is by self-construction that individuals can learn things that have durability. Anything that is self-taught is learned once and for all. During the process of constructing, individuals actually sense, master, and feel the inner structure of values. Some individuals might think that constructing values is interesting only as a game and that individuals are more fascinated by the game than they are by the possible outcome of the struggle. This is a valid doubt that is applicable to some individuals. Conceding that there are actual individuals who behave without values, I nevertheless wish to think about those cases in which there is no concern with games but more concern with values.

Human beings, when given actual opportunities, are value creating. As value creators, they are the potential sources of hitherto unknown ways of living, of novel ideas, and of infinite visions. True, just because ideas are novel, they are not thus useful and worthy of our attention. The danger with labeling ideas before they take root, however, is that by labeling ideas, we indirectly obstruct their potential to inspire us to listen, see, and be awakened from our deep sleep. We human beings are incapable of fully knowing who we are, what we can create, and how we must act. It is the nature of action not to fully disclose its intentions, and so human beings as value creators are incapable of anticipating the moral/rational consequences of their actions. During the process of self-construction, the individual moral actors are incapable of knowing the consequence of their actions. Individuals can only act; they act for the sake of creating values. They can never act, though, for the sake of values that are societally approved of as normal, acceptable, and healthy. I am not saying that individuals should completely reject tradition. In fact, there are sectors of tradition that are truly worth preserving and must be critically appropriated. What I am saying is that tradition cannot exhaust the capacity to create values and that new values can be created only through self-construction, guided by what I call *reflective presence*, under the atmosphere of *existential seriousness*.

Tradition, customs, habits, etc. can indeed be used effectively in self-construction. Individuals can readily and richly draw from traditional experience-tested ways of life. Tradition, we might say, can be worked on with an emancipatory intent. Tradition, however, can also be used with a conformistic intent; typically it is used non-emancipatorily.

One of the merits of self-construction is that it aims at the ideal of autonomously producing values—values that are intrinsically unpredictable. The initial stages of producing these novel values is always difficult and frustrating. The first experience of value creation is certainly more trying than would be the experience of following models or simply imitating the values of others. Novel values, as opposed to the values of tradition, are more risky and more frightening. Consequently, individuals are less prone to construct novel values. They prefer, instead, to conform to existing standards of being. Novel values are also tragic. During the initial phases of value-creation—the phases that depart from the familiar terrain of tradition—individuals do not know what they are doing; they tend to harm themselves.

Creativity, I must stress, is not painless. Like the road to knowledge, creativity is always painful, risky, and frightening. Constructing values, which as a rule goes beyond assembling the readily available components of tradition, is also risky and painfully trying. Human beings, without engaging in the self-construction of values, might always be overcome by the powerful winds of prejudice, closed-mindedness, thoughtlessness, and guidance by self-proclaimed experts. Such experts try and often succeed in persuading individuals to remain dependent, imitative, and unwilling to create anything new. This trend is particularly prominent during modernity.

Question 19 was: What has modernity done to truth, language, and desire that the other historical periods did not do?

In a disturbing sense, modernity, certainly much more than antiquity, has accorded too much importance to the presumptuous thesis that rational knowledge is the foundation of action and that it is those who "know" who must show those who do not know—but who ceaselessly desire—how they must lead their lives. I call this thesis—a thesis that distinctly captures the modern attitude—presumptuous because it unjustly and arrogantly accords too much power to the experts of modern rational-scientific knowledge. Modernity, as the age of experts and discipliners, takes away from ordinary individuals the capacity to learn, the capacity to learn and develop their hidden potential (the potential for self-construction) by listening to the silent voices of their own inner reason and conscience rather than to outside advisors. The experts of knowledge, in the modern age, even have the dangerous power to decide what is right for individuals when these individuals are not rationally and morally persuaded by the experts. In modernity, the experts are distinctly privileged to discipline the "irrational desires" of the maladjusted ordinary individuals.

The quest for a foundation or a ground that does not universalize a false particular or a one-sided vision is an admirable project. Such a project deserves our support, recognition, and objective admiration. The project ought to be self-imposed by all reflective individuals as an absolute duty, an absolute obligation; it is the absolute duty of a human being as an inherently metaphysically disposed being. It is this silent metaphysical disposition toward uncovering a ground that makes us markedly human. I wish that the modern attitude had it in abundance. The foundation of modernity is not the metaphysical disposition as I wish it would be, but instead is arrogant, one-sided science. It is this ground that I am challenging. I am also attacking modernity's tendency to accord unlimited powers to particular worldviews and visions, including many that are morally questionable, power-centered, and proudly one-sided. These visions with the hidden will to power, in the name of foundational knowledge and founding experts, prevent ordinary individuals from ever becoming mentally and morally mature individuals. There is too much leadership by experts and too little growing; there is excessive protectiveness of the helpless individual by those who think for him/her and very little trust in the individual to self-construct durable values. It is, in short, the right of the individual to trust his/her immediately felt desires and styles of existence that I have been attempting to defend philosophically. I wish to defend this thesis further with the following arguments.

Human beings are potentially and communicatively active, metaphysically disposed inquirers, critically philosophic and existentially serious. Human beings, who are communicative, inquiring, critical thinkers—if they are trustfully and respectfully given an opportunity—can responsibly act on their immediate desires. In the course of desiring, they can learn the important virtue of self-control—the self-control that may allow them to enjoy life without either excess or unnecessary austerity. The ability to govern one's own innermost desires makes any expert an unneeded guide. Human beings, to the extent that they visibly rule themselves, do not need others to guide them. Rather, they need other human beings to recognize their struggle to truly become autonomous; they need others to continuously and honestly encourage them to cut the umbilical chord of dependency which is moral and mental slavery. Self-empowered individuals do not *dominate* others; they confer power on others, thus empowering themselves and all others with whom they are destined to live.

Human beings can learn how to desire only if they are given the minimal opportunity to experience desire for their immediate wants, perceived as pleasure giving. The capacity to inquire, to engage in metaphysical wondering, to be communicatively active, and to be critically philosophic can emerge out of *the desires* themselves. Human beings, from what I have attentively observed, are not just immediate desirers. They are also critical judges of their immediate desires, and quite capable of abandoning some of their pernicious desires. Human beings are desiring beings in another sense. The transcendental activities of inquiry, communication, and critical thinking are sought after only to the extent that they are pleasure-giving activities or the activities are pleasurable themselves. I am, of course, not claiming that all human beings are born this way; I am, however, claiming that human beings can learn to grow to appreciate the life of thinking and the critical moral power involved in constantly dominating the desires by self-control. Rarely do human beings desire to inflict pain upon themselves or others as a pleasurable activity or a way of life. It is a fact that there are spiteful human beings. But we truly do not know that cruel behavior gives them pleasure; we only assume that it does. We should at least question that assumption. There are individuals who, instead of giving pain to others, attempt to give joy instead; such individuals actively desire the good, the just, and the happy, although they never attain it.

Styles of existence, as grounded upon the desires, cannot be apriori accepted or dismissed, or normatively disciplined, by the screening power of rational-scientific knowledge. The will to rational-knowledge, like the will to trust immediately appealing sense-knowledge, is also grounded upon other forms of desire, that is the desire of intuitive-aesthetic knowledge and the knowledge of the religious sentiments. To deny that the will to rational-knowledge is desire-seeking is really to sacrifice honest communication to ideological mystification.

At best, we must concede a hermeneutical circle here and not a foundational superiority of one vision over another. We can, if we want, recognize several inherently different ways of comporting ourselves in the world—all of which are humanly rich ways of sensing and thinking about our common physical world. There are no superiorities here—only differences that allow the self-constructing moral/rational subjects to meaningfully value the world and human beings. It is out of these differences that values grow, norms arise, and horizons fuse.

Unless we heed a hermeneutical circle here, we will mislead ourselves into thinking that we thereby are not using the arbitrary language of modern science against the claims of moral/rational thinking and that we are pitting modern rational-scientific knowledge against the humble wish of the desires to be and to know.

Furthermore, the desires are, in a fundamental sense, expressions of human beings to determine how they ought to live their lives, what they must do, what they should desire, and finally how they must act. The will to self-determination cannot be guided by the experts of rational-scientific knowledge or even by the self-proclaimed representatives of God. The desires are the ultimate origins of freedom, a freedom that is expressed in the language of human speech. Desires in their formative stage are immediacies; they are initially informed by imme- diate intuitive knowledge which is articulated in the language of myth, super- stition, art, and poetry. Modernity's quick dismissal of these rich sources of our humanity is really shocking. Modernity, with the aid of the modern disciplines of anthropology, psychology, and sociology, has progressively emptied human beings of their complex and often unclassifiable human constitution. The clas- sification of human beings into human types is really the beginning of their slow death. Perhaps without our intention, we have already killed human beings by religiously and scientifically denying their right to be, their right to create new values, and their right to learn by constructing. The right to determine the way one should lead his/her life loses its moral/rational power if it is assumed by representatives of any kind. Freedom, as the expression of possibility, cannot be represented; it can only be participatively created by conscious and consci- entious human beings.

Modernity, however, continues to use rational-scientific knowledge as a cri- terion by which certain orientations to the world are elevated to the status of normal knowledge and others are systematically eliminated as modes of knowl- edge, styles of existence, and ethics of living. Language is systematically and subtly used and abused in this process of accepting and rejecting forms of knowledge, styles of existence, and ethics of living. Certain ways of living never blossom to full maturity; they are killed on the level of silent cries, murmurs, and faint voices of the oppressed, the humiliated, resentful, spiteful, and mad inhabitants of the underground. Raw human desires, regulated by self-generated reason, which might as well be the source of a potentially comprehensive and tolerant reason—are not even given a chance. It is Foucault's monumental con- tribution that he intelligently showed us how modern science has disciplined the self by highly politicized uses of power as domination.

At the immediately everyday level, to the extent that modernity judges the desires as necessarily dangerous, it is blocking the road toward self- determination, the road toward truths, and the truths of human beings in their effort to uncover the nature of Being. Being, true Being, is the totality of beings. But the Truth of Being can be manifested only in the truths of beings. Modern- ity's arrogant refusal to recognize the paths of truth toward Being is to defend unreason in the name of the reason of science.

Throughout the book, up until now, I have not raised the question, which is central to this book: Are power and domination the same? Both Foucault and Habermas, but particularly Foucault, tend to think that power by definition is domination. I want to argue against Foucault that power and domination are not the same.

Foucault tests the interpenetration of power and domination in his provocative deconstruction of the history of sexuality from the Greeks up to the early Christians. His chief conclusions of his intellectual journey may be summarized as follows.

The thinkers of antiquity—Socrates, Plato, Aristotle, and Xenophon—used language to categorize modes of conduct as normal and/or abnormal. Aphrodisia (sexuality) was one of the modes of conduct that was critically judged as abnormal insofar as its role in (1) generating fear, (2) functioning as a model of conduct, (3) providing an image of stigma, and (4) serving as an example of abstinence.[14]

As Foucault put it, for the ancient thinkers, it is "the relationship with the self that enabled a person to keep from being carried away by the appetites and pleasures, to maintain a mastery and superiority over them, to keep his senses in a state of tranquility, to remain free from interior bondage to the passions, and to achieve a mode of being that could be defined by the full enjoyment of oneself, or the perfect supremacy of oneself over oneself.[15]

Plato and Aristotle associated sexuality with a force, an *energia*, that was prone to excess. Thus, they both called for a severe restraint of sexuality lest it lead the self as well as the community in which the self lives to inevitable destruction. Unregulated sexuality is a tyrant that ought to be resisted by the stringent laws of the community. In this way sexuality was systematically problematized by the ancients. To help the inner self to effectively hamper unregulated sexuality, Plato and Aristotle proposed that wisdom, courage, moderation and knowledge should serve as the guides for the self's struggle to overcome the tyranny of the pungent passion of sexuality.[16]

Those who succumb to the passion of sexuality are slavish. They are unfit to rule. Power and sexuality are intimately related. Those who can control themselves are destined to rule others as well. The litmus test of sexuality is the relationship between adult males and boys. For Plato, Foucault contends, the love of boys was unnatural. Those lovers of boys who pursue their loves for the sake of sexuality are inauthentic. Their love is not the disclosure of truth, the truth that emerges from the relationship to boys, boys as epitomizers of wisdom. True love, as the love of boys, is an erotic relationship. The love should not consummate in the unnatural form of aphrodisia.

When love of boys is sexualized, then who penetrates whom becomes poignantly important. *Penetration is an act of power, power as domination.* Artemidorm, for example, examined dreams as relationships of power, domination, and submission.[17] The significance of sexual dreams is entrenched in ideas of who is penetrating whom, therefore who is ruling whom. The ruler penetrates and the ruled is penetrated. In this particular sense, sexuality is made a focus of power. *Note that power is experienced not as self-empowerment but rather as the vehicle of domination.*

Furthermore, the frequency and modes of sexuality that are oriented toward pleasure without procreative ends becomes a subject of medical discussion. Thus, Plato, Aristotle, and Galen wrote about sexuality extensively and gave advice to its careless practitioners. Some typical pieces of advice are (1) sexual acts must consummate in the production of children, (2) sexual acts must closely follow the seasons so that they can be done properly, (3) the soul must be in a good condition in order to restore the health of the body, (4) good diets are the key to good sexual life, (5) excess of any kind must be avoided, (6) sex must be performed within the context of marriage between members of the opposite sex or else the sexual act is unnatural. Thus, the love of boys was judged as abnormal and unnatural. John Rajchman is right when he wrote, "according to Foucault, in Greek ethics, there was nothing like our 19th-century category of deviancy. Despite an elaborate code of courtship to regulate the relations between men and boys of good families, nobody was constituted as a homosexual, nor, therefore, as a heterosexual, kind of person. . . . Greek ethics was not morality of normalizing populations. Nor was it a Kantian morality of obedience to universalisable rules."[18]

For Foucault, of course, it is question 6 that is the most problematical in that it naturalizes a relationship between the sexes that is otherwise a historical act conditioned by the power of language, a language that arbitrarily denaturalizes the love of boys.[19] Thinkers such as Pseudo-Lucian have actually argued that the love of boys is a direct cosmological, political, and moral violation of nature. Consequently, the sexual practice ought to be systematically suppressed for the sake of the fortitude and decency of community.

All the above developments led Foucault to the inevitable conclusion that styles of existence are deeply penetrated by power. Even the ancients who were extolled to be the most tolerant observers of human sexuality broke the ground for modern science to specifically focus on forms of sexuality as supportive of community (monogamous, heterosexual) and destructive of community (homosexual, lesbian). In this fashion, Foucault concludes, "These new erotics organizes itself around the symmetrical and reciprocal relationship of a man and woman, around the high value attributed to virginity, and around the complete union in which it finds perfection."[20]

I, too, am going to return to the ancients, as did Foucault. Unlike Foucault however, I am going to focus on the way they conceived of power, particularly in regard to its relationship to domination. Before I study the ancients, however, I want to reflect on the relationship between power and domination. Are power and domination the same? My immediate response to the question is: no, they are not the same. They can be and ought to be distinguished. It is this thesis that I wish to defend below.

NOTES

1. The constructivist tradition is intelligently presented by John Rawls in his highly acclaimed work, *Political Liberalism* (New York: Columbia University Press, 1993). See lecture 3. I am grateful to his creative articulations of constructivism in moral philosophy. My views, to which I came on my own, are remarkably similar.

2. I have attempted to contrast the tradition established by Strauss and further popularized by Alan Bloom in *The Closing of the American Mind* from the constructivist tradition, in Teodros Kiros, "Self-Construction," *Journal of Social Philosophy* 25, no. 1 (1994): 104–105.

3. A major part of Plato's *Republic*, as I argue in chapter 3 below, idealizes the harmony of the body and mind. I am in agreement with Plato on this theme.

4. For a rich articulation of the sources of moral action, see Charles Taylor's distinctly Hegelian work, *Sources of the Self* (Cambridge: Harvard University Press, 1989). See also David A. Hollinger, *Postethnic America* (New York: Basic Books, 1995).

5. One of the most useful and systematic presentations of self-realization as an expression of self-determination is Ernst Tugendhat, *Self-Consciousness and Self-Determination* (Cambridge: MIT Press, 1986). See pp. 200–219. For a systematic treatment of the notion of self-determination, see Teodros Kiros, "Self-determination," *Journal of Social Philosophy* 22, no.1 (Spring 1994): pp. 50–65.

6. Here I am essentially disagreeing with Alan Bloom's interpretation of Plato as an educational elite who distrusts ordinary selves to think for themselves.

7. I disagree with Aristotle and those who interpret his moral philosophy with the arguments that I am developing here through the working out of the notion of self-construction as an act of freedom. See also John Dewey, *Freedom and Culture* (New York: Capricorn Books, 1939), pp. 3–50.

8. I read all of Kant's moral theory as an attempt to free human beings from tutelage to values that they did not construct through self-developed principles of legislation. See Kant's "What is Enlightenment" in *On History* (New York: Bobbs-Merrill, 1963) and his *Foundations of the Metaphysics of Morals* (Indianapolis: Bobbs-Merrill, 1963).

9. Seyla Benhabib, *Situating the Self* (New York: Routledge, 1992), pp. 178–203.

10. Amy Gutman, ed., *Multiculturalism* (Princeton: Princeton University Press, 1994), p. 7.

11. Hannah Arendt has compellingly analyzed the prepolitical nature of force as opposed to power, which is distinctly political in her *The Human Condition* (Chicago: University of Chicago Press, 1958).

12. In *Political Liberalism*, John Rawls has masterfully put religion in the private sphere of comprehensive doctrines that cannot be employed to justify unreasonable political principles of Justice. I agree with Rawls's analytic separation of rationality and reason. It is the conflating of the two that could produce terroristic civil wars in the name of rationality. See *Political Liberalism*, pp. 47–86.

13. I have developed this theme in Teodros Kiros, "Doing African Philosophy," *New Political Science* Vol 2, no. 32 (Summer 1995): 95–117.

14. Michel Foucault, *The Use of Pleasure* (New York: Vintage Books, 1986), p. 5.

15. Ibid., p. 31.

16. For an extensive treatment of the theme of sexuality in the works of Foucault, see

Rebecca Comay, "Excavating the Repressive Hypothesis," in *Michel Foucault: Critical Assessments*, ed. Smart (New York, London: Routledge, 1994).

17. Michel Foucault, *The Care of the Self* (New York: Pantheon Books, 1986), pp. 24–25.

18. John Rajchman "Ethics After Foucault," in *Michel Foucault: Critical Assessments*, ed. Barry Smart (London and New York: Routledge, 1994), p. 232.

19. Ibid., pp. 100–208.

20. Ibid., p. 232. For a penetrating analysis of the ethical dimension of sexuality in Foucault's work as a whole, see Rajchman, "Ethics after Foucault."

3

Self-Construction and the Desiring Subject: Power and Domination

WHAT IS DOMINATION?

The dominator and the dominated occasionally really wish to like one another. In reality, they truly cannot. They cannot because both, by virtue of the asymmetrical positions they hold, are put in spaces that foster hatred. Their positions project the negative memories of the reality of domination. Their ever present unequal positions are constant and living reminders of the horrible reality of their inequalities.

The dominator and the dominated are fundamentally human beings. This rather trite fact is easy to state. The dominator and the dominated are so conscious of this fact that they assert it thoughtlessly and automatically. It is startling to see that human beings, in the course of asserting this trite statement, betray the imperative implicit within it. This imperative is frequently violated by the practice of killing, harming, and abusing another person. The dominator asserts statement A and simultaneously does non-A action. The hypocrisy is truly shocking.

What is domination? Let the following definition serve as a working conceptualization of domination. When two human beings A and B are interacting within community C, their interaction ought to be that of equals since they are equal in their human power to think, their sincere efforts to seek practical knowledge, their need for food, shelter, and clothing, and their moral power to care for themselves and all others within community C. When A and B are equal in the above sense, one can infer that there is a minimum will to dominate. When the power of thinking, the striving toward practical knowledge, the availability of food, shelter, and clothing, and the exercise of the moral power of care are unequally possessed by A and B, the will to dominate becomes an inevitable tendency.

Domination has something to do with the capacity to think, possess practical knowledge, own the tools of wealth, and be able to act with moral power; but domination is also the direct consequence of the will, that is, the disposition and conscious struggle to act on what would otherwise remain abstract abilities. It is a disciplined struggle that wishes to change potentiality into actuality. Domination's nature is starkly disclosed in the realm of the actions, stances, and existential choices made by A and B as members of community C. I said above that the nature of domination is disclosed during the moments in which A is doing something to B, and that the effect—whatever it may be—discloses the true nature of domination.

Imagine the following case. Individual A finds it considerably easier to treat his friends selfishly and insensitively. At the same time, he knows that true friendship necessarily excludes a selfish and insensitive treatment of a genuine friend. But A's moral and intellectual soul structure—in spite of himself and what he wishes to be toward his friend—is pervaded by the will to dominate. Selfishness and insensitivity are manifestations/expressions of the will to dominate. A knows or is aware of the fact that friendship—genuinely understood—and A's practices in his interactions with his friends are not what they ought to be. The abstraction of friendship and the practice of selfishness and insensitivity are in deep conflict. They are contradictorily juxtaposed. A's life, which is grounded on a universal abstraction that calls for care and sensitivity, is contradicted by selfishness and insensitivity. A's soul is characterized by the absence of self-mastery because selfishness and insensitivity are dominating A's potential powers of care and sensitivity. A wants to overcome this contradictory life. What must or what can he do?

It seems very easy for individuals to selfishly, thoughtlessly, and insensitively do the bad rather than struggle to do the good, or at least, to do what is perceived to be the good, according to Aristotle.[1] Doing evil seems to come to human beings rather smoothly, naturally. There are no walls to be jumped, no roadblocks to be removed. While it seems natural to do what is perceived as bad, it does not seem as natural to do what is perceived as good. Doing perceived good seems to require a transnatural effort to begin doing it. To do good seems a burdensome venture into the exceedingly difficult task of going against our natural selves—the selves that readily move toward insensitivity and thoughtlessness. In short, we have to overcome our will to dominate others in order to emerge as human beings capable of overcoming the domination of reason by some of our spontaneous impulse of selfishness and insensitivity. A's project is located within a circle encompassing the will to dominate the other and the silent pressure between dominating and masking the will to dominate. What must she/he do?

Various individuals would conceive of their projects differently. A is no exception. A, if he/she so wishes, can do the following. A first has to make the firm decision that treating others thoughtlessly and insensitively is a tendency to be overcome. A honestly says to himself, ''I must struggle against the moral vices of insensitivity and thoughtlessness.'' Then taking the second step, A says to himself, ''I am going to struggle against myself.''

The next step is characterized by a period of struggle in which A is struggling against A. Initially, and even after a little while, this phase of the experience is quite trying. We know that A has decided to struggle against himself. There is an external power to which A can appeal when the road gets overwhelmingly difficult. A's ultimate appeal is inner reason, and if A is religious, inner reason is further guided by the power of rational faith. Inner reason and rational faith may occasionally show A what he must do and not do. The correct paths may thus be disclosed to A; given the disclosure, A decides rationally and morally. Just because an individual is reasonable and faithful, it does not follow that the correct decision will be revealed to him. What is certain is that on the road to the struggle against oneself—if such a struggle is warranted—the correct path to follow is the product of a relentless, perpetual trial and error. The emancipation of A from his dominating passions is decidedly a product of the truth resulting from this relentless and perpetual trial and error. At some future date this struggle may result in the victory of the self to conquer its passions.

When individual A engages in relentless and perpetual trial and error, it may be said that he/she is searching for some ''objective'' rational/moral principles that may guide him/her in the course of leading his/her life. These principles may after all be the paths that A is after. Those paths may in turn be the road maps[2]—not necessarily the brightest, the straightest of possibilities. By possibilities, I mean that the road maps may one day become truly bright, straight, rational/moral principles that many, if not all, thoughtful and sensitive individuals may choose to follow.

Domination over one's passions is a sincere, serious attempt in which an individual, such as A in our example, comes to realize that some of the ends that he/she chose are objectively not good for him/her, and that some of the pleasure that he/she chose as ends are not worthy of him/her. Consequently, he/she has decided to struggle against those pleasures that he/she now thinks are not good for him/her. Domination is A's struggle against part of his/her constitution. A wants to master those pleasures that are seeking to control his/her everyday life. Self-mastery is the end which A wants to choose. Note that it is A who studied and diagnosed that his/her soul is defective and guided his/her own prognosis by deciding to try to emancipate his/her soul from the undue guidance of excessive pleasures. A wants to begin caring for his/her soul. No external agent has coerced A to examine his/her soul; it is A who has examined A; and it is A who will struggle with A by engaging in a relentless and perpetual trial and error—a trial and error that is in search of authentic rational/moral principles. A, by his/her own decision, has become a quester, a wonderer, a searcher, an inquirer, a creator—a thinker in despair. For A, self-mastery has become a noble end. By domination, A understands a situation in which A is not in control but is instead severely controlled by another power that he/she hopes to master. That power, whatever else it might be, did not generate internally from the ocean depth of A's soul. Rather, it is external to A, an external power that is dominating his/her existence, the very moment of his/her passions. A's struggle against A is precisely a struggle against that external power. It is not, as ordinarily perceived, a struggle against the elimination of power per se. There may be healthy forms of power—a point that I wish to develop in the second part of this book on power—that are worth nurturing very carefully. I will argue later in part 2 that self-empowerment, if internally generated, which is distinct from external power—the power in which domination originates—is a precious value that we must cherish.

Now that I have digressed a little, let me return to my reflection on domination by external power, a power that is outside of the self.

IS DOMINATION A FACT?

Facts by definition are empirical, therefore the obvious answer to the question is: yes, to the extent that one could carefully identify individuals who dominate others, one infers that domination—the domination of B by A—is a fact that can be empirically identified. In this sense, domination is a fact. However the obvious fact that A dominates B does not necessarily tell us much about the nature of domination.

By the accidents of history, individuals are born to the world. The world is based on (a) some structures that are already ordered, (b) others that have yet to be ordered, (c) structures that are partly ordered, and (d) structures that seem to be completely ordered but are themselves incomprehensible and unfathomable. Domination as a fact has something to do with all of the above, but it is also particularly affected by (a), (c), and (d).

To a significant extent, the world to which human beings are born is already structured. Laws and customs, as many great thinkers have argued, are two of the chief features of the perennial structures of the everyday world. To say that A is born to world B is to imply that the customs, laws, and even life styles in the world of B are already determined, articulated, and institutionalized in the political, cultural, and social life styles and ways of living. The content of laws and customs—the flesh and blood of life—in a world that is already structured has been fleshed out, defined, and judged as good by those who hold power. The laws and customs have also been eternally judged as absolutely good for those who are still unborn, yet to come, yet to live and struggle. Laws and customs in an already structured world *dominate* by their very abstract claim to universality, eternity, and ahistoricality.

As members of the everyday world governed by universal laws and customs, human beings become dominated by those whose formations, definitions, and design they did not choose, determine, and form by the concrete struggle of mind and body. Any forced attachment to anything external, such as laws and customs, deprives human beings of involvement and the chance to struggle.

The norms, values, and beliefs that individuals adopt are not always chosen by them. More often, individuals are subtly encouraged to live their lives in certain ways. Hitherto untested modes of existence are carefully screened out from the realm of seriousness, from the arena of human attention, from the region of the possible. If all human beings were equally morally and rationally powerful insofar as their ability to choose styles of life, ethics of existence, and principles that govern their everyday conduct, then it would not make much sense to assume that within an already structured world, the content of choice is already determined and decided by others. To the extent that individuals are morally and rationally powerful, they are by virtue of an impenetrable moral/rational power capable of fully resisting the pressures and manipulations of others, enabling them to hold their ground. Unfortunately, human beings' biographies and formations are so varied that we can never intelligently assume that all individuals are capable of overcoming the compelling presence of hegemonic ideas, values, norms, and beliefs. In this particular sense, the world to which individuals are born is already structured for them. There are *very limited spaces* in that world for novelty, creativity, discovery, retrieval of values, norms, and philosophies of life.

The empirical world, however, is not completely ordered. There is, thus, room for creativity. There are limited spaces that can be fruitfully inhabited by the morally/rationally independent and courageous. Individuals are not completely determined by the circumstances in which they find themselves. In this sense, circumstances—families, friends, peer groups—do not prevent individuals from becoming truly autonomous, authentic moral/rational agents. I must stress that the will to be autonomous does not always lead to autonomy. There are deep roadblocks to be removed. At times beloved families, intimate friends, and peer groups stand in the way. There is also the frightening possibility of loneliness that may await the solitary and autonomous person. Each of the above makes it profoundly difficult for fragile human beings to determine our own destinies, engage our rational/moral power, or activate our wills and passions to choose what we truly want. It is as if circumstances completely order, in a determining way, our path of growth and our will to mature.

The empirical world thus indeed offers a limited space that is not completely ordered. Those who wish and will to determine the content of their lives can do so. Courage and the resolve to retain their freedom and dignity may help them in their incessant struggle to create and bring forth novel values to the empirical world. An example would be a struggle to construct a nonracist and nonsexist moral community.

How does one become courageous and resolute? This is a difficult question to answer; in fact, we may not even be capable of fully answering it. However, I wish to try to explore some tentative answers. The clearest and quite persuasive view to many is that courage is a cardinal virtue that is delicately cultivated within the right family in the form of habit. A given individual becomes courageous to the precise extent that he/she is rightly raised. Note, however, the deficiency of the view. Nowhere in that view is asked the ultimate question: What is courage and how and when do we know that we know it before we raise the question of family upbringing?

One does not become courageous by simply deciding to become so. The meaning of courage must first be thoroughly understood by the person who wishes to attain it. The resolve to become courageous must be preceded by the knowledge of what courage is. When I say that courage is grounded upon meaning, and meaning itself is squeezed out of knowledge, I mean that the acts that pass the exemplifications of courage are deeply penetrated, not by the language of authentic truth, but rather by the arrogance of the language of power, particularly the language of one-dimensional desire. Thus, for most individuals war is a courageous act, whereas peace is not. War is a conventionally compelling instance of courage.

I wish to conceive of courage in the following nonconventional way. By courage, I understand the internal power that a human being has and with which he/she can confront the most difficult experience—for example, the inevitable possibility of death for the sake of a noble cause. Such a person prefers death with honor to life with shame and guilt. For such a person, shame and guilt are vices by which he/she wishes not to be contaminated; whereas caring for others, not taking advantage of the humble and decent, or speaking, writing, and thinking on behalf of the silent, the voiceless, the overburdened and the poor are virtues that he/she resolves to courageously defend. Courage, for this person, is the self-initiated responsibility to defend public virtue, even when these actions may be accompanied by the ever present possibility of death. Yet, the courageous person acts in spite of the danger that he/she sometimes clearly perceives.

Thus, the ends of courage, such as the possibility of authentic self-gratification resulting from a particular courageous act and from an honestly lived life make it worthwhile for some people to cultivate the internalization of courage as the meaningful knowledge of the public acts of caring, thinking, speaking, and even writing on behalf of a harmonious soul. By a harmonious soul, I mean a soul that is self-ordered and thereby is in a solid condition to silently and joyously help others. The harmonious soul knows precisely when it ought to engage its courage, its impressive moral power, to swim against the current social stream of detached indifference. The voice and conscience are effective when non-showy and absolutely non-paternalistic. If the voice and conscience are motivated by the selfish desire to get noticed and admired, they lose profundity and the force to move anyone. Courage is more moving if it is veiled. The veil of courage should be uncovered only during an action or event, a happening that speaks directly without the noise and announcement of the common rational/moral agent. It is the stance, the orientation, the worldview of the courageous rational/moral actor that should tell us what courage is. It is from the courageous action itself that we can one day draw a cumulatively formed theoretical meaning of what courage is; and it is through the act as well that the royal road toward the conception of courage as knowledge is traveled. A series of morally/rationally moving acts, events, and occurrences may one day result in allowing us to develop a standard conception of courage, a form of courage that could serve us as a guide to those who wish to become courageous but truly do not know how. Note here a crucial distinction between saying that one becomes courageous by simply following the example of courageous heroes as a model that blindly and mindlessly follows what one sees but does not deeply comprehend, and saying that one becomes courageous by doing acts. Repeatedly doing what is not always pleasant and fighting the hidden but powerful will of the dominating appetites that compel one to do cowardly and frivolous deeds can produce courageous acts. Repeated and not always pleasant actions can germinate a knowledge of courage. The ultimate house of courage as a form of knowledge is not (a) blind habituation to the models of courage—that is, the revered moral/rational heroes that empirical history glorify (such as the warlords of antiquity, the so-called decisive, thoughtless, and cruel killers of modernity, and even the suprahuman saints of Christianity) nor is it (b) a theoretical definition of courage as founded by the super-intelligent. It is rather a repeated practice of the difficult, the seemingly impossible. It is the self-constructing subject who really is capable of courageous acts.

The house of courage is action, but it may more precisely be called that undetermined space in human social reality where we can freely choose to work in order to construct a novel value creatively. It is courage that precisely makes it possible for us to choose the most difficult task of going against ourselves, in the quest to become morally and rationally extraordinary human beings. I conclude then that the empirical world is not completely ordered, nor is it the dream of a fool, of a naive and immature idealist to think that human beings can free themselves from self-inflicted domination that leads to surrender or resigning oneself to the power of the world. There is a social space in the empirical world, which by the repeated and relentless practice of certain acts can definitely house courageous acts. Domination by our appetites, which blocks the emergence of the courageous revelations that human beings can be potentially extraordinary, is then not a fact that cannot be changed. There is, in fact, a way of undoing what history has done to most of us; one such way, I have argued, is the road of the conscious and resolute cultivation of courage. It takes exceptional courage to develop the public virtues of caring for oneself and for others, generosity, responsibility to oneself and others, and even love, the love of all human beings. These sublime public virtues are not beyond the realm of human grasp. They are potentially reachable and cultivable virtues by those who wish to courageously confront them so as to possess them as permanent virtues that accompany their alert everyday existence.

Individuals may also be born to structures that seem to be completely ordered but are incomprehensible and unfathomable. Domination is crucially and disturbingly affected by this dimension of the world. The individual who sincerely attempts to desubjugate himself from the force of external power is destined to confront this incomprehensible and almost mystical experience. It is in this realm that ''moral evil,'' for example, is located—a point that I will develop in relation to Aristotle.

IS FREEDOM FROM POWER AS DOMINATION A FACT OR A PERMANENT POSSIBILITY?

In some ways, this question is related to the question of evil that I briefly introduced at the end of chapter 2. I now wish to return to that theme first before I proceed to struggle with the question: Is freedom from domination a fact or a permanent possibility?

Freedom from domination is a fact for those who have accepted domination as natural to those who dominate and those who get dominated. I wish to elucidate the proposition above with an example.

Consider the following group interaction in a classroom composed of ten students, male and female. The group is discussing a text that was assigned to be read with maximum care. The group meets to discuss the text; the reading has been done. As the professor, I had repeatedly emphasized in class that since all students were advised to seriously read the text and, as a consequence, would comprehend the reading, they could, if they so chose, confidently participate in discussions. To the great disappointment of this instructor, *not* all students participated. Of course, shyness and lack of experience were contributing factors in the absence of a significant level of participation. But there are other factors that I observed that are equally worth thinking about in the quest to comprehensively understand the roots of power as domination.

One image still stands out in my mind. The image is that of a male student present in that group. He was short and handsome, articulate and aggressive, talkative yet not consistently substantive, nervous, deceptively warm, and unwilling to listen to others, including myself, the instructor, unless I aggressively overwhelmed him, at which point he became too timid to utter any thoughts and began to submit to me. All his initial confidence and arrogance began to melt, and he became as scared and as innocent as a child. He completely changed his personality. The group did not seem to notice all of these changes, for reasons that I wish to share with you later.

The group in which the talker prevailed was dazzled by him. For the group, the talker was a symbol of strength: power, aristocratic values, coldness, detachment, normality, nobility, aggressiveness, relentlessness, the dominating instinct.[3] The intimidated, servile, fascinated men and women were positively responding to those symbols of strength. The talker was the visible expression of those values. His presence there was a definite value. In fact, he was value himself—domination, a symbol of strength, was *the* value. Domination as positive, aristocratic, noble, and good has become internalized by the group as a value. This is my judgment, of course, judgment that I believe has the merit of enabling us to understand the genealogy of the value of domination.

The way others perceive us is as important as the way we perceive ourselves, and sometimes even more important. Thus the impressive talker, contrary to his own self-perception, which as I described above was not consistently positive, was perceived as noble, heroic, knowledgeable. The group's silent positive judgment became the source of the talker's power. The young man sensed their judgment as the group, by its silence, handed power to him. He covertly converted this power into a tool of domination.

Power and Domination Are Not the Same

Power, I wish to argue, can be self-producing. When power is self-producing, it thereby becomes an end. The self employs power as a *means* that aims at the cultivation of an *end*. In this process of a self-guided activity, there is neither the need nor the occasion to use power as a tool with which to dominate anything or any person. Domination is simply not a feature of power when power is normally and healthily fit into a scheme of novel language games, new ways of perceiving the world.

The talker needed power not as a self-produced end aiming at a normal value but rather as a devious tool of dominating the silent, humble, thoughtful, uncertain others. I will now examine in detail the crucial experience of how some dominate and others are simply dominated along with the interpretations of some Greek thinkers who have carefully reflected on the question of the nature of domination and power. My thesis is that in the otherwise careful thoughts of the philosophers, power and domination are not carefully distinguished. A change is reflected in recent theorizing by feminist writers who have made some measurable contributions toward separating power and domination. Before providing my own constructive theory of power as self-empowerment, I think it is worth struggling with the reflections of some of the most seminal Greek and non-Greek thinkers, as Foucault did brilliantly.

THE OBSTACLES TO FREEING ONESELF FROM THE FACT/POSSIBILITY OF POWER AS DOMINATION

Roots of Domination: The Arguments of the Philosophers

Plato

Plato's major thesis about the human roots of domination is fully articulated in his truly stunning portrayal of the tyrannical disposition in human character found in the ninth book of the *Republic*. Plato's thesis may be summarized as follows.

For Plato, it is a democratic regime that becomes a necessary condition for the emergence of a tyrannical regime.[4] Similarly, the tyrannical person is an outgrowth of the democratic person. Tyranny then is a negative value to the extent that it is a transformation from democracy. Democracy itself, which for Plato is a regime where liberty is abused, is also a negative value.[5] Plato characterizes tyranny in this way. Central to a deep understanding of the tyrant—someone whose self-constitution involves the need to dominate others as well as his/her helplessness due to domination by the external force of unnecessary pleasures—is Plato's unique insight into the nature of desire.

In a major passage, Plato wrote:

Of the unnecessary pleasures and desires, there are, in my opinion, some that are hostile to law and that probably come to be in everyone; but, when checked by the laws and the better desires, with the help of argument, in some human beings they are entirely gotten rid of or only a few weak ones are left, while in others stronger and more numerous ones remain.

"Which ones do you mean?" he said.

"Those," I said, "that make up in sleep when the rest of the soul—all that belongs to the calculating, tame, and ruling part of it—slumbers, while the beastly and wild part, gorged with food or drink, is skittish and, pushing sleep away, seeks to go and satisfy its dispositions. You know that in such a state it dares to do everything as though it were released from, and rid of, all shame and prudence. And it does not shy from attempting intercourse, as it supposes, with a mother or anyone else at all—human beings, gods, and beasts, or attempting any foul member at all, and there is no food from which it abstains. And in a word, it omits no act of folly or shamelessness."[6]

For Plato, human beings are desiring beings who gravitate toward the apparently good and move away from the apparently nondesirable (or bad). This movement constitutes a major portion of human activities. When human beings move toward the desirable, however, they generally do not pause to critically and judiciously evaluate the merits of the different objects of desire. Plato makes the major observation that although human beings tend to tenaciously follow their instincts when they seek to gratify the objects of their desires, because desiring as such is "natural," it does not necessarily follow that they are right to do so. Rather, Plato seeks to awaken us to the radical idea that desiring each and everything without making a self-generated decision to examine the nature of desire itself is ultimately destructive. Yet we often choose not to open our power of inquiry to the problem of desire.[7]

For those who wish to be thinking people, human existence is too precious for them to let themselves be guided by the meandering of goal-less desires. Existence is generally goal-directed (for example, toward happiness) as are the desires upon which existence is anchored. Rarely, however, are we aware of this basis for our existence.

For Plato, not all desires are equally admirable. Some are excellent, others are very good, still others are simply bad. Some desires are absolutely necessary for our human existence: food, shelter, clothing are good examples; and some other desires, for example, excessive alcohol, drugs, etc. are objectively harmful to the human body and spirit. Those desires that are excellent are so because they have become subjected to the regulative direction of self-imposed law. Desires that cannot be directed by the regulative power of self-imposed law necessarily become bad as do the characters of human beings who live their lives chaotically.

Plato contends that the desires that destroy human beings are those that are particularly active during sleep. In the sleeping state, anything is desirable. The objects of desire in the dream state are boundless, lawless, shameless, ungovernable, impervious to regulated direction by reason or the solemn state of inquiry. What is even more frightening is the fact that these desires feel wild, and ruthless, even to those who relish the feeling of freedom released by the demonic charm of boundless desires. These are unnatural desires that need to be controlled.

Furthermore, "a man becomes tyrannical in the precise sense when, either by nature or by his practices or both, he has become drunken, erotic and melancholic."[8] The tyrant would pursue the most unnatural desires when fancy and an exaggerated need compel him. Thus Plato writes, "Is it your opinion that for the sake of a newly-formed lady friend and unnecessary concubine such a man will strike his old friend and necessary mother, or that for the sake of a newly-found and unnecessary boy friend, in the bloom of youth, he will strike his elderly and necessary father who is no longer in the bloom of youth and is the oldest of friends, and that he will enslave his parents to them if he should bring them into the same house?"[9]

Drunkenness, eros, and melancholy are human vices for Plato. They are vices that describe the fallen state to which the tyrannical self enters when it surrenders its will to unnatural desires—desires that deliberately and shamelessly transgress the boundaries set by the inquiring or reasonable self. Drunkenness, eros, and melancholy are either products of nature, in which case they are outside human control but themselves become controlling forces, or are constructs of habitual practice, in which case they are directly but over a long period of time caused by human beings against their own selves. In short, the vices of drunkenness, eros, and melancholy are both natural and social. Naturalness and sociability are deeply involved in what humans do and do not do, what humans are and are not, what human beings have actually become and can overbecome. Plato characteristically vacillates between nature, the permanently unchangeable power, and the social, the ceaselessly in flux—fluid, dynamic, product of conscious human choice.

The desires then are potentially deep sources of a tragic form of life, found, for example, in the classic Greek literature of the Oedipus myth, where all human values are shamelessly transgressed for the sake of lustful desires seeking an outlet in raw sexuality. For Plato, the desires, however, are also equally healthy wells of a longing for a peaceful life. This life contains moments of eros and aphrodisia, love and sexuality, which consummate in the births of human beings, destined to propagate the human species. This form of life, neither tragic nor paradoxical but a healthy blend of the two moments, is what thinkers of all ages have longed for, so far to no avail. The wondering, the quest, the refusal to dream and not to dream are all bound up with the potential of human desires, the potential of human beings to destroy, regress, imagine, and create. Imagination to construct and the will to destroy. Drunkenness, eros, and melancholy are thus destructive powers as well as constructive human gifts, of which Plato was critically aware.

For Plato, the drunken and erotic tyrant is the worst enemy of his own self. He/she does not have a friendly attitude toward his/her own self; he/she does not profoundly love himself/herself. Because he/she is not a friend to himself/herself, we can safely infer that he/she is equally incapable of entering into friendship with other human beings. Plato put it thus: "Therefore, they live their whole life without ever being friend of anyone, always one's master or another's slave. The tyrannical nature never has a task of freedom or true friendship."[10]

Plato and others have provided some important insights about the nature of freedom and friendship that have a subtle bearing on the nature of domination. Plato is right when he asserts that the tyrant is neither free nor friendly. Freedom and friendship are foreign to his/her character. They are nonvalues to the tyrant. At a minimum, the tyrant must either deny or completely dominate others in order that he/she may feel free. He/she, in turn, although not consciously, is dominated by the thoughtless and irrational desire to dominate others. Dominating others is a necessary condition for the tyrant to feel free. Note that for the tyrant, what is really important is not that he/she is actually free as much as that he/she feels free. The freedom that he/she feels is actually the absence of freedom of those others who are dominated by his/her experience. A tyrant's freedom is so dominated by thoughtlessness that he/she is prevented from ever disengaging himself/herself from the will to dominate in order to consider why someone would dominate others.

For Plato, the structure of the tyrant's character is the key we must turn to enter their inner depths. The soul or psyche of the tyrannical inner regime is upheld by three foundational pillars: reason and unreason with the desires suspended in between. A mature and truly balanced character must have a well-blended mix of these three foundational pillars. A character can be said to be reasonable if his/her desire for gain, honor, and prudence is fundamentally dominated not by gain or honor, but rather by the erotic desire for prudence. Such a character is considered to be the true aristos (king). He or she is capable of intimate self-governance and can correctly choose the appropriate wants and subsequently satisfy the objects of human desire. The kingly or aristocratic inner regime is guided by prudence; gain and honor are consequently subordinate to prudence. The inner regime is not mesmerized by gain and honor as is the tyrannical inner regime.

The tyrant is the exact opposite of the aristocrat. Whereas the aristocrat is captivated by prudence or reason, the tyrant is intoxicated with the desires for unlimited monetary gain or the honor of power, and an imprudence that erases the power of choice has been erased. The intoxication with gain and honor leads the tyrant to reduce all his/her relationships with others, including friends and loved ones, to means. A tyrant would even enslave himself to others by belittling himself if the others could be made to serve for his/her well-planned future scheme. For the tyrant, human beings are not intrinsically lovable or worthy of love. They are either useful or useless instruments for his own pleasure.

The tyrant is not free. He/she is a slave of gain, money, status—each of which germinates from the depth of the pillar of desire undirected by reason. The tyrant does not use his/her critical powers of prudence or inquiry, therefore he/she is inexperienced in dispassionately thinking about the objects of desire. Any desired object is impudently and thoughtlessly pursued. Thus, in the tyrant's eyes, even one's own mother could be a sexually desired object, if that enables the tyrant to get his/her way. The values of right and wrong, good and evil, justice and injustice, friendliness and hate are all judged as equal, without intrinsic differences that stir the human mind and heart to be deeply concerned about the human condition. The tyrant unconcerned about the well being of others, cannot be moved by anything except gain.

The tyrant cannot enter into friendship because true friendship demands love, compassion, patience, limitless time, and, above all, a sense of justice. The tyrant who is enslaved by self-centered desires cannot provide other-oriented virtues such as love, compassion, and patience. Only those who are free can be compassionate when others demand freedom, just as it is easier for those who have loved to return love when it is demanded from them. The tyrant cannot give either freedom or friendship to others precisely because he/she has never experienced the flares of freedom and friendship. The tyrant is a tragic figure in that he/she has never loved his/her own self. The tyrant experiences life not as self-empowerment but strictly as the will to power.[11]

Aristotle: "Evil" as Power to Dominate

Aristotle does not directly speak to the question of tyranny with the honesty and straightforwardness of Plato. Aristotle certainly did not write a whole book—as Plato did—to examine the soul of the tyrant. But I wish to contend that where Plato spoke about the tyrant, Aristotle addressed himself to the question of moral evil. To the extent that Aristotle was aware of moral evil, he was deeply knowledgeable about the character or soul of a morally evil self. The tyrant and the morally evil person, I wish to argue, are remarkably similar if not identical. Moral evil, or a long practice of it, could easily result in the birth of Plato's tyrant—the tyrant who is habitually erotic, drunk, and melancholic. The morally evil person dissipates his/her energy on the will to dominate others, without shame or remorse.

What is moral evil for Aristotle though? It is in Book III of *Nicomachean Ethics* that the question of moral evil is raised. He theorizes as follows. Human beings are acting beings. As such they act voluntarily and involuntarily. All actions are neither exclusively voluntary or exclusively involuntary. Actions that are voluntarily done, for example, drunkenness, exact our approbation. We condemn drunks with the conviction that if they should strongly will, they could avoid getting drunk. Their power to drink is equal to their power not to drink. The action as such is within the sphere of the controllable. Aristotle's concept of biology does not include an awareness of a genetic disposition that may cause alcoholism. Aristotle insists that all actions that are voluntarily done can also be voluntarily refrained from.

For Aristotle, voluntary actions are done under compulsion or ignorance. There are some actions, however, that take place because of fear of a real tyrant. Such actions are not easily judged either as voluntary or involuntary.[12]

Aristotle's strong claim is that the power to do action A voluntarily implies that there is also the power not to do action A voluntarily. Where there is a power to act, there is a power not to act. As just stated, actions may be considered voluntary even when done under compulsion and ignorance, and one may voluntarily submit to compulsion and ignorance to do something that one would otherwise not be willing to do. Compulsion and ignorance could be used to explain individual acts, but cannot be persuasively used to justify some socially undesirable acts. To explain an action is not to justify it. Aristotle writes: "In some cases again, such submission though not praised is condoned, when a man does something wrong through fear of penalties that impose too great a strain on human nature, and that no one could endure. Yet there seem to be acts which a man cannot be compelled to do, and rather than do them he ought to submit to the most terrible death: for instance, we think it ridiculous that Alcmalon in Euripides' play is compelled by certain threats to murder his mother."[13]

Above, Aristotle adds to the argument that compulsion and ignorance do not justify an undesirable act, such as killing one's mother under the threat of death. The new argument is that the actor's strength of character should also be taken into account when we examine why some individuals submit to the fear of death, and others prefer to die instead of committing a heinous act that is not worthy of them. According to Hutchinson, for Aristotle, "A man's character, then, is that aspect of his soul which possesses these common features; it is good or bad according to whether it is obedient or not to the voice of reason."[14] Aristotle's puzzle is why, when individuals are directly confronted with the possibility of death as the consequence of an ignoble act, do they still do it.

His general answer seems to be that the motives of character give us a strong clue to understanding why an individual chooses death to protect a principle, as opposed to choosing life to protect nothing. Nobility is a value for such an individual, and the motive of nobility is what is being protected.

Voluntary actions that are done through ignorance are of two kinds. There are cases in which an individual has acted voluntarily afterward regrets the consequences of the action; in this, "we think that he has acted involuntarily."

If he does not regret the act, however, "we may call him a 'non-voluntary' agent."[15]

For Aristotle, just because an individual could act through ignorance, it does not mean that the individual is acting *in* ignorance. Acting *through* ignorance is not the same as acting *in* ignorance. Thus, we can say that the drunk is not necessarily unaware of the bad consequences of drinking, and yet he/she chooses to drink excessively. He does not drink *in ignorance* of the consequences of drinking, but drinks in spite of the consequences. The drunkard is not drinking involuntarily, or in ignorance, but is voluntarily drinking because he/she has become habituated to a non-restrained behavior.

There is a special type of ignorance, Aristotle teaches, that is most applicable to the discussion of moral choice.[16] One is ignorant when one does not know what he/she should do before he/she does anything. Let us call this the ignorance of moral principles. There is a second type I wish to call the ignorance of particular circumstance, facts, events, etc. It is the second type that is directly relevant to an examination of the nature of moral evil.

The second type of ignorance deals with particular circumstances. They are (1) the agent, (2) the act, (3) the thing that is affected by the act (4) the instrument, for example, a tool used to effect a result, (5) the intention of the act, and (6) the manner, for example, gently or violently.[17]

A human being who is still sane can claim ignorance in all the six circumstances when accused of committing a heinous crime, such as the brutal treatment of a fellow human being, or enslavement, torture, or subjecting others to sophisticated psychological abuse. Discussion of the second type of ignorance helps us to elucidate the meaning and scope of the nature of choice. Before examining the character of the morally evil person as a chooser, we need to first analyze the nature of choice.

Choice is intimately connected with character. Thus, the chooser, in the act of choosing, is developing a particular kind of character. He or she, we may explicitly but modestly say, is becoming a person, cultivating virtues or vices, as the case may be.

As we recall, actions are voluntary and involuntary. Involuntary actions in particular are concerned with the knowledge or ignorance of particular kinds of circumstances, facts, and events. Choice, too, is a kind of action. For Aristotle, "choice is manifestly a voluntary act."[18] Choice and action are, of course, not the same. Action is wider than choice. However, action is something that all individuals can do. Very young children are said to act when they move their hands to grab the leg of a chair. They have acted but not chosen. Choice, as opposed to action, deals with the acts of mature adults.

Furthermore, choice is mistakenly identified with (1) desire, (2) passion, (3) wishes, or (4) some form of opinion.[19] Aristotle argues that children, for example, could act desirously, passionately, wishfully, or even opinionatedly, but just because they so act, it does not follow that they have chosen the way in which they have acted. Not just children but also individuals with defective characters, could be said to be "not" choosing because they have acted under the guidance of desire, passion, wishes, or opinion. An individual with a defective character could act but not choose. G. E. Mure is quite right when he states that, for Aristotle, "the really bad man is a perverted, not simply a defective, moral agent."[20]

Choice runs counter to desire because the desiring person may have a defective character; choice is counter to passion because the passionate individual may be irrational, as Plato's excessively erotic tyrant; choice is opposed to a wish because some wishes are wishes for the impossible, for example, the wish not to die; and finally, choice cannot be based on opinions, which are too unstable and vulnerable to fluctuating tides.

If choice runs counter to desire, passion, wishes, and opinion, what does it encounter? Choice is indeed a kind of "voluntary action preceded by deliberation, since choice involves reasoning and some process of thought."[21] Choice is preceded by deliberation—deliberation by a sensible individual. Surely, the objects of deliberation are too many to be fully known. We cannot deliberate about the eternal, nor about the order of the universe, or about numbers.

According to Aristotle, deliberation is very specific. We deliberate about objects in our control that are achievable by action. We do not deliberate about ends but about means. It is we who deliberate about what we should do and not do in order to become particular kinds of persons. Thus, the person who has chosen an evil end chose the end because he/she deliberated about the means to attain that particular end. When he/she chose to enslave, torture, manipulate, etc., he/she fully considered particular circumstances: the dignity of the person, the act, the effect of the act, the instrument, the intention of the act, and the manners of the act before he/she proceeded to choose. He/she deliberated his/her action in the realm of choosing. He/she did not involuntarily act in ignorance of the circumstance but rather chose through the ignorance of the circumstance; he/she chose in spite of the knowledge of the circumstance, perhaps fully convinced of his/her belief that there is nothing wrong with acting in those particular ways towards certain kinds of persons and objects.

Aristotle writes:

Therefore virtue also depends on ourselves. And so also does vice. For where we are free to act, we are also free to refrain from acting, and where we are able to say No, we are also able to say Yes; if therefore, we are responsible for doing a thing when to do it is right, we are also responsible for not doing it when not to do it is wrong, and if we are responsible for wrongly doing it. But if it is in our power to do and to refrain from doing right and wrong, and if, as we saw, being good or bad is doing right or wrong, it consequently depends on us whether we are virtuous or vicious.[22]

For Aristotle, the individual is responsible for the outcome of his/her own choices. I wish to extend this general argument to specifically apply to the moral choice of moral evil. I argue with Aristotle's thesis that the morally evil person is nonvirtuous precisely because he/she deliberated and chose moral evil as a way of life. At the minimum, to choose evil over and against good presupposes the acceptance of viciousness as a way of life. However, viciousness itself may be invisibly guided by what I wish to call thoughtlessness[23] or a nonmeditative disposition toward the world—particularly toward those six circumstances that Aristotle so rigorously mapped out, namely, the importance of the agent, the act itself, the effect of the act on the agent, an object and other human beings, the instrument that is used to effect an action, the intended consequence of an action, and finally, the manner of the action, gentle or violent. The individual who chooses to do evil, we could argue, overlooks the importance of carefully considering the circumstance when he/she feels like harming someone other than himself/herself.

In fact, it is crucial for the individual who is set to harm another that he/she consciously violates the humanness of another human being by refusing to acknowledge others as possessing an intrinsic dignity that should not be violated. The individual who deliberately chooses to transgress the first circumstance (the importance of the agent) finds good reasons to do so without shame, guilt, remorse, or even a moment's thought. The violated other is seen as inferior to the violator. Given this inferiority, the violator deliberates and justifies his disposition of violence (moral/psychological, physical) toward the other. He comes to believe that this other deserved the harsh treatment. The morally evil person has chosen an end that is a consequence of calculated deliberation, however thoughtless and unreflective such deliberation might be in the eyes of those who view thinking as a meditative and not a calculative activity, particularly when applied to the worth of human beings. The morally evil person does not consider himself/herself blameworthy for the evil ends he/she is habitually practicing. Morally evil practices become justified practices. There is nothing wrong with them; they are just ways of being human. For Aristotle, though, vice as such is a moral disease. He himself writes: "for vice resembles diseases like dropsy and consumption, whereas unrestraint is like epilepsy, vice being a chronic, unrestraint an intermittent evil. Indeed unrestraint and vice are entirely different in kind, for vice is unconscious, whereas the unrestrained man is aware of his infirmity."[24]

Note that if I am right that the morally evil person is vicious and that moral evil itself is a vice, it becomes readily apparent—thanks to Aristotle—that the morally evil person does not choose evil because he/she is overwhelmed by his/her unrestrained passions, and that he/she does not enjoy this moral weakness, but rather that the practice itself is freely and happily chosen. Of course, there are institutional factors that complicate the way individuals choose. It is conceivable that for some individuals, subjecting others to one's whims and arbitrary desires is a joy-giving pleasure and that some individuals actually enjoy inflicting pain upon others. It gives them joy, power, a delicate feeling of superiority, so they practice it.

How does one become evil? This is of course a difficult question to answer definitively. One such answer may be the following. One might not be born evil but could be nurtured from early on in the habitual practice of doing evil, due to the repeated and unchallenged practice of certain actions, such as indifference toward the needs of others, self-centeredness, selfishness, pride, arrogance, conceit, etc. If one, as a matter of course, repeatedly practices all of the above, it becomes considerably easier to overlook or even not acknowledge the preciousness and value of human beings and their right to not be violated but be treated with the deepest respect we are capable of giving to others. The morally evil person, I wish to argue, is not willing to embrace any such orientation toward the world. A sense of duty toward others, in particular, is not within his/her purview. Such an orientation is not a value, norm, or principle. Evil then can be taught; it need not be merely natural. The disposition toward choosing evil may be natural, but the actual practice itself is a product of careful and long nurture. I will have Aristotle speak for himself on the question of evil: "For it is our *choice* of good or evil that determines our character, not our *opinion* about good or evil. And we choose to take or avoid some good or evil thing, but we opine what a thing is, or for whom it is advantageous, or how it is so."[25] (Italics mine.)

Thus, individuals do not choose evil as an end because they do not know what they are choosing. Individuals do not innocently choose what seemed to be good to them, then turned out to be evil. A person's character must be disposed in a certain way for that person and not for them to make this choice. It is not a valid excuse to say I chose A (potentially evil) and not B (harmless choice) because I had the wrong opinion. Opinions are not in a strong sense relevant justifications of wrongs that are involuntarily committed. Human beings may be opinionated but not fully knowledgeable of the nature of what they choose. Therefore, where opinions are helpless to guide us toward the choice of noble ends, the disposition of our character may be all that is left to us in our struggle to choose correctly. How we choose when we are confronted with tempting choices is not a function of the correctness of the opinions we hold as much as it is by the function of the strength of our character. Character is strengthened not by succumbing to our desires, passions, and opinions but by listening to our inner reason. In our capacity to reflect intelligently, we can make the resolute decision to fight the will to dominate others. Evil as an end would be chosen by the character who listens not to the voice of inner reason but to vicious and unrestrained passions. The morally evil person can shamelessly dominate others precisely because he/she is dominated by the absence of a meditative disposition. A meditative orientation toward the world and all beings in that world is not given a moment's attention by the morally evil person. The morally evil person experiences others, including friends, not as autonomous human beings worthy of his/her deep respect, but rather as objects of domination. Self-constructing moral subjects are advised to be critically aware of the creeping presence of evil which has to be combated by thought and action.

Epictetus

The fundamental insight into the nature of human beings as choosers is that rarely do humans intelligently and carefully distinguish between events that are within the sphere of their control and those that are outside their control. This axiom is fundamental to Epictetus in his impressive attempt to make us humans master the challenges of moral choice—the choice between good and evil, the bedrock of power and domination.[26]

Before we choose anything at all, the philosopher argues, there is a prior question that we should all ask. Are the things that I wish to have things that I can have, things within my sphere of control (in a sphere of free action) or outside of that sphere? When reflected upon, this question makes it easier for human beings to recognize the external forces that control them and push them to desire (a) objects which they *cannot* have, (b) objects which they *should not* have, and (c) objects that confusedly tempt them *to have and not to have them*. These confusions arise from the inability to distinguish between the spheres of the controllable and uncontrollable.

One of the formidable obstacles to the wish to be freed from the domination of external forces—for example, the irrational compulsion to accumulate a mass of commodities, in the process risking one's life to obtain them—is the human tendency, according to an Epictetean insight, to not really think through the nature of the things and events that one chooses. Human beings, as desiring beings, wish to have anything and everything—that is to say that they do not distinguish between what they can have and what they cannot and perhaps should not, and this provides a pivot to the consideration of domination that uses power to acquire access to anything and everything.

I am a bit puzzled about humanity, particularly about those who interminably desire in quest of things that is both within and outside our control. The philosopher, by introducing these two spheres, wants to ease our burden, so that we do not have, in the name of freedom, to seek things that we cannot and perhaps should not even have.

Indeed, Epictetus may be doing just that—easing the burden. By so doing, he is not depriving us of our freedom to desire whatever we want, with or without reasons. Suppose that some individuals consider the two spheres to be nothing more than arbitrary distinctions made by philosophers, not applicable to the question of desire. To them, Epictetus would say: "It is for this reason especially that we need education, so as to learn how, in confronting with nature, to adopt to specific instances our preconceived idea of what is rational and what is irrational. But for determining the rational and the irrational, we employ not only our estimates of the value of external things, but also the criterion of that which is in keeping with one's own character."[27]

Perhaps, but how do I know whether I have the right or wrong character to be worthy of abiding by the sphere of choice? For Epictetus, genuine education is education toward the development of a solid character. A given character is solid to the extent that its content is in conformity with comprehensively reasonable principles. But this begs the question: What are principles? Whose principles? These are very difficult questions. Nevertheless, I will try to think them out with the help of Epictetus's perspective.

A solid character is guided by principles, instructs Epictetus. Principles are the providers of moral purpose. A given individual has moral purpose when we see him/her struggling to free himself or herself of dominating desires that are determined by the force of external things like money and goods. A morally purposeful human being is free from domination by external things when he/she constructs a lifelong project of continuous self-cultivation that aims at moral progress. We know that a person is morally purposeful and is guided by principles when we see him/her doing the strikingly right things. Moral progress then is visible not in the grandiose claims of theoretical principle but in the simple, decent, and yet extraordinary actions.[28] Principles then are knowable as effects, actions as such and not necessarily as theoretical claims.

Moral purpose is effectively present—almost unmistakably—when it is realized in concrete deeds. The greater the absence of domination by external things, the greater the amount of moral progress, manifest in good choices.

How would anyone know that he/she is following a correct moral purpose? Besides, what is a correct moral purpose per se? To begin with, a correct moral purpose shows awareness of the distinctions between the two spheres that I established earlier, namely, events that are within the individual's sphere of control and events that are outside of it. Once an individual recognizes the distinctions, he/she is on the path of moral progress. Moral progress is possible only within the sphere of the controllable. The uncontrollable is left to the divinities. Furthermore, moral progress itself is not an easy task and is, in fact, a lifelong project. Many individuals hastily embark on it, thinking that it is easy. Upon taking a few steps, they discover that it is a demanding project. For many, it is a burden. For others, it is a challenge. To a considerable number, it does not exist; they are not even aware of its presence.

To those for whom it is a challenge, here are some suggestions from Epictetus that they may wish to consider. Moral progress is a goal. Goals, however, are not so easily definable that individuals may confidently pursue them. Goals are in a crucial way conditioned by external things in that our sense impressions are affected by external things. Our sense impressions are affected by external things in at least four ways, according to Epictetus. When we perceive things and choose values, we perceive them insofar as we think (1) they are or so seem to be, (2) they are not or so seem not to be, (3) they are but do not seem to be, and (4) they are not yet seem to be.[29] Given that this is how we perceive the world through the prism of external things, we rarely know which goals to pursue and which to avoid. Thus, good and evil tend to overlap, and in the absence of precise criteria, it is exceedingly difficult to steadfastly and consistently choose between good and evil on the long path of moral progress.

In moral discourse, the term progress implies that a road is being traveled—a road with a point of departure and an explicit destination. Education mediates this road. On the road of moral progress, the self is continuously confronted with external impressions of external things in which being and seeming to be play a decisive role. As a consequence, the self has to struggle to choose correctly. The above notion is fundamental to Epictetus' impressive insight into the nature of moral progress.

Consider the following instructive statement, in which Epictetus teaches us the method by which, if we so choose, we could embark on the exceedingly difficult task of overcoming the power of external impressions, those which block the possibility of becoming good.

Every habit and faculty is confirmed and strengthened by the corresponding actions, that of walking by walking, that of running by running. If you wish to be a good reader, read, if you wish to be a good writer, write. If you should give up reading for thinly(?) days one after the other, and be engaged in something else, you will know what happens. . . . In general, therefore, if you want to do something, make a habit of it; if you want not to do something, refrain from doing it, and accustom yourself to something else instead. . . . For it is inevitable that some habits and faculties should, in consequence of the corresponding actions, spring up, though they did not exist before, and that others which were already there should be intensified and made strong.[30]

The passage is full of profound insights, from which I wish to present the consequences of the following central concepts. They are:

1. Habit is a crucial way of nurturing moral ideas;
2. A repeated struggle to become a certain kind of person leads to a kind of moral progress;
3. To do something is just as strong as not doing it—it is really a question of resolve.

Consider the following example that Epictetus uses to test his notion of moral progress. He writes: "For when once you conceive a desire for money, if reason be applied to bring you to a realization of the evil, both the passions stilled and our governing principle is restored to its original authority; but if you do not apply a remedy, your governing principle does not revert to its previous condition, but our being aroused again by the corresponding external impression, it bursts into the flame of desire more quickly than it did before."[31]

Let us pause for a moment and really reflect on this message in the context of the concepts of (1) habit, (2) repeated doing, and (3) resolve.

Money for Epictetus is an external power that subtly imposes itself on us by overpowering us. For some individuals, it is a value they will die for—it is deeply "stilled" in the very nerves of their bodies. They feel its power and they respond to it by doing anything within their disposal to acquire it. Some even enslave themselves to it. Acquiring money as a value becomes a firm habit that some individuals consciously and proudly practice. Money, for them, is a power in itself. Through it, they could attempt to acquire other values, such as friends, fame, stature, honor, respect, immortality. Money, as an external impression, deeply penetrates everyday existence; individuals naturally, therefore, habitually enjoy its effects, such as comfort, security, and prestige. Its effects are as powerful as the desire for it.

An individual who repeatedly and almost mechanically performs this habit obviously sees no flaws worthy of his/her attention. Everything is as it ought to be. It is positive to die for money, given its enjoyable effects. The individual has already intellectually and emotionally unthinkingly justified the desire for money as an absolute good. Suppose that another individual with different values challenges the money monger with the following argument: Succumbing to the ideology of acquisition is not worthy of an authentically free human being, and to the extent that he/she is a begetter of money, one is not free but rather a slave. In short, slavish are those who are overpowered by money, although they may not know it.

Repeated performance of a habit, such as seeking money, leads to the solidification of the habit to a point that one is unable to break it. No matter what the counter arguments against the habit are, including the attribution of slavishness to those who are obsessed with the habit, the individual does not accept them. The counter argument could easily be dismissed as a value or norm that the money lover does not share. Some moneymakers even go to the extent of attributing laziness, cowardice, stupidity, and lack of ambition to those who think that money making is a vice. Note that instead of feeling regret, blameworthiness, and challenge, the moneymakers refuse to listen to arguments that could make them critically examine the habit. Reflection or the possibility of reflection is replaced by defensiveness, stubbornness, and even viciousness. These responses are not worthy of human beings who ought to wish to travel the long and difficult road of moral progress.

A repeated action such as money seeking can surely blind the mind to the need of examining the grounds for a habit, to see if there is any reason for the habituated actor to need change at all. Rather, repeated doing, stimulated by the convenient and conservative force of habit does not lead to critical inquiry or the wish to inquire, but to arrogance, firmly supported by happy self-righteousness. When an individual is habituated in this sense, and the habit makes repeated action a workable virtue, the habituated is convinced that critical inquiry is not for him/her but only for the softhearted and soft-minded.

The moneymaker then has a problem only in the eyes of those for whom money-making is not a positive value. To the moneymaker himself/herself, money is a power, a symbol of achievement, a crown of honor, a virtue of the aristocrat. How is one to convince him/her that none of his/her claims are true? It is certainly possible to be able to think critically even when one is enveloped by the warmth of comfort. Even human beings who have never suffered in their lives may know the difference between the experience of wealth and the unbearable burden of poverty. The money-getter has surely enjoyed the benefits of money and knows them directly. What they have never directly experienced or seriously thought about is the ugly and disgraceful insult of being poor.

It is the moneyless who feel the insult and absolute ugliness of poverty. All others may at best be sympathetic with the condition of the poor. Others may not be capable at all of expressing any sympathy. Worse of all is the fact that some rich persons really think that the poor are poor because they do not know the value, importance, and privilege of having substantial amounts of money.

For the rich and successful, the acquisition of money is a supreme habit—a habit worth glorifying. The habit is the virtue of virtues. The money owner is absolutely convinced that his/her habit is a good and that he/she is free, and not, as Epictetus contended, a slave to an external force.

Slavish are the rich, contend those who are either cursed by the creator to be perpetually dependent on the rich or those who have miserably failed at the market where only the fittest survive and the unfit surrender to destitution and poverty. Free are those who have survived the struggle and become conspicuously rich, respected, and highly envied members of society.

Epictetus challenges the above views root and branch by developing a truly courageous and original conception of freedom. His main thesis is that any person who submits to an external force as such is unfree. Epictetus speaks for himself in the following sentence: ''He is free who lives as he wills, who is subject neither to compulsion nor hindrance, nor force, whose choices are unhampered, whose desires attain their end, whose aversions do not fall into what they would avoid.''[32]

Freedom, according to Epictetus, is the total power of the human self to determine the form and content of its desires, wants, and needs. Freedom is also the power to avoid choosing what should not be chosen, not wanting what should not be wanted, not desiring what should not be desired. Freedom then has a positive aspect, namely, the power to determine the content of all human experience; its negative aspect is the power to avoid all that is not good for the self. As Epictetus put it in a truly splendid way, ''No man is free who is not master of himself.''[33] By this criterion, the rich are not free. They are the slaves of money.

Most individuals rather axiomatically believe that freedom is merely the ability and willingness to ''satisfy yourself with what you desire.''[34] Epictetus radically disagrees with that popular conception. If freedom means anything at all, it entails the absolutely imperative condition that not all that is desired should be satisfied. In fact, freedom entails the destruction of desire as such.[35] This is no doubt a strong and deceptively phrased argument, which I will challenge later on.

The destruction of the desires, according to Epictetus, is a supreme act of self-purification that removes all that defiles the emotions. The impure self is not fit for freedom, is not even aware of its lack of freedom; and in this total lack of awareness lies the bedrock of this condition. The destruction of the desires then is the keystone of the meaning of freedom understood as emancipation from the self-imposed domination by an individual over desire.

Epictetus speaks for himself: "Purify your judgments, for fear that lest something of what is not your own may be fastened to them, or grown together with them, and may give you pain when it is torn loose. And every day while you are training yourself, as you do in the gymnasium, do not say you are "pursuing philosophy" [indeed an arrogant phrase!] but that you are a slave presenting your emancipator in court."[36]

The important question to be put to Epictetus is this. If freedom is merely emancipation from the dominating presence of desire, in what sense could the self be free if it is permitted to be guided by desire, given the fact that all selves are desiring beings? One answer is that Epictetus seems to be claiming that man is not only a desiring being but also a being traveling on the long and strenuous road of moral progress. In fact, man himself is moral progress. What Epictetus means by the cryptic phrase "man is moral progress" may be reconstructed to mean the following: moral progress is liberation from desire, for example, the desire for the acquisition of money for its own sake.

To say that man is moral progress means that man is a being who evolves from some kind of morality to another—from some kind of person toward another. The word progress itself is an evolutionary and therefore transformative term. Man as a morally progressing being is transformed by progressive education and experience. It is very important, however, to stress that the education is self-chosen and self-guided. Of course, educators can and do play a role as models after whom those who will educate pattern themselves. It is crucial that education be self-guided, if education is to have—as it desired—a lasting impact on human beings. Education and the possibility of moral progress are importantly related.

Man, whose main telos is moral progress, can evolve from one way of being toward another. That evolution is itself an educational experience, a kind of moral progress. The content of moral progress is human desire, and it is the desires that are affected during the process of education. It is the desires that are the real stuff that moral progress seeks desperately to transform. As one example of this transformation, the desire for sex with moderation is reasonable and should be carefully nurtured by education.

It is typical of human beings, as Epictetus understands their character, that they do not methodically distinguish events under their control—for example, their judgment of the desirability of an external impression such as money, from the facts of human nature, such as the fragility of the body. Human beings wrongly worry about both to the same degree. It is the inability to distinguish the two that constitutes human misery. Therefore, genuine education could play a decisive role here. If people wished it to, education could teach the value of distinguishing the controllable from the uncontrollable. One of the central moments of an authentic educational experience is—given the distinction between the controllable and uncontrollable—pursuing desires that are worth pursuing, those that (a) apply only to the controllable sphere, (b) are controllable themselves, that is to say that they are not excessively liked because anything excessive is dangerous, and (c) are directed and willed by the divine, who makes it possible for human beings to will what He wants them to will.

Unfortunately, unlike Aristotle before him, and Foucault much later after him, Epictetus does not say that not all desires are necessarily bad. Nor does he state that human beings need not prohibit themselves from all desires. On the road to moral progress, human beings are also desiring beings, and moral progress and desires are not totally incompatible. In fact, there may be desires within the controllable sphere that are worth developing and purifying by reflective self-education. It is very unreasonable and unfair to human beings to deprive them of all desires. Epictetus is right that not all desires are objectively good for human beings, but he is disappointingly wrong when he claims that true moral progress is emancipation from desires as such.

To claim as Epictetus does that freedom is really emancipation from the desires is to violate the biological constitution of humans as beings who desire both material things, such as food, shelter, clothing, and nonmaterial ends, such as God, freedom and thought. Human beings are by no means free when they somehow train their bodies—if this is doable and desirable—to be emancipated from desires for material and nonmaterial things. If Epictetus is really arguing for this sense of freedom, he is depriving human beings of their right to happiness, which is fundamentally both a material and nonmaterial experience. I will go into more depth on this topic when I reflect on the question of power that does not dominate, but rather transcendental power which enriches human beings to profoundly examine and understand themselves as very complex beings. A powerful passage from Epictetus reminds us, ''The man who exercises himself against such external impressions is the true athlete in training. Hold unhappy man; be not swept along with your impressions! Great is the struggle, divine the task; the prize is a kingdom, freedom, serenity, peace. Remember God; call upon him to help you and stand by your side, just as voyages in a storm, call upon the Discourse.''[37]

Kant

Kant's enterprise is remarkably similar to that of Epictetus. Like Epictetus before him, Kant is not very favorably disposed toward the desires, or, as he prefers to call them, the inclinations. Kant's radically original conception of freedom seeks to locate the possibility of becoming free in the demanding and most difficult task of freeing the reluctant self from its zealous attachment to the inclinations. Freedom, for Kant, begins precisely at the point in which the self experiences attachment to the inclinations as a serious problem and not as a virtuous habit. To elaborate, I now wish to provide an exposition of the general thesis as elaborated in Kant's *Foundations of the Metaphysics of Morals*.

Any action worthy of its name is free—objectively free—if and only if it is firmly anchored upon the *good will*. The good will is absolutely good if and only if it anchors a particular action that is objectively free in such a way that the good will is analytically the cause and effect of a free action.

The good will is good in itself. It constructs the condition of its goodness and it simultaneously constructs effects that are visibly good. It is in this sense that the good in itself resembles an analytical statement for Kant. Nothing that is visibly good is caused by anything that is either internal (guided by the inclinations) or external (such as a law that commands obedience by fear) to the acting self. Rather, anything that is absolutely good is caused by the good will and its effect is goodness. Insofar as the cause and effect of an objectively free action are derivable from the good will, the good will is analytical.[38]

A good will is good in a deeper sense because it is a will that objectively follows the self-constructed faculty of *pure reason*. When pure reason applies itself to free action, it becomes practical reason—reason that guides action. Practical reason is most operative in the concept of duty. Duty is authentic when the self undertakes an action that is frequently opposed by the power of the resistant desires (or inclinations), overcomes the resistance, and undertakes the action in spite of the resistance. The power of a freely chosen internalization of a sense of duty enables the self to decide against the desires and for the sake of the purity of the imperative of pure reason. Kant puts it thus: "Now as an act from duty wholly excludes the influence of inclination and there with every object of the will, nothing remains which can determine the will objectively except the law, and nothing subjectively except pure respect for this practical law. This subjective element is the maxim that I ought to follow such a law even if it thwarts all my inclinations."[39]

Thus, for Kant, "The first proposition of morality is that to have moral worth, an action must be done from duty. The second proposition is: An action performed from duty does not have its moral worth in the purpose which is to be achieved through it but in the maxim by which it is determined."[40]

The concept of duty is not an empirical one, that is to say, it is not derived from actual human experience. There may not have existed actual human beings who conducted their actions in accordance with the sense of dutifulness. Even if there has not existed a single human being who lived dutifully, one can still conceive of a dutiful self metaphysically. The rational/moral concept of duty is a metaphysical concept independent of empirical history. Duty is a metaphysical concept that is a priori derived from the depths of pure reason. This argument is truly new with Kant. True, Plato hints at it with the idea of the Forms, but even Plato does not entirely detach the Forms from experience. Rather, Plato conceives of the Forms as derivable from human beings before human beings become deeply alienated from themselves.

Kant, unlike Plato, consistently insists that the concept of duty is underivable from human practice. It is derived solely from pure reason, if not as a realizable idea, certainly as a regulative ideal—the ideal of human perfection.

Kant speaks for himself:

Nor could one give poorer counsel to morality than to attempt to derive it from examples. For each example of morality which is exhibited to me must itself have been previously judged according to principles of morality to see whether it is worthy to serve as an original example, i.e., as a model. By no means could it authoritatively furnish the concept of morality. Even the Holy one of the Gospel must be compared with our ideal of moral perfection before he is recognized as such; Even He says of himself, ''why call ye (whom you see) good? None is good (the archetype of the good) except God only (whom you do not see).'' But whence done have the concept of God as the highest good? Solely from the idea of moral perfection which reason formulates a priori and which it inseparably connects with the concept of a free will.[41]

The point is simply that duty, like the idea of God, is not compellingly believable because it cannot be seen, touched, etc. Rather, the idea of duty compels us by the sheer power of its intelligibility, just as the idea of God is absolutely convincing precisely because it is invisible. The intelligible—the realm to which God and duty belong—are derivable from the invisible source of reason and never from the visible source of empirical practice, the realm of phenomenal examples. In Kantian jargon, duty is a noumenal and not a phenomenal concept.[42]

For Kant, human beings are rational beings, and rationality is a faculty that enables human beings (a) to will only the good will; (b) to practice dutifulness as the effect of the following of the good will; (c) to manifest their duties in the form of maxims, such as the maxims:

1. ''Act only according to that maxim by which you can at the same time will that it should become a universal law.''

2. ''Act as though the maxim of your action were by your will to become a universal law of nature.''[43]

3. ''Act so that you treat humanity, whether in your own person or that of another, always as an end and never as a means only.''[44]

For Kant, the key to the possibility of envisioning a self that is capable of living in accordance with the concept of duty, and thereby determining its destiny, is the concept of freedom—freedom from the unbearable burden of the desires.

It will be recalled that the good will generates causes and effects. Causality, we may say following Kant, is the property of the good will, just as freedom in turn is the property of causality.[45] By the latter statement, I think Kant means this: An action is objectively free if and only if it is self-caused. For example, I chose not to eat chocolate, although my desires were pressuring me to eat chocolate, which I have come to learn is objectively not good for my health. Note that the action I have willfully chosen is my own, given the good reasons I have for doing one action (not eating chocolate) as opposed to another (eating chocolate). My self-developed reason helped me to decide on my course of action. There is no other "foreign" reason that I did not freely choose that persuaded me to go against my desires. In this instance, both the cause (the existence of reasons) and the effect, the action I chose, were self-caused. In this sense, free action is the property of causality. None of the above claims are empirically demonstrable, however, as Kant repeatedly insists. They are claims that are established on the behalf of pure reason in its practical form.

To be a human being, Kant repeats, is among other things (1) the power to will; (2) the practice of duty; (3) the construction of maxims; (4) the unusual task of being free—free from desires so as to be in a position to judge objectively.[46] All human beings, insofar as they are able to exercise the powers in (1), (2), and (3) above, are qualified to be called rational beings. All rational beings are capable of being objectively free, insofar as they exercise their power of judgment freely. The idea of freedom then is an objective fact for rational human beings. Freedom is not an illusion. It is rather a fact that human beings can retrieve from the depth of pure reason, which they can then practically apply to realize freedom.

Kant is not saying that given the power to judge freely, one could easily produce a freely chosen action. No. Kant knows that the desires, which are constitutive of human nature, are going to resist any counseling of reason. Nor is he explicitly arguing that the desires should be dominated by reason. I think that the idea of domination destroys the very idea of the realizability of freedom. I think Kant knows this. If he is not aware of this, then he is certainly contradicting himself, because freedom cannot be reconciled with domination, not even domination by reason. Just what is Kant saying?

Kant is actually aware of the fact that desires, in the form of impulses and incentives, are constitutive parts of our humanity. We are nothing without our desires, but at the same time, human nature is much more than the desires. Although it is exceedingly difficult for us, we can surmount desire if we really want to and allow good will to aid us in deciding objectively, therefore universally, that it is not only a choice for us but also for all other members of the universe.

The fact that our sensuous nature gets easily affected by our desires need not preclude the possibility that we can also be rational beings capable of acting dutifully, in opposition to desires. On the one hand, as sensuous beings, we are guided by desires under the spontaneous leadership of our wild instincts. This makes us phenomenal beings, beings firmly attached to the world of appearance, and subject to its unstable laws, laws which produce ever changing human beings.

On the other hand, as rational beings, we are also capable of transcending the world of appearances and heading toward the world of things in themselves, things that never change. This would make us noumenal beings, who live in a noumenal world through our imagination. As noumenal beings, we are subject only to the world of freedom. When we fully exercise this freedom, we become autonomous beings. As Kant puts it, "The concept of autonomy is inseparably connected with the idea of freedom, and with the former, there is inseparably bound the universal principle of morality, which ideally is the ground of all action of rational beings, just as natural law is the ground of all appearances.''[47] When we act objectively and freely, we do so only as noumenal beings who are fully capable of ''disregarding all desires and sensuous attractions.''[48]

We have come full circle. In the able and disciplined hands of Emmanuel Kant, the long tradition of revolt against desires that began with Epictetus obtains a systematic defense on behalf of the possibility of becoming objectively free. In the hands of Kant, desires are finally given a severe criticism resulting in the view that freedom is not obtained through the realization of all that is desired. Rather, if freedom means anything at all, it is attainable only by disregarding everything sensuous that blocks the passage of pure reason toward the practical.[49] It is from Kant that I learned how crucial the power of self-construction is for the idea of self-constructing any human values; moreover, it is from Kant as well that the idea of self-legislation, as a limiting condition of constructing values, came.

The Psychological Roots of Domination

Dostoyevsky

It may not be an exaggeration to state that in world literature (at least the segment with which I am familiar) Dostoyevsky's name shines like a lonely star in its relentless struggle to discern the depths of human desires—particularly that dimension of the desires that harbors the unfathomable and bewildering phenomenon of evil.[50] The idea of self-construction which I am developing here will be incomplete unless informed by the notion of power as domination as Dostoyevsky presents it so powerfully.

The phenomenon of evil is one of the central themes in Dostoyevsky's short but intense career. *Notes from Underground* and *The Possessed* are devoted to the discernment of the origins of power, ideology, and tyranny. In that persistent and disarmingly honest project, the meaning of desires is one of the keystones to the understanding of human nature. The phenomenon of evil looms large in his analysis of human nature. In what follows, I wish to succinctly formulate some Dostoyevskian insights about desires that are scattered through the pages of *The Possessed* in particular, and, to a lesser extent, *Notes from Underground*.

The central chapter in *The Possessed* which forcefully and directly examines the phenomenon of *evil* and through it the nature of the desires is chapter 9 of part 2 entitled ''At Tikhon's (Stavrogin's Confessions).'' In this chapter, Dostoyevsky's aim is to demonstrate the existence of the devil, the father of evil by examining Stavrogin's dream. Stavrogin, we are told, saw something in his dream. He saw the devil himself. Here is how Stavrogin relates his dream to Tikhon, as Dostoyevsky narrates it: ''And then, briefly and so abruptly that many words were almost unintelligible, he told Tikhon that he was subject to strange hallucinations, especially at night; that he seemed to be or feel close to him some evil creature, mocking and 'rational,' which took on a variety of personalities and characters, but which he knew was always the same creature— 'and it always makes me furious.' "[51]

Stavrogin continues: "So let me tell you to start with that there is nothing I am ashamed of! And now, to make up for my bluntness, I will declare openly and unblushingly that I do believe in the Devil; that I believe canonically in a personal, not an allegorical devil. And I would also like to assure you that I do not wish to extract any secrets from anyone. Well, I suppose that covers it."[52]

Stavrogin's life itself is patterned after this model of evil. His is a life filled with evil desires, devilish plans, indulgent impulses, brutal instincts, intriguing designs, cruel love affairs, recklessness, selfishness, and thoughtlessness. At every step of the way, Stavrogin abuses the desires, and the desires in turn darken the joys of life for him. The great Kantian possibility of autonomy is foreign to Stavrogin's soul, but he shares with Kant the great idea of "radical evil."

Stavrogin's confession to Tikhon was that he was responsible for the horrible rape and murder of a truly innocent twelve-year-old girl, Matryosha. It was in the heat of intense passion, at a moment of the intoxication of the desires, at a time in which Stavrogin had totally lost control over himself that he committed the horrible rape. Stravrogin was possessed by the devil when he enacted this crime, or so he confesses to Tikhon. During the time that he led the girl to murder herself, he was not, as we may assume, beside himself, temporarily mad. No. Shocking though it may be, he was in full control of his senses. He knew what he was doing. He was cold, reasonable, and lucid. He raped soberly and willfully. He was so lucid that he confessed to remembering every detail of the incident. He was of sound mind and fully responsible for his actions.

Evil, the potential source of power as domination, Dostoyevsky seems to instruct us, does not reside in madness or the loss of self-control. It resides in the quite lucid will to coldly, therefore reasonably and often joyfully, inflict suffering and death upon others. In a portrait of Stavrogin, Dostoyevsky himself said: "He had more viciousness in him than both those men put together, but his viciousness was cold and controlled and, if it is possible to say so, reasonable—the most repulsive and dangerous variety there is. So let me repeat once more: I considered him then just as I consider him today (when everything is over) as the type of man who, if struck in the face of receiving a similar insult, would kill the offender then and there, without challenging him to a duel."[53]

Dostoyevsky's portrait of Stavrogin becomes complicated. There is no doubt that Stavrogin, the possessed, is a heinous and cold-blooded killer. Stavrogin's lack of a meditative cast of mind by and large accounts for the lax way in which he inflicts torture upon others. This much is readily apparent in Stavrogin's personality as Dostoyevsky depicts it. But there are more wrinkles to this man's personality.

After Matryosha's death, we see Stavrogin struggling against himself and against those desires that overcame him and made him the cause of another person's early and unexpected death, while he himself lingers in a tortured, restless, meaningless, and sometimes guilt-ridden existence. Since Matryosha's death, life has definitely become a prolonged adventure and an unbearable burden, rather than a joyous path with frequent mishaps.

Although Stavrogin has difficulty accepting the fact, he is frightened, haunted by "remorse." He committed to memory every single detail of the incident that proceeded Matryosha's death. He keeps on recalling the fists that threatened him, full of hate, marked by intense anger—the terrifying fists of the little girl. He struggled to forget, but the memory was too deeply engrained and he simply could not. It is this, the refusal of memory to die, that scared him to death. The source of his great fear is the possibility that he may never be able to forget. He struggles to kill the memory, but the memory keeps killing him instead. His project, which is rather a hopeless one, is to rid himself of this fear. Tikhon, the psychologist, knows this but does not dwell on it.

Dostoyevsky has Stavrogin say:

I had never experienced anything like it before. I remember sitting like that until night. I didn't stir and had no idea of the time. Now I would like to explain clearly what happened. Was it what they call remorse or a feeling of guilt? I can't answer that even today. But I know that I can't bear to see that figure, and precisely when it stands in the doorway, yes, and just at that moment, not a second earlier or later, just when she shook her head and threatened me with her tiny raised fist. Now her gesture and the threat in it were no longer comic but terrifying. I pitied her and my pity tended into madness, and I would have given my body to be torn to pieces if only it could be undone. It is not my crime that obsesses me; it is not even that I regret her dying so deeply. What I cannot stand is that moment, and since then I have relived it almost every day, and I know perfectly well that I am doomed. It is that vision that I cannot bear just as I couldn't bear it even then, although I didn't know it. And this apparition doesn't come to me by itself—I call it forth and I can't help doing so, although it makes life impossible for me. Ah, if only I could see her when I am awake, even if it was nothing but a hallucination! I wish she would look at me with her big feverish eyes, just as they were then that she would see—but it is just a stupid idea, and nothing of the sort will ever happen![54]

Clearly then, Stavrogin is not like Kant's ideal self, obsessed with the desire to overcome a profoundly disturbing feeling of moral shame and having the subsequent rational resolve to reemerge as a moral/rational hero fully committed to acting only out of a sense of duty and never out of a sense of impulsive feeling. Stavrogin certainly does not fit the Kantian framework of being. He is a man of the flesh and aware, as Aurelius would say, of the sins of passion and desire, or aware of their existence only to the extent that he sins spontaneously, willfully, and powerfully.

Stavrogin is certainly not like Dostoyevsky's underground man, the chief character in *Notes from Underground*. The differences are quite striking. Stavrogin's disease, I have argued, is the fear of not facing himself—facing the consequence of his evil actions. He is power-seeking, selfish, cold, thoughtless, malicious, proudly obsessed with himself in a morbid way. He is certainly not embittered or resentful. In fact—and this connection with the underground man is important—he is the cause for the resentment and vindictiveness of numerous human beings toward characters among whom he is the most exaggerated symbol.

The underground man comes into being precisely because vicious characters like Stavrogin become the seed that produces resentment, spite, hate, and alienation. The character, Stavrogin, enjoys inflicting suffering upon others; the underground man, as the living consequence of the infliction of suffering, begins to enjoy suffering as such.

The underground man, for Dostoyevsky, symbolizes man as "affected by progress and European civilization,"[55] that is, as hyperconscious, peace loving, logical, utilitarian, and advantage seeking.[56] The underground man has fully internalized the above social complexes which seem to preclude the possibility of greatness due to an excessive consciousness that blocks the kind of action that produces greatness. Ralph Matlow is profoundly right when he writes, "Suffering, and the necessity for suffering become a mainstay of Dostoevsky's philosophy. In the *Notes*, he introduces one of his most brilliant discoveries, that suffering can become an object rather than a result."[57] Too much thinking, and the hesitations that typically result from it, can easily generate a mediocre, a socially conscious man who is without authentic individuality.

Contrary to the commonplace notion that civilization has tamed man, civilized man in fact has become wilder, more blood-thirsty, more expressive of his genuine desire for "wealth, prosperity, freedom, peace."[58] The more civilization attempts to tame man, to soften him, the more his desires revolt, the more wild he becomes. Man, as envisioned by Kant, is inauthentic—he is paralyzed, impoverished, without the freedom to choose, without desires and passions, or so Dostoyevsky thinks.

But man without desires is nothing for the narrator. The undesiring man is a man without character, vitality. A characterless being is a being who cannot choose, and a person without the freedom to choose is essentially a slave. The narrator movingly writes: "For what is a man without desire, without free will and without choice, if not a stop in an organ?" Furthermore, the narrator continues:

H'm! you decide. Our choice is usually mistaken through a mistaken notion of our advantage. We sometimes choose absolute nonsense because in our stupidity we see in that nonsense the easier means of attaining an advantage assumed beforehand. But when all that is explained and worked out on paper (which is perfectly possible, for it is contemptible and senseless to assume in advance that man will never understand some laws of nature), then of course, so-called desires will not exist. After all, if desire should at any time come to terms completely with reason, we shall then, of course, reason and not desire, simply because, after all, it will be impossible to retain reason and desire something senseless, and in that way knowingly act against reason and desire to injure ourselves.[59]

The narrator runs completely counter to the Epictetean and Kantian conceptions of the self in which the self, it was argued, would be freed after it is emancipated from the sins of desire, the chief source of the self's profoundly mistaken conception of freedom. The narrator argues the opposite case quite forcefully. In a dramatic form, the argument may be reconstructed in the following way.

The authentic self is free when it desires everything and anything—including the disadvantageous, the explicitly harmful, and above all, the senseless. One is not free when he/she is reasonable. On the contrary, one is free when he/she knowingly desires the unreasonable, the irrational. True, it is good to desire the reasonable. But reason satisfies only the rational dispositions of human beings. Will, on the other hand, satisfies both the rational and the impulsive dispositions since human beings are both reasonable and unreasonable.[60] Human beings are completely free if and only if they are allowed to desire what is objectively good for them as well as what they stupidly desire. Again, human nature is composed of intelligence and stupidity; consequently, the desires themselves are disposed toward good and harmful objects. This fact about human beings cannot be changed. No reform of man can change this fact. We may better understand human beings if we accept this fact than if we attempt to change them. By changing them, we may make them even more miserable, more pitiful than they already are. The various attempts at changing man, which began the Enlightenment and continued through and after the era of socialism, have crippled, impoverished, and worsened the human condition.

Modern man, of which the underground man is a paradigmatic example, is a miserable being—a being who cannot choose, cannot desire, cannot be unreasonable, cannot destroy, and yet he/she wants to choose, to desire, to be unreasonable, and to destroy. Above all, he wants and enjoys suffering.

The underground man experiences life as a series of catastrophes, a pile of dirt and dust. He is erudite, "civilized," bookish, proud, and intelligent. But in the eyes of the rich, the accomplished, the powerful, and the famous, the underground man's erudition, civilization, pride, and intelligence are nothing of any value. Consider, for example, the scene at the bar, the bar where the underground man goes to get even with his rich and accomplished friends. He imposes himself on them. He lectures them and yet they ignore him like a fly, and he, in turn, is "crushed and humiliated." As the literature puts it: "I scanned them all insolently with my dulled eyes. But they seemed to have forgotten me altogether. They were noisy, vociferous, cheerful."[61]

The underground man, as man in his honest moments, needed recognition. Those powerful men, by whom the underground man wished to be recognized, refused to extend it to him. By their relentless inattention, they crushed and humiliated him. He desperately wished to be recognized, and they, tenaciously and deliberately, withheld that recognition from him.

The Stavrogins of the age enjoyed inflicting pain upon their underground slaves, of which this particular underground person of the "abstract and intentional" city of Petersburg is the most dramatic metaphor—the metaphor of life as catastrophe, of the marked absence of community.

In spite of the underground man's disposition toward intense anguish, his internalization of resentment, and his wish to explode and get back at others, he also attempts to revitalize his sad soul by attempting to love. As Vyacheslav Ivanov put it, "the 'Underground Hero,' although repulsive in his manner of life, is capable of clear sighted and lofty meditation."[62] The bar conversation with the young Liza points in that direction, although, it turned out to be a direction without a destiny or a goal. It was a direction with a promising stand in that it excites the reader's expectation. But it is a very short excitement, because the underground man uses his great power of speech not to really communicate his feeling to his beloved, as Plutarch would have it, but to test his power. The underground man is not sure of himself. He is anxious, unhappy, and cannot fall in love, even if he wants to. I will let the narrator speak about the underground man's conception of love: "Love is a holy mystery and ought to be hidden from all others' eyes, no matter what happens. That makes it holier and better."[63]

The underground man preaches to young Liza to change herself. He insists that she abandon the profession of prostitution. Witness the power of his words as he preaches, with words that really reduce her to nothing. He powerfully denudes her of her identity. Here are those words:

But when will you be free? Only think. What are you giving up here? What is it you are making a slave of? It is your soul, together with your body; you are selling your soul which you have no right to dispose of! You give your love to be outraged by every drunkard. Love! But after all that is everything, but after all, it is a jewel, it is a maiden's treasure, love—why! After all a man would be ready to give his soul, to face death to gain that love. But how much is your love worth now? You can be bought, all of you, body and soul, and there is no need to strive for love when you can have everything without love.[64]

These are not easy words. They seem to be the words of a true believer. They are so powerful that they could crush a person's self-worth. The more sensitive the person, the deeper the words penetrate. Liza is destroyed by them—she yearns for change. She is willing to be transformed into the underground man's apparent conception of a true self. But the underground man does not mean what he says, he only knows how to say what could be profoundly moving. He himself says this much: "I felt for some time that I was turning her soul upside down and breaking her heart, and the more I was convinced of it, the more I wanted to gain my end as quickly and as effectively as possible. The sport, the sport attracted me; yet it was not merely the sport.''[65]

Earlier, in Chapter 1, we learned from the speech act philosophers that language can be used prelocutionarily, that is for the rhetorical purpose of persuading. Here, the narrator has given us a model of that particular usage. He does not mean what he says, but can say it so persuasively that he deceives us into believing that he means what he says. He himself, not to mention us the innocent reader, is stunned by the power of his speech. He has learned and mastered the craft of his age, an age that subtly used words, the most divine gifts of humanity, not to inspire sincere, truthful thinking, as Habermas dreams, but rather as a tool of domination as Foucault has bitterly argued.

The underground man is not merely a victim of suffering. No. That would be too simple. Rather, he himself is intoxicated with power—the power that gives power to oneself by destroying the other. He has fallen in love with the image of power. He is seduced by the prejudices and cultures of his age, which he so masterfully tested against Liza. Liza herself is a metaphor of those who are easily deceived by whoever does it sensitively, delicately, and, when needed, brutally. Liza is a metaphor of the unconscious, that part of the unconscious that is most vulnerable to manipulation by the language of the ego. The narrator is a master psychologist. He seems to understand the desires of the power hungry as well as the desires of those who are powerless but who hunger for power. The underground man is an amalgam of both desires, and he could use them appropriately. In this sense, the underground man is like Stavrogin in that he enjoys inflicting suffering upon others. He is unlike Stavrogin in that he is objectively powerless in the eyes of those who could crush him. He could crush only those who are absolutely powerless: the sick, the young, the wretched, etc.

Did the underground man fall in love with Liza? If we look at his words, the answer seems to be NO. The narrator tells us that what the underground man wanted was not love, but power—''Power, power was what I wanted then, sport was what I wanted, I wanted to bring out your tears, your humiliation, your hysteria.''[66] Furthermore, ''I am a blackguard because I am the nastiest, stupidest, pettiest, absurdest, and most envious of all worms on earth.''[67] Finally, in an immortal passage that rings with the language of truth, the narrator writes:

I know I shall be told that this is incredible to be as spiteful and stupid as I was; it may be added it was strange that I would not love her, or at any rate, appreciate her love. Why is it strange? In the first place, by then I was incapable of love, for, I repeat, with me, *loving meant tyrannizing and showing my moral superiority.* I have never in my life ever been able to imagine any other sort of love, and having nowadays come to the point of sometimes thinking that love really consists in the right—freely given by the beloved object—to be tyrannized over. Even in my underground dreams, I did not imagine love in any form except as a struggle. I always began it with hatred and ended it with moral subjugation, and afterward I could never imagine what to do with the subjugated object.[68]

I wish to ask my readers if the underground man, like Stavrogin, is not also possessed. Is it not really the highest sin of the desires to appeal to human vulnerabilities—namely, their sentiments and sometimes their stupidities—to convert them into our image, and then, after we do that skillfully, abandon them to despair, anguish, and suffering? Is it not this that the underground man in particular—because he is more subtle, more educated than Stavrogin, the brutal killer—does to the victim of love, the weak, the overburdened, precisely because others have also previously victimized the underground man? Has not the underground man internalized the experience of oppression from which he has learned not the power of forgiveness but rather the power of resentment? Is not the human condition a paradoxical amalgam of darkness and light: hate and love, vengeance and redemption? Is there a way out for us human beings from the paradox of our nature?

I wish to examine some of these questions through the eyes of Freud, my next focus of interpretive reflection.

Freud

Earlier I argued that Dostoyevsky, the writer, was also a master psychologist. His characters, Stavrogin and the underground man, as well as many, many others, are very intriguing from a psychological point of view. These characters, in the able hands of Dostoyevsky, challenge us to examine our own human makeup. They sometimes terrify us when we master the courage that it takes to look inside; at other times, these characters provoke us to examine our dogmas when they show us novel ways of living our lives; sometimes they simply inspire us to think about the unfathomable world of the unconscious, the world in which the capacity to do evil is hidden.

Freud builds upon this tradition, a tradition that is deeply rooted, as I argued earlier, in Plato's immortal portrait of the tyrant in each one of us—the tyrant who lives in the quiet of night when all guards of the self are loose. In his own original way, Dostoyevsky too rediscovers Plato through the remarkable similarity of their insights. Where Plato spoke about the irrational tyrant, Dostoyevsky spoke about evil, and Foucault in his own way spoke about ''minimal domination'' as a facet of the human condition.

Freud joins the discussion with his impressive concept of the unconscious, the world of the psyche; where Plato spoke about the soul, Freud penetrated the structure of the soul, which he called the mental apparatus. In what follows, I wish to restrict my reflections to the desires, as Freud understood them, by making an extended interpretation of two relevant texts: *Beyond the Pleasure Principle* and *Civilization and Its Discontents*. In exploring these two texts, my aim is to restrict the discussions to Freud's conceptions of the human desires as focuses of the plays of power.

The human mental apparatus, for Freud, is compartmentalized into conscious, preconscious, and unconscious aspects. The unconscious aspect, in particular, is the house of unrestrained instincts. A central aspect of the unconscious, the house of the instincts, escapes that world, and in the form of the ego becomes conscious; that is to say, the ego becomes an expression of reality by developing a reality principle—a principle that is explicitly guided by doing deeds that are allowed and by not doing actions that are prohibited.

A crucial aspect of the unconscious, characterized by the awesome presence of the natural instincts, is governed by the pleasure principle, or if you like, by the desires and passions of the self. The pleasure principle, unlike the reality principle, does not recognize boundaries. The pleasure principle, if it could, would abolish the humanly/linguistically constructed distinctions between the real and the unreal, the doable and the undoable, the acceptable and the taboo, the normal and the abnormal, the human and the bestial.

The pleasure principle derives its name from the existence of the desires and the sense in which the desires are conceived to be the beginnings and ends of pleasure and, therefore, the realization of unrestrained human happiness. I have said all of the above by way of preface to Freud.[69] I will now closely follow Freud's mind.

The mental apparatus, contrary to public opinion, is not dominated by the pleasure principle. The most that could be cautiously said about the pleasure principle is this: "There exists in the mind a strong tendency toward the pleasure principle, but that tendency is opposed by certain forces or circumstances, so that the final outcome cannot always be in harmony with the tendency towards pleasure."[70] The rival enemy of the pleasure principle, as it aggressively seeks to assert itself, is none other than the reality principle, which makes its regulative presence felt through the language of the ego. These two rival tendencies in the mental apparatus compete for domination. According to Freud: "The pleasure principle long persists, however, as the method of working employed by the sexual instincts, which are so hard to "educate," and, starting from those instincts, or in the ego itself, it often succeeds in overcoming the reality principle, to the detriment of the organism as a whole."[71]

Freud will later explain what he means by the cryptic phrase, "to the detriment of the organism as a whole," which he simply throws at us here. I will leave it at the ambiguous stage for now.

The pleasure principle attempts to overcome the commanding pressure of the authoritative ego. It often crucially fails. A significant number of pleasures are repressed. Therefore, the process of repression begins, a process that is critical for the development of the happy individual. Repression is a denial of freedom of the unrestrained pleasures.[72]

When certain pleasure-giving desires are repressed, repression is the result. Some of the displeasure that results from repression is perceptual, even illusory; some other displeasures, though, are real and have real sources. For example, some powerful individuals may conceive of our desires as a real danger to society[73] and repress us from freely realizing perceived pleasures. Individuals who are victimized by such explicitly repressive measures internalize a deep hatred of the repressors. Dostoyevsky's underground man became resentful, vindictive, hateful, and cruel precisely because he could not and would not forgive his repressors. The underground man is a paradigm example of the unhappy individual from a Freudian psychoanalytic perspective.

For the individual, as Freud understands, the possibility of being happy is deeply dependent upon the unrestrained expression of the pleasure-guided instincts, and it is precisely this vital need that the reality principle, in concert with the upholders of the "normal" and the allowable, deny to the pleasure principle. But what is denied the pleasure principle is not forgotten by the individual. His or her pleasurable demands retreat to the depth of the unconscious, where they are retained by memory which denounces, accuses, and disturbs the moral world of the ego. The pleasure principle, in the name of happiness-giving pleasures, indicts the reality principle by invoking the happy past as a yardstick that judges the present form of life as miserable, repressive, ungratifying. The past is idealized and the wish to repeat it, hence the process of the eternal return, is emphasized. Equally significant is the unhappy individual's forward-looking production of new, more progressive forms of life. By viewing the reality principle historically, the present is attacked through the idealization of the past as well as a novel vision of the future. The past and the future, eternal return and the not-yet, conspire against the frozen present.[74] The pleasure principle then does not experience all life as nothing but death, destruction, suffering, and decay. Life is also the begetter of life, the harbinger of continuity, the consummation of joy. It is Eros. It is not just and only Thanatos. The pleasure-giving instincts are not just destructive but also constructive; they repeat as well as create. Repetition and creation are two sides of the human condition.[75] Freud himself writes: "We, on the other hand, dealing not with the living substance but with the forces operating in it, have been led to distinguish two kinds of instincts, which are perpetually attempting and achieving a renewal of life."[76]

The biological study of life advances the strong hypothesis that we are destined to die a natural death, and in this sense there are instincts that lead to death. Freud's hypothesis of the existence of the death instincts, which is anchored upon psychoanalysis, is collaborated by biology, a fact that Freud seems to happily welcome.[77] What are some of the pragmatic consequences of Freud's theory so far with respect to the issue of the desires and the fact of domination?

1. The desires are the sources of the need for pleasure, a need that is firmly grounded upon life or sexual instincts. The sexual instincts themselves are life-giving when they are healthily enjoyed. They could also serve a destructive purpose when they are perverse. Freud mentions sadism and masochism as examples of perversities.[78] In this sense, the desires could be potentially dangerous to the self, harbingers of self-abuse in the name of happiness.

2. The sexual instincts are also paradoxically life-giving powers. In this form, they take leave of Eros, which is based on a true love of the beloved without a mixture of hate and on respect, sensitivity, care and trust. In this instance, desires serve a constructive purpose for human beings. They teach them the difficult art of love and genuine care of the other.

3. Life then, as Plato long observed, is an interminable struggle between suffering and joy, destruction and harmony, repetition and creation.

4. The vicissitudes of life itself are reflected in the ups and downs of the instincts themselves. The central conflict is played out between two authoritative instincts: the death instincts to which encompass both the sexual and the life instincts. The pleasure principle is essentially trapped between these instincts themselves, as reflected in the concrete struggle of Stavrogin, Martyosha, and the underground man of exemplary Dostoyevskian literature.

In *Civilization and Its Discontents*, Freud continues his preoccupation with the pleasure principle. For Freud, civilization per se came into being precisely because it skillfully, albeit cruelly, mastered the importance of the destruction of the pleasure principle. Civilization's self-imposed project then was the systematic repression of the pleasure-giving desires. At the very least, civilization does not encourage people to satisfy their desperate need for joy, happiness, less work, more free time, and the unmitigated free expression of desires and wants.

Human beings demand of life, as Freud puts it: "happiness; they want to become happy and to remain so. . . . This endeavor has two sides, a positive and negative aim. It aims, on the one hand, at an absence of pain and unpleasure, and on the other, at the experiencing of strong feelings of pleasure. . . . What decides the purpose of life is simply the program of the pleasure principle. This pleasure dominates the operation of the mental apparatus from the start.[79]

The demand of human beings for happiness is a threat to the growth of civilization as it is understood by the civilizers, or as Foucault would have it, by the norm and value givers. It is they who explicitly and implicitly discipline the wild, savage, and uncultured demands originating in the id—the house of both the life-giving and the sexual instincts. Civilization houses the demands of the ego via the guidance given by the reality principle. This guidance becomes authoritative in the hands of the state and civil society: the family, family tradition, the ethos of the collective culture, the church and its teachings, the educational sphere lead by the experts of culture along with the disciplining power of the social sciences. The final and most authoritative part of the mental apparatus is the super-ego, a function that is crystallized both by the state and by civil society. Civilization works and realizes the project of the civilizers through the concrete works that are visible in the activities of the state and civil society. These works are empirically identifiable.[80]

Freud was aware that although human beings yearn for happiness and would do anything to avoid pain, our very "constitution" condemns us to the fact of unhappiness and suffering as Dostoyevsky before him was acutely aware. The brutal work of civilization through the concrete subapparatuses of the state and civil society is only one of the three sources of anxiety, suffering, anguish, and pain. For Freud: "We are threatened with suffering from three directions: from our own body, which is doomed to decay and dissolution and which cannot do without pain and anxiety as warning signals; from the external world, which may rage against us with overwhelming and merciless forces of destruction; and finally from our relations to other men. The suffering which comes from this last source is perhaps more painful to us than any other.''[81]

For self-constructing subjects who have concretely realized the tragic dimension of life—tragic because there are some powerful forces that mitigate the demands of the id in its relentless effort to overcome the facts of decay and death, the power of the reality principle, and the presence of evil and nonreflectiveness embodied in tyrannical and demonic human beings, the self begins to surrender and moderate the aggressive demands of the pleasure principle.

Freud does not seem concerned about the effects of civilization on human beings who desire, even though they may desire things that are dangerous to them. The idea of self-construction by potentially principle-originating beings, a concept that I defend in this book, is a meaningless worry to Freud. I will return to this point much later as I attempt to defend power as a value—a value which along with the will to construct principles, may give us a vision of human beings who are spiritually and materially powerful, fully vigilant, engaged and engaging, reflective, and full of character in tune with their own individual souls. *Such human beings I wish to call principles-originating and humbly communicative, those who can be trusted to construct human values.*

I will return to Freud's reflections on the question of civilization and its discomforting effects.[82] For the sake of argument, I will assume with Freud that human beings have willfully chosen to be cautious, that have thereby moderated the pleasure principles, have became a reality principle. I will now ask a question that a pragmatist would ask: What is the consequence of the reality principle?

Freud argues that averting suffering instead of enjoying it, as Dostoyevsky's characters often do, has the value of enabling people to cope with life without having to face themselves to deal with good and evil things or events. Human beings, Freud tells us, develop several means of averting suffering from (1) their own body, (2) the pressures of external reality, and (3) some bad human relationships. Freud identifies four modes of coping. They are (1) the killing of the instincts, for example, yoga; (2) sublimation of the instincts, for example, the replacement of sexual desires by intense cerebral focus on the life of the intellect; (3) breaking off with reality completely, for example, the hermit who retreats to wilderness and thus escapes the displeasures of the reality principle under civilization; (4) finally, and the most potent weapon of fighting the inevitability of suffering, is love—the wish to love and be loved completely, a love that is accompanied by the resolve to forgive the sins of the desires and the passions. One example is the love of beauty, a love that does not always consummate in sexual encounters but rather in the Plutarchian notion of spiritual love—a love that combines the demands of Aphrodisia with the noble aims of Eros—a synthesis of thought and rational desires. Beauty, when spiritually and materially understood, is thus the highest synthesis of spirit and matter, thought, and passion.[83]

Human beings, for Freud, are primarily pleasure seekers. Hence the role of the pleasure principle is the key to the mysteries of our existence. As was noted in my treatment of Dostoyevsky's anguished characters, the quest for pleasure even leads some human beings to neglect reason in the name of the pleasurable freedom of destroying themselves. Such is the power of the pleasure principle, such is the power of its presence in the midst of our everyday life. Civilization is acutely aware of the power of the pleasure principle, and it systematically attempts to hamper its intervention.

The various modes of coping with the deeply felt needs of the desires, which are expressed through the pleasure principle, are relative. Each person chooses the appropriate mode of coping. Yet, one of the most unfortunate and dangerous coping modes that civilization seeks to universally impose on individuals, in spite of the uniqueness of their desires, is institutionalized religion. Religion, writes Freud, "restricts this play of choice and adaptation, since it imposes equally on everyone its own path to the acquisition of happiness and protection from suffering. Its technique consists in depressing the value of life and distorting the picture of the real world in a delusional manner—which presupposes on intimidation of the intelligence."[84]

Note that for Freud, and here I agree with him, religion's conception of freedom does not allow for the realization of needs arising out of desires and passions but rather through repression of the dangerous life instincts. It is the presence of these instincts and the individual's acute awareness of them that produce the unhappiness of the individual, and it is the freezing and killing of these instincts that is going to reduce unhappiness and neuroses. Repressive and false expectations and desires may ultimately lead to the happiness of the individual, although it may also lead to the development of a nonintelligent human being.

Freud contended earlier that we suffer so tragically because we are simultaneously hit from three directions: (1) the fragility of our body and the fact of our death, (2) the powerful role of the reality principle in its war with the pleasure principle, and (3) the concrete presence of thoughtless and cruel human beings. There is very little that we can do about (1) and (2). As Epictetus beautifully phrased it, they are forces outside the sphere of human control. We simply surrender to the facts of existence. The third condition is in our sphere of control. Freud speaks for himself:

If we cannot remove all suffering, we can remove some, and we can mitigate some: the experience of many thousands of years has convinced us of that. As regards the third source, the social force of suffering, our attitude is a different one. We do not admit at all; we cannot see why the regulations made by ourselves should not, on the contrary, be a protection and a benefit for every one of us. And yet, when we consider how unsuccessful we have been in precisely this field of prevention of suffering, a suspicion dawns on us that here, too, a piece of unconquerable nature may lie behind—this time a piece of our own psychical constitution.[85]

If we take the effects of the third direction as seriously as Freud does, we find a particular picture of civilization emerging. To begin with, I must now ask a question that should have been asked earlier. What is civilization after all? For Freud, it is a particularly privileged mode of organizing the world. The ''civilized'' mode of organizing the world is composed of (1) order, (2) beauty, (3) cleanliness, (4) religion, (5) abstract intellectual, scientific, and artistic powers, and (6) social relationships among human beings. Of the above parts of civilization, the sixth component, which as you may recall, a result of the third direction of suffering, is the most crucial dimension.

The sixth part, if you wish, constitutes what I will call the political dimension of psychoanalysis. It is political because it is directly concerned with the way power works—the power that some human beings have over others. Power in this sense becomes visible in the social relationships of human beings as members of the state, for example as political officials invested with authority to execute orders by promoting, demoting, recognizing, rejecting, and harassing human beings; as members of the family, for example as fathers, mothers, perpetuators of family tradition; as founders of Ethos; as lovers; as neighbors, etc. At every step, civilization attempts to see to it that a particular strong individual does not dominate all others. There is an obvious attempt on the part of civilization to dispense justice as fairness to all individuals. According to Freud: ''The power of this community is then set up as 'right' in opposition to the power of the individual, which is condemned as 'brute force.' This replacement of the power of the individual by the power of community constitutes the decisive step of civilization.''[86]

One decisive implication of this is that the law of the community subordinates the individual's power to decide on the great questions of life. Civilization presents the nurturance of what I call the *existentially serious person*. A concern with existence, which is the ultimate freedom of the individual, is subordinated to the increased legally sanctified power of the community to decide on the behalf of the helpless, neurotic, pleasure-seeking, and dangerous individual who is incapable of cautiously determining the desires of the self. As we recall (in chapter 1), Foucault convincingly argued against this particular contrivance. The life instincts feel increasingly deprived. They experience community as an oppressive power over their freedoms. The institutions of civilization, such as the state and civil society, are not sensed as protective and productive of happiness but as a cruel, alien force that must not be obeyed. Crucial war begins between the individual and his/her anger. The great struggles of humankind center around the perennial question: What is due to the individual and what is due to civilization? This question, as Freud brilliantly observed, has yet to be resolved. Civilization, Freud argues, is built up upon a renunciation of instinct.

Earlier, we considered various modes of coping with the inevitability of suffering. The fourth mode was love. In love, human beings discover genital love as intensely satisfying. Genital love, for certain human beings, becomes the beginning and end of love. When this happens, human beings expose themselves to love's dangers; unfaithfulness, rejection by the beloved, and, ultimately, the death of the beloved. Some human beings—as Plato and Plutarch wisely observed—with great effort transcend the sexual dimension of love by seeking its hidden spiritual foundation. For example, Saint Francis of Assisi, located in love a deep power that leads to happiness; for him, love did not consummate in sex. He inhibited the sexual instinct.

Inhibition of the sexual aim is quite conducive to the inner purposes of civilization in that the energy of the libido which would otherwise be expended in sex can be transferred to work. Work, not pleasure, is the goal of civilization.[87] A severe curtailment of sexuality does indeed serve civilization well by giving it energetic—albeit sexually frustrated—workers. Pychoanalytically, sexual inhibition results in the cultivation of neurotics. Neurotic people, according to psychoanalytic work, cannot tolerate sexual inhibition.[88] Civilization seeks to subordinate the individual and all his/her urges to that of the group, the team, etc. But love cannot tolerate subordination to any group. At the peak of any love experience, the presence of a third person is a threat. The lovers are sufficient to themselves. Civilization, however, cannot tolerate this sufficiently:

[Civilization that] aims at binding the members of the community together in a libidinal way as well employs every means to that end . . . it summons up aim-inhibited libido on the largest scale so as to strengthen the communal bond by relations of friendship. In order for these aims to be fulfilled, a restriction upon sexual life is unavoidable. But we are unable to understand what the necessity is which forces civilization along this path, and which causes its antagonism to sexuality. There must be some disturbing factor which we have not yet discovered.[89]

Civilization demands of its abstract citizens what does not come naturally to them: love, friendship, and care for strangers. If they were willing to love or befriend anyone at all, it would be the members of their immediate family. On the contrary, Freud notes that individuals may be more inclined to wish for the suffering of those whom they can never love. In a footnote, Freud quotes Heine whose wishes were: (1) a humble cottage with a good bed, good food, fresh milk and butter; (2) flowers on his window; (3) a few fine trees; and (4) "if God wants to make my happiness complete, he will grant me the joy of seeing some six or seven of my enemies hanging from those trees."[90]

The last wish is an extremely important point psychoanalytically. In fact, the "disturbing factor" suggests the probable existence of an aggressive instinct, the death instinct, which Freud analyzed in *Beyond the Pleasure Principle*. He returns to that theme, which deserves a close analysis since it has an important bearing on the nature of the desires that self-constructing subjects are fated to battle. As Freud put it:

Men are not gentle creatures who want to be loved, and who at the most can defend themselves if they are attacked; they are, on the contrary, creatures among whose instinctual endowments is to be reckoned a powerful share of aggressiveness. As a result, their neighbor is for them not only a potential helper or sexual object, but also someone who tempts them to satisfy their aggressiveness on him, to exploit his capacity for work without compensation, to use him sexually without his consent, to siege his possessions, to humiliate him, to cause him, to torture and kill him.[91]

Civilization draws a bitter lesson from the above observed facts: human beings' inclinations toward aggression far outweigh their inclinations toward becoming autonomous and reasonable. In this book, I have attempted to show how Dostoyevsky's characters symbolized the first and Kant's philosophic arguments powerfully articulated for the possibility of the second. Here, Freud is struggling to give us a psychoanalytic interpretation of Dostoyevsky's characters on the levels of the unconscious, the invisible, the world of the desires.

When civilization sensed the potentially dangerous power of the aggressive instincts, it attempted to put to work equally powerful forces to hold them down. One such method is the repression of love aimed at sexual consummation. These repressive methods of civilization, needless to say, were not happily received by the modern subjects. These methods were intensely hated, and this hatred was deeply internalized in the depth of the unconscious—a concept Milan Kundera brilliantly captured when he wrote of the refusal of memory to forget and of the forgetting that history attempts to instill in its laughing modern subjects, which the hate-filled and hurt subjects intensely resist by refusing to forget. This was summarized in Kundera's truly brilliant statement: "The struggle of man against power is the struggle of memory against forgetting."[92]

Civilization developed a yet more subtle method of quieting down the unhappy aggressive instincts. I will let a compelling literary stylist articulate what the method is:

What happens in him to render his desire for aggression innocuous? . . . His aggressiveness is interjected, internalized; it is, in point of fact, sent back to where it came from—that is, it is directed toward his own ego. There it is taken over by a portion of the ego, which sets itself over against the rest of the ego as Super-ego, and which now in the form of "CONSCIENCE," is ready to put into action against the ego the same harsh aggressiveness that the ego would have liked to satisfy upon other, extraneous individuals. The tension between the harsh super-ego and the ego that is subjected to it is called by us the sense of guilt; it expresses itself as a need for punishment. Civilization, therefore, obtains mastery over the individual's dangerous desire for aggression by weakening and disarming it and by setting up an agency within him to watch over it, like a garrison in a conquered city.[93]

In this remarkable passage, Freud seems to have given a remarkable twist to the religions as well as to a Kantian philosophic interpretation of conscience and guilt. Particularly, for Kant, conscience is the human faculty appealed to in order to extract the decision to act from a deep sense of duty. The inner dialogue between the self and the self through the medium of conscience is intended to develop the potential power of human beings to become reflective in a way that may help them to protect themselves from the temptation of the "selfish and destructive desires," as Freud later called them. Kant sets thought against desire; and in that set conscience is a positive power. Reflectively autonomous human beings activate the faculty of conscience not out of a sense of guilt but out of the belief that in moments of great decision, it is thought as care and not self-ishness or thoughtlessness that must guide them. This was at least Kant's ideal conception of the pure self—the self that holds an interminable dialogue with conscience, which is the inner light of reason and passion.

Civilization proceeds in the opposite direction. It appeals to conscience not to activate reason, but rather to activate fear, intimidation, and self-hatred. Civilization says to individuals:

1. If you do not act justly, you will be judged and excommunicated by others;
2. If you do not act justly, you will be punished by the law;
3. If you do not act justly, you will be punished in the next world;
4. If you do not act justly, you will be hated by others;
5. You will be happier if you entirely renounce the instincts for your own sake; if you repress them;
6. Be guided by the community's standards; the community is your true other. Renounce your own selfish individual standards;
7. Love your neighbors even if they hate you. Love them as your own self;
8. Seek the happiness of the community. That ought to be your ideal—an ideal that humanizes you although it may make you individually unhappy.

If one does not follow the above commandments of civilization, one is fated to suffer. Civilization essentially rules not through dialogue but through the technique of the diffusion of guilt. Individual resistances are ignored, or treated as pathological, a fact that led Freud to assert: "In the severity of its commands and prohibitions, it troubles itself too little about the happiness of the ego in that it takes insufficient account of the resistance against them—of the instinctual strength of the Id. . . . On the contrary, it assumes that a man's ego is psychologically capable of anything that is required of it, that his ego has unlimited mastery over his Id. This is a mistake. . . . If more is demanded of man, a revolt will be produced in him or a neurosis, or he will be made unhappy."[94]

Under the intense pressure of those severe commands, what civilization will have on its hands are unhappy and even potentially dangerous individuals who have only internalized their repressed desires. My attempt at reconstructing a theory of power that does not dominate begins here. Dreams, I argue, by interpreting Freud, are rich sources of desires that empower as well as desires that push the self in the direction of Dostoyevsky's *paradoxical and dualistic* characters. The challenge is to balance both proclivities in the self. Dreams that empower are those that aim at the future, that give us images of possibilities.

Dreams that disempower, on the other hand—against which the self must be protected—are the ones that must be carefully regulated by the reflective presence. They are dreams that teach us about the future through the symbols of evil. Both dream forms are crucial for a total understanding of the self.

The Desires in the Form of Dreams

In this section, I wish to argue, by reconstructing Freud, that civilization does not only repress the so-called pathological/abnormal eccentrics—the murderers, rapists, and truly "sick souls" of the scientific age—but also certain ways of being. These repressed ways surface in the form of fragments, chaotic hopes and wishes, confused images, unreachable ideals, surrealistic visions and re-visions, all of which have been evaluated by Freud, for (a) their prophetic value, (b) their visions and re-visions; and (c) their symbolic meanings. These dreams are interpretable because each dream is a result of imagination and imaginations are full of meaning—even the most seemingly meaningless dreams constitute a meaning that must and can be interpreted.[95] Freud's interpretive originality lay in his emphasis on exposing the internal inadequacies of commonplace methods of symbolism and coding. He builds upon the achievements of these methods by adding his own hermeneutics of interpretation, which are a synthesis of critical sensitivity to sense impressions and relaxed self-observation. Added to critical sensitivity and self-observation is the power of memories that refuse to die and stay alive themselves in the depth of the unconscious, which we experience as dealt with by the phenomenon of forgetting. Freud discussed these concepts in *The Interpretation of Dreams*, which was published in 1900—twenty years before the publication of *Beyond the Pleasure Principle* which, as noted earlier, also contained these ideas. We noted as well the importance of the theme of guilt and its internalization in the foundation and maintenance of civilization in *Civilization and Its Discontents*. All these themes are products of Freud's "mature" period.

In his youthful period, Freud explored the intriguing concept of wish fulfillment, through which he deeply penetrated into the world of the unconscious—the true home of the desires. The phenomenon of repression, which as we know is one of the pillars of psychoanalysis as Freud understands it in his later works, was already discovered by him in *The Interpretation of Dreams*. A dream, Freud succinctly argued, is a disguised fulfillment of a suppressed or repressed wish. To prove his point, Freud gives numerous analyses of dreams to illustrate the role of wishes and counter-wishes in them.

Before I proceed to provide an interpretation of dreams as an expression of desires in the form of wishes, I need to explain why I did not begin my analysis of Freud's conception of domination by desires, particularly the aggressive instincts, via his earlier work. My reason is that a deep understanding of the beautifully articulated "doctrine" of psychoanalysis in the later works, with which I began, could be illuminated in a rich and open way through Freud's own exploratory, less rigid, and meditative insights into the nature of human desires. Freud himself, in the preface to the third (revised) English edition, wrote: "This book, with the new contribution to psychology which surprised the world when it was published (1900), remains essentially unaltered. It contains, even according to my present-day judgment, the most valuable of all the discoveries it has been my good fortune to make. Insight such as this falls to one's lot but once in a life time."[96]

I fully agree with Freud. It is through his unusually penetrating insight into the nature of the desires and his valuable unfathoming of the meaningful dreams in which desires manifest themselves that we get an anatomy of "human nature." What human beings desire in dreams in a profound sense is an expression of who they are. In this sense, dreams are disclosers of the meaning of human existence—particularly *who* we are. Who we are, if we ever succeed in discovering this fully, gives us a clue to what we can and cannot become. For example, (1) Do our dreams disclose the wish to dominate, or be dominated, or both? (2) Is domination a value to me, and, if so, why? (3) Do dreams contain elements of "truth"? If so, what kind? (4) Are dreams based on thought, or are they unrelated to thought? (5) If they are the latter, what is their status as a path to truth? (6) Are dreams simple fantasies without thought? (7) What is being represented in dreams? This last question in particular was so crucial to Freud that he allotted a substantial space to the subject, which I wish to explore here. In fact, I will begin with the discussion of this question and make my way to reflecting about the others, particularly the question: Do our dreams disclose the wish to dominate, or be dominated, or both?

What is being represented in dreams? The obvious answer to Freud is: thoughts, dream thoughts, or if you will, dream desires. These desires are manifestly expressed in interpretable, therefore meaningful dreams, whose meanings are buried in those latent thoughts. Dreams then as a rule have manifest and latent meanings. Furthermore, dreams are not about a particular consistent theme. They are rather clusters of disparate images, a plurality of themes, a mass of confusing opposites: red-blue flowers, strong-weak candles, hot-cold water, up/down stream, etc.; they are hidden presences of the ego, the self, in the form of another person. The "other" in a dream is always the self. At this point, I will have Freud speak for himself:

It is my experience, and one to which I have found no exception, that every dream deals with the dreamer himself. Dreams are completely egotistical. Wherever my own ego does not appear in the content of the dream, but only some extraneous person, I may safely assume that my own ego lies concealed, by identification, behind this other person; I can insert my ego into the context. . . . Thus my ego may be represented in a dream several times over, now directly and now through identification with extraneous persons.[97]

Dreams then do not have a clear and consistent meaning; if they did, they would not require an interpreter. Dreams by definition are impregnated with multifarious meanings. They are complicated further by the complexity of the natures of the dreamers: human beings. Further still, to the great credit of Freud, he was the one who woke us up to the fact that dreams hide psychological meanings. Sometimes, the manifest meaning of a dream is contrary to the dream thought. The manifest meaning reverses the latent thought. Dreams are characterized by contraries, contradictions, reversible meanings. According to Freud: "For instance, in the case of a young obsession neurotic, there lay concealed behind one of his dreams the memory of a death-wish dating from his childhood and directed against his father, of whom he had been afraid. Here is the text of the dream: HIS FATHER WAS SCOLDING HIM FOR COMING HOME SO LATE."[98]

The latent wish as opposed to the manifest one, according to Freud, is that the neurotic wished the death of his father—that was the latent dream thought.

Dream thoughts are represented by symbols, according to Freud. He lists and analyzes, with amazing penetration, the symbolic meaning of dreams. For example, a hat symbolizes male genitals; a "little one" as the genital organ. "Being run over" in a dream symbolizes intercourse; buildings, stairs, or shafts symbolize the genitals; landscapes symbolize female organs, and persons symbolize male organs; the up and down movement of staircases symbolizes "the rhythm of the sexual act and its up and down motion."[99] Freud refuses to concede to the critics' resistance to psychoanalysis's reluctance to distinguish between normal and neurotic persons' symbolic dreams. Freud's critics had argued that it is only the neurotic whose dreams are symbolic of latent unhealthy (nonsexual) meanings. The normal ones do not have sexually symbolic dreams at all. Freud cited the text of a dream of a prudish girl. The text was this: "I arrange the center of a table with flowers for a birthday."[100] The flowers were lilies, violets, pinks, carnations in a valley. Lilies symbolizes purity; violets violent rape; carnations freshness, and a centerpiece represents virginity.

Note that every word in the dream was a sexual symbol. Dreams, Freud argues, are also affective. The affects that one genuinely experiences in the dream world of uninhibited desires during wakeful state encounter the powerful presence of external reality. Reality's function is to repress the explosive desires. Dreams are themselves self-censuring. There are dreams that resist the crucial revelation of certain chains in a dream. The absence of these chain links complicates the task of the psychoanalyst as an interpreter, but not to the point that the dream is uninterpretable. The fact that there are roadblocks to be overcome in the quests of interpreting a dream was itself a major discovery made by Freud—a discovery that psychoanalysts should remember when they are struggling with patients' resistance to recalling their dreams. Freud insisted that forgotten dreams can be reconstructed without the patient's help by a highly skilled psychoanalyst.

Dreams are often forgotten. Forgetting is an integral aspect of dreaming. Human beings forget their dreams partly because of the untrustworthiness of the power of meaning. One technique that Freud used to enable patients to recall their dreams is to ask them to repeat them. When Freud did so, he discovered that the patients used different terms to express their dream each time they repeated them. Freud would link the different terms to derive meanings that could constitute the whole dream. Each fresh term stood for a fragment of a whole dream. Through this technique, a dream's whole meaning can be approximately reconstructed.[101]

We have established the argument that patients forget parts of their dream because memory fails them. That is one plausible reason. There is another intriguing reason, however. Patients seem to forget fragments of a dream that they do not want to face. Fragments that disturbingly reveal the features of themselves that are "infantile" or "abnormal" may be repressed by memory. Patients resist these revelations. The task of the psychoanalyst then is (a) to alert patients to the sad fact of the untrustworthiness of memory—a reminder of our finitude; (b) to alert them as well to the fact that the aspects of a dream that have been lost have been deliberately hidden and that patients are resisting the disclosure of a truth about themselves that they cannot resolutely face; and (c) to help them overcome their resistance. Freud's conclusion at this point is that if (c) is successfully undertaken, a dream can be fully interpreted.

I wish to argue with Freud that dreams indeed originate in the *unconscious—the house of the desires, from which the self-constructing moral subject draws some of the content of human values*. The truly fantastic things about which human beings dream have an origin which can be traced. Freud agrees with Nietzsche's assertion that in dreams: "some primeval relic of humanity is at work which we can now scarcely reach any longer by a direct path; and we may expect that the analysis of dreams will lead us to a knowledge of man's archaic heritage, of what is psychically innate in him."[102]

This is one chief origin of dreams. Dreams could also originate in (1) the desires of the day that seek fulfillment in the night; (2) the desires that originated in the day but were "repudiated" and consequently seek fulfillment in dreams; (3) the desires that remain suppressed in the unconscious and struggle to make it to consciousness.[103] The above three reasons are consciously desired and as such function as instigators of the wish to dream.[104]

Freud concurs with the ancients, Plato and Aristotle in particular, for whom dreams were thoughts that take place in the night. A dream, Aristotle remarks and Freud agrees, is "a thinking that persists (in so far as we are asleep) in the state of sleep,"[105] to which Plato ironically proposed that "the virtuous man is content to dream what a wicked man really does."[106] As we recall, I had earlier attempted to show that the tyrannical self, for Plato, is precisely a wicked self. Importantly, this self is incapable of recognizing the important boundary between what can only be dreamt but cannot be lived without risking self-destruction, which is the dream of the wicked tyrannical self, and what can be dreamt as well as be lived, which is the disposition of the virtuous self. I will defend this thesis as crucial to the concept of a self that empowers itself in a healthy way via the power of constructive desires—desires that enrich and humanize the self.

The ancients in their own way recognized the existence of the unconscious but not to the level of precision and depth uncovered by Freud. For Freud, the unconscious may not be a material reality as it was for the ancients. The unconscious is a psychic reality that instigates a reality in the form of dreams, which are expressive, symbolic, and disclosing of human fantasies. As Nietzsche penetratingly perceived, reality is always ready to return—the return of the repressed, the haunting of memory, the longing that refuses to be silenced, resists death.

I will terminate my reflections on Freud with a passage that beautifully summarizes his immortal defense of the unconscious—the love of the desires:

If we look at unconscious wishes reduced to their most fundamental and truest shape, we shall have to conclude, no doubt, that psychical reality is a particular form of existence not to be confused with material reality. Thus there seems to be no justification for people's reluctance in accepting responsibility for the immortality of their dreams. When the mode of functioning of the mental apparatus is rightly appreciated and the relation between the conscious and the unconscious understood, the greater part of what is ethically objectionable in our dream and fantasy lives will be found to disappear. . . . And the value of dreams for giving us knowledge of the future? There is of course no question of that. It would be truer to say instead that they give us knowledge of the past. For dreams are derived from the past in every sense. Nevertheless, the ancient belief that dreams foretell the future is not wholly devoid of truth. By picturing our wishes as fulfilled, dreams are after all leading us into the future. But this future, which the dreamer pictures as the present, has been molded by his indestructible wish into a perfect likeness of the past.[107]

I am now in a position to articulate a pragmatic conception of power that is grounded upon my belief that the self-constructing subject can actually be trusted to exercise power as self-empowerment. The self-empowered subject can be freed from experiencing power as domination.

NOTES

1. See Aristotle, *Nicomachean Ethics* (Indianapolis: Bobbs-Merrill, 1962).
2. Ludwig Wittgenstein, *Philosophical Investigations* (New York: Macmillan, 1945), par. 653.
3. I borrowed these nouns from Friedrich Nietzsche's *On the Genealogy of Morals*, ed. Walter Kaufmann (New York: Vintage Books, 1969), pp. 34–57.
4. See Alan Bloom's penetrating remarks on book 9 in his essay at the end of Alan Bloom, *The Republic of Plato* (New York: Basic Books, 1968).
5. Bloom, *The Republic of Plato*, p. 251.
6. Ibid., p. 251.
7. John Rajchman has some subtle points to make about the nature of desire and the problematic of self-constitution in "Ethics After Foucault," in *Michel Foucault: Critical Assessments*, vol. 1, 1994. See pp. 198–200.

8. Ibid., p. 253. See Gregory Vlastos, ed., *Plato: A Collection of Critical Essays* (Notre Dame: University of Notre Dame Press, 1971).

9. Ibid., p. 255.

10. Ibid., p. 256. The theme of Plato's self-mastery is brilliantly handled by Charles Taylor, *Sources of the Self* (Cambridge: Harvard University Press, 1989), pp. 115–127.

11. For an illuminating discussion of "evil," see Harold Cherness "The Sources of Evil According to Plato," in *Plato*, ed. Vlastos.

12. See Aristotle, *Nicomachean Ethics* (Indianapolis: Bobbs-Merrill, 1962), p. 119.

13. Ibid., p. 121. For a very useful general introduction to Aristotle's ethical universe see D. S. Hutchinson, *The Virtues of Aristotle* (London, New York: Routledge and Keagan Paul, 1986). See also G.R.G. Mure, *Aristotle* (New York: Oxford Press, 1964).

14. Hutchinson, *The Virtues of Aristotle*, p. 73.

15. See Aristotle, *Nichomachean Ethics* (Cambridge: Harvard University Press, 1982), p. 123.

16. See Hutchinson's beautifully presented discussion of moral choice in *The Virtues of Aristotle*, pp. 88–107.

17. See Aristotle, *Nichomachean Ethics* (Cambridge: Harvard University Press, 1982), p. 125.

18. Ibid., p. 129.

19. Ibid.

20. Mure, *Aristotle*, p. 149.

21. See Aristotle, *Nichomachean Ethics*, p. 133.

22. Ibid., p. 145.

23. One can read Hannah Arendt's conception of evil as a disturbing absence of thought, to which I am arguing choice adds a very much needed ingredient, as I read Aristotle to be arguing.

24. See Aristotle, *Nichomachean Ethics* (Cambridge: Harvard University Press, 1982), p. 419.

25. Ibid., p. 133.

26. See Epictetus, *The Discourses I* (Cambridge: Harvard University Press, 1979), pp. 7–15.

27. Ibid., p. 17. For a penetrating examination of Epictetus as an ethical thinker who influenced the stoical thoughts of Marcus Aurelius, see R. B. Rutherford, *The Meditations of Marcus Aurelius* (Oxford: Clarendon Press, 1989), pp. 225–255.

28. This vision was central to the moral thoughts of Hannah Arendt, as articulated by Seyla Benhabib's *Situating the Self* (New York: Routledge, 1992). See pp. 89–121.

29. See Epictetus, *Discourses*, p. 171.

30. Ibid.

31. Ibid., pp. 349–350.

32. Ibid., book iv, p. 351.

33. Ibid., p. 477.

34. Ibid., p. 305.

35. Ibid., book ii, p. 357.

36. Ibid., p. 287.

37. Ibid., p. 283.

38. See Immanuel Kant, *Foundations of the Metaphysics of Morals* (Indianapolis: Bobbs-Merrill, 1959).

39. Ibid., p. 17. Of the huge body of literature on Kant, it is John Rawls's interpretations that I am closely following here. I attempt to read Kant following my own reasoning as well. See John Rawls, *Political Liberalism* (New York: Columbia University Press, 1993).

40. Ibid., p. 16.

41. Ibid., p. 25.

42. For a brief explication of the concept of autonomy, see Teodros Kiros, *Toward the Construction of a Theory of Political Action* (New York, Lanham, London: University Press of America, 1985), pp. 251–261.

43. See Kant, *Foundations*, p. 39.

44. Ibid., p. 47.

45. Ibid., p. 64.

46. For a recent discussion of linking the power to judge objectively (the theme of *The Critique of Pure Reason*) and the equally objective existence of freedom, given the power to judge freely, see the lucid arguments by Hannah Arendt.

47. See Kant, *Foundations*, p. 71.

48. Ibid., p. 77.

49. See Kant, *Essays on History* (New York: Bobbs-Merrill, 1956). The essay is a succinct formulation of the destructive potential of the natural instincts, unless they are directed by reason.

50. There is a vast literature on Dostoyevsky. For the purposes of my limited focus here, see the recent work by Roger B. Anderson, *Dostoevsky: Myth of Duality* (Gainesville: University of Florida Press, 1986).

51. See Dostoyevsky, *The Possessed* (New York: Signet Classics, 1962), p. 410.

52. Ibid., p. 411.

53. Ibid., p. 195. For Anderson, in *Dostoevsky*, Stavrogin is not so much evil as he is a victim of hubris. See pp. 100–105.

54. Ibid., p. 430.

55. See Dostoyevsky, *Notes from Underground and The Grand Inquisitor* (New York: A. Dutton Paperback, 1960), p. 13.

56. Ibid., p. 19.

57. Ralph E. Matlaw, trans., introduction to *Notes from Underground and The Grand Inquisitor* (New York: Dutton Press, 1960), p. xv.

58. Ibid., p. 19.

59. Ibid., p. 24. See Matlaw's instructive analyses of these themes in his introduction to *Notes*.

60. Ibid., p. 25. Some readers of Dostoevsky have accused him of nihilism. For a defense against those charges see Joseph Frank, *Dostoevsky: The Stir of Liberation 1860–1865* (Princeton: Princeton University Press, 1986).

61. Ibid., p. 67.

62. Vyacheslav Ivanov, *Freedom and the Tragic Life* (New York: Noonday Press, 1960), p. 134.

63. Dostoyevsky, *Notes*, p. 85.

64. Ibid., pp. 87–88.

65. Ibid., p. 88.

66. Ibid., p. 108. A subtle analysis of the role of duality and conflict in Dostoevsky is given by Roger B. Anderson, *Dostoevsky* (Gainesville: University Press of Florida, 1986), pp. 12–27.

67. Ibid., pp. 108–109.

68. Ibid., p. 111.

69. For a succinct summary of Freud's psychoanalytic contributions, see Freud, *An Outline of Psychoanalysis* (New York: W. W. Norton, 1969).

70. See Sigmund Freud, *Beyond the Pleasure Principle* (New York: W. W. Norton, 1961), p. 4.

71. Ibid.

72. Ibid. For a remarkable and critical interpretation of Freud's pleasure principle, see Herbert Marcuse, *Eros and Civilization* (Boston: Beacon Press, 1955).

73. Ibid., p. 5.

74. Ibid.

75. Ibid., p. 40. For a radically original interpretation of Eros and the human condition see Herbert Marcuse, *Five Lectures* (Boston: Beacon Press, 1970), pp. 1–28.

76. Ibid., p. 31.

77. Ibid., p. 40.

78. Ibid., p. 47.

79. See Freud, *Civilization and Its Discontents* (New York: W. W. Norton, 1962), p. 23.

80. Ibid.

81. Ibid., p. 24.

82. See Jürgen Habermas, *Knowledge and Human Interests* (London: Heinemann, 1972). Habermas has some interesting philosophical remarks about psychoanalysis and the possibility of purifying language from distortions. See also Paul Ricouer, *Freud and Philosophy* (New Haven: Yale University Press, 1970).

83. See Freud, *Civilization and Its Discontents*, pp. 25–31.

84. Ibid., pp. 31–32.

85. Ibid., p. 33.

86. Ibid., p. 42.

87. Ibid., p. 52. Herbert Marcuse has put this question into serious doubt in *Eros and Civilization*.

88. Ibid., p. 55.

89. Ibid., p. 56. For a hypothesis that advances an economic/ideological interpretation of the disturbing factor, see my own interpretation of Gramsci's essay, "Fordism and Americanism," in Teodros Kiros, *Toward the Construction of a Theory of Political Action* (New York, Lanham, London: University Press of America, 1985), pp. 168–175.

90. See Freud, *Civilization and Its Discontents*, p. 57.

91. Ibid., p. 58.

92. Milan Kundera, *The Book of Laughter and Forgetting* (New York: Penguin, 1980), p. 3.

93. See Freud, *Civilization and Its Discontents*, pp. 70–71.

94. Ibid., p. 90.

95. See Freud, *The Interpretation of Dreams* (New York: Avon Books, 1965), pp. 35–127. For a critical response to Freud's celebrated psychoanalytic interpretation of dreams, see Ludwig Wittgenstein "Remarks on Freud," in *Philosophy and Psychoanalysis*, ed. Brian Farrell (Toronto: Macmillan College Publishing Company, 1994).

96. Ibid., p. xxxii.

97. Ibid., p. 358.

98. Ibid., pp. 63–64. In a probing essay Wittgenstein has questioned the explanatory

status of dreams. See *Philosophy and Psychoanalysis*, ed. Brian A. Farrell, pp. 59–72. See also Jean-Paul Sartre, "Bad Faith," in the same book.

99. Ibid., p. 405.

100. Ibid., p. 409.

101. Ibid., pp. 552–555.

102. Ibid., p. 588. See Erich Fromm's remarkable development of this theme in *The Anatomy of Human Destructiveness* (New York: Holt, Rinehart and Winston, 1973).

103. Ibid., pp. 589–590.

104. Ibid.

105. Ibid., p. 588.

106. Ibid., p. 658. The ontological status of the "unconscious" is brilliantly examined by T. R. Miles in "The Unconscious," in *Philosophy and Psychoanalysis*, ed. Farrell, pp. 17–27. See also M. H. Erdelyi, "Modeling the Unconscious," in the same book, pp. 17–43. Finally, Habermas also has rigorous remarks in "The Interpretation of a Case," pp. 43–50.

107. Ibid, pp. 659–660.

4

Self-Empowerment and Self-Construction: Power in the American Pragmatic Tradition

WILLIAM JAMES: POWER IN THE AMERICAN PRAGMATIC TRADITION

The essays that I wish to use to articulate a powerful defense of the desires—those desires that make a real difference in the way human beings conduct and construct their lives—are James's "Humanism and Truth" and "What Pragmatism Means."[1]

To begin with, what does pragmatism mean for James? The pragmatist will not seek to ask the unfathomable question that continues to haunt philosophers: What are desires? Rather, pragmatists, true to their humanistic bent, will reconstruct the question to read: Whatever the desires are, what concrete difference would their unrestrained practice make in individuals' real lives? There is then what I wish to call a pragmatic conception of the desires—a conception that does not pass a prejudicial judgment on the desires as much as seek to understand their concrete effect on our human existence.

For James, there are as many truths as there are individuals willing to construct them. Truths do not exist a priori, given, ready to be discovered by individuals, as much as they are ways of orientation to the world—ways that arise out of human experience.[2] The experiencing of truths concretely means the repeated testing of orientations and concepts that work and orientations and concepts that do not work, an ideal orientation for self-constructing subjects. As James boldly put it:

The serious meaning of a concept, says Mr. Pierce, lies in the concrete difference to some one which its being true will make. Strive to bring all debated conceptions to that "pragmatic" test, and you will escape vain wrangling: if it can make no practical difference which of two statements be true, then they are one statement in two verbal forms; if it can make no practical difference whether a given statement be true or false, then the statement has no real meaning. In neither case is there anything fit to quarrel about; we may save our breath, and pass to more important things.[3]

Let us recall that in the section on self-construction, I defended a thesis that went as follows. Individuals as such are potentially capable of constructing truths.[4] Truths of course can be developed (a) by the emulation of models, (b) by imitation, (c) by self-construction. Self-constructed truth is the most powerful way of producing endurable values and norms precisely because in constructing values, for example, the individual not only knows (a) how enviable models do things and (b) how repeated imitation produces certain habit(s), but also (c) fundamentally masters the inner architectonic along with the detailed logics of the values themselves. I now wish to add that in the construction of values, there is a special kind of care that the self attaches to what I have called one's deeply revered gift of existence.[5]

The various values and norms that form the layers of styles of existence and ethics of living are also humanistic, as James and later Dewey argue. They are humanistic because not all styles of existence and ethics of living are necessarily of the same weight and importance. To argue so would be too irresponsible and even dangerous. Some styles of existence reflect an awareness of the gift of existence and the fragility of that gift. Others are simply not that intelligently sensitive to the gift and the preciousness of the privileges of existence. Such people squander their lives meaninglessly and tragically. They have no goals, purposes, or aims. The historicity and temporality of goals, purposes, and aims, however, is a shallow excuse for not having any. We ought to struggle diligently to live our short lives with some self-constructed norms and values as guides in the forms of ideal goals, purposes, and aims. Pragmatism as humanism is deeply aware of the above practical facets of existence that complete us as potentially thoughtful human beings who take their existence as seriously as they are able to.

James put the point succinctly: "All that the pragmatic method implies, then, is that truths should have practical consequences. In England, the word has been used, more broadly still, to cover the notion that the truth of any statement consists in the consequences, and particularly in their being good consequences. . . . I think that Mr. Schiller's proposal to call the wider pragmatism by the nature of 'humanism' is excellent and ought to be adopted."[6]

The norms and values that are most cherishable, when pragmatically understood, are the ones that give us guides to what we must do and how we can do it. Pragmatism may indeed fail us in that it does not give an ultimate justification of our actions when we choose to act. But that is not the point behind action, as we learned from Aristotle. An action need not be comprehensively judged before the pragmatic subject acts. As we recall, none of Dostoyevsky's characters knew the justifications of their actions. However, it would be a gross misunderstanding of pragmatism if we construct it to justify any action—such as the actions of Stavrogin in *The Possessed*. Stavrogin, as a rule, never stopped to think out the consequences of his evil actions. He simply acted under the shadow of evil, the horizon of the dark. Pragmatically speaking, it is not enough for the pragmatic subject to act. He/She must act under the shadow of the humanely good. An action, however, is not good because (a) it reproduces the wishes of the divine, or (b) it approximately corresponds to the good of the divine. No action is good (only) because it has been deemed to serve the concrete practical needs of the pragmatic subject both as a discrete being and as a social being destined to live within a community of other pragmatic subjects with practical needs. The pragmatic subject is in touch with himself/herself and other practically in need human beings. At stake is needing to recognize the other as practically in need of food, shelter, clothing; needing of friends; and needing of the desire to think, to be free, and to contemplate deeply and comprehensively.[7]

The search for "truth" is not necessarily independent of the role of the subjective desires—desires for the practical needs of life, as well as desires for the loftier needs which together represent disparate and often chaotic styles of existence and ethics of living. If "truth" means anything at all, it has something to do with the concrete struggles of life. Truths guide life. Truths guide life justly—because they are relative to the passions and desires of concretely different human beings. There is not an imposing, all-encompassing, absolute and tyrannical "truth," which must correspond to what human beings should want; there are truths that announce their presence by testing themselves against the multifariously practical, aesthetic, religious, and psychic needs of human beings. There is no single truth independent of experience and beyond time, space, and history. For pragmatic humanism, truth is dependent on context, circumstance, history, and time. Truth guides but never rules—it does not rule by silencing dissent and by denying difference. The search for truth provides an environment for the emergence of beings who question by reflecting, who learn by testing, who become wiser by growing, who mature within the context of time and history.

I will let James speak for himself again: "Yet at each and every concrete moment, truth for each man is what that man 'troweth' at that moment, with the maximum of satisfaction to himself; and similarly, abstract truth, truth verified by the long run, and abstract satisfactoriness, coincide. . . . The fundamental fact about our experience is that it is a process of change. . . . But, owing to the fact that all experience is a process, no point of view can ever be the last one."[8]

To summarize, for pragmatic humanism, there is not single truth but many truths. The main points of humanism, according to James, are:

1. An experience, perceptual or conceptual, must conform and not correspond to reality in order to be true.

2. By "reality," humanism means "the other conceptual or perceptual experiences with which a given experience is mixed up."

3. By "conforming," as opposed to "corresponding," humanism means taking account of in order to gain a practically and intellectually satisfactory result.

4. To "take account of" and to be "satisfactory" are not definable, but can be worked out in order to be usable.

5. Vaguely speaking, "we take account of" something by preserving reality in its unmodified form as much as possible; for reality to be satisfactory, the reality must not contradict other realities. We must minimize contradictions as much as possible.

6. A given truth is good for its time, and later judgments may conform to it. "Yet, virtually at least, it may have been true previously."[9]

I will now move on to John Dewey's pragmatism.

JOHN DEWEY: POWER, CHOICE, AND MORAL LIFE

At the outset, I wish to indicate that Dewey's references to the pragmatic method are not as frequent as James's. The infrequence, however, is not an indication of the fact that Dewey did not think much of pragmatism. In fact, I think that what Dewey does, the type of life-guiding philosophy that he practices, is directly pragmatic according to the strict definition of pragmatism that James gave us. Dewey, it could be safely argued, is a pragmatic humanist.

As we recall, pragmatic humanism is concerned not merely with consequences, but with *good* consequences. The question of goodness—the goodness of the moral self—was a central pillar of Deweyan pragmatic humanism. The question of the moral self—a self that is morally empowered to lead its destiny—is systematically developed in John Dewey's *Theory of the Moral Life*, the essentials of which I will interpret below.[10]

To be a self presupposes that one needs a formative experience. The self, for Dewey, is at all times a construction. The construction of anything is really the putting together of parts, and the whole that emerges is composed of parts. The parts are just as important to the whole as the whole is to the parts. The self, in this sense, is an act of self-construction. The parts of which the self is made are desires. These desires are expressed in the form of preferences—preferences for the A, B, C, D of everyday living. Some prefer marriage to coupling; some prefer male partners to females, etc. These preferences are guided by impulses and wants for A but not B, C but not D. Preferences themselves are acts of selection, and selections are expressions of discriminate choices. Preferences, in a deeper sense, are also acts of self-determination that are anchored upon norms and values. The norms and values, however, are sometimes self-constructed; at other times, they are inherited from tradition and are simply acquired from habit. As Dewey put it, "We are so constructed that both by original temperament and by acquired habit we move toward some objects rather than others.''[11] These preferences, however, are not always consciously—that is, reflectively, chosen. They are preferences that are organically accumulated from habit. It is only when preferences compete with each other and we have to choose among preferences that reflection become necessary. Self-constructing subjects are inevitably confronted every day with preferences from which variety they have to choose. The need to reflect then does not precede preferences. Rather, the completion of preferences and the imperativeness of choosing among them produces the need to reflect. Dewey puts it aptly: ''We have to make up our minds when we want two conflicting things, which of them we *really* want. That is choice. We prefer spontaneously, we choose deliberately, knowingly.''[12]

The empirical self always prefers. It orients itself to the world through its impulses and wants. The self-constructing self uses preference to develop into a self that deliberately guides its impulses and wants. The self that chooses curiously attempts to satisfy the needs of impulses and wants, the products of habit, and new wants and needs that may arise of deliberate choosing. Dewey here struggles to reconcile the human propensity to satisfy both habits and new wants and needs.

How we choose among preferences, for Dewey, gives us a clue to the formation of selfhood or character. Those preferences we choose, among competing preferences, disclose who we really are.[13] For Dewey, impulses and wants may not be enough to prefer A over B; in this sense, impulses and wants are mere means. Impulses and wants, as expressions of desires, are important in a deeper sense. They are indispensable points of departure for the art of self-construction. Impulses and wants function as motives or interests that give everyday living a poignancy that it would otherwise not have. They become human interests. Kill the interests, then you will kill the human being. The self will have no interest in learning how to reflect—that is, how to choose. If desires are crushed, so is the self that chooses through desires. Desires then are integral aspects of choice. As Dewey puts it: ''A motive is not then a drive *to* action, or something which moves *to* do something. It *is* the movement of the self as a whole, a movement in which desire is integrated with an object so completely as to be chosen as a compelling end.''[14]

Impulses—such as selfishness, benevolence, care—are not organic dispositions. They emerge out of the way we are consciously educated to choose. Alfonso J. Damico is surely right when he writes, for Dewey, ''Morality finally comes down to the question of which habits or forms of conduct the individual possesses.''[15] Dewey thus says, ''Selfishness and unselfishness, in a genuinely moral sense, thus finally emerge, instead of being native 'motives.' ''[16]

Responsibility and accountability are important features of self-construction. The need to responsibly prefer and choose forms our selfhood, our character. We do not become this person or that merely by wishing to be. The selves that we form are products of the ways in which we have preferred and chosen.

Responsibility is closely linked with freedom. Freedom, Dewey rightly argues, "is connected with possibility of growth, learning and modification of character, just as in responsibility."[17]

Growth, on the behalf of one's self, is a mode of power—self-empowerment. To grow is to outgrow something; it is to abandon one way of life for the sake of another; it is to surrender one habit for a better one. The out-growing from something, the abandoning and surrendering are all done by the self that is forming itself—a self that is humanizing itself for its own sake. To be free, for Dewey, is to grow. The self is not born to freedom; it rather grows to freedom. Becoming responsible is a way of growing to freedom, as is becoming accountable to one's own preferences and choices. Growth produces a new self. For Dewey, the self is not static. It is dynamic. It is so dynamic that not only could it acquire new information, it could be programmed. The self can truly change by growing new tendencies, habits, values, and desires. Each tendency, habit, value, and desire is self-empowering. It is a way of truly consciously guiding our preferences—to better ourselves. The self is a constant becoming. It is ceaseless change, endless growth for the better or worse. "There is no such thing as a fixed, ready-made, finished self."[18]

The pragmatic ideas of James and Dewey are crucial in my development of the idea that the self-constructing subject can experience truths only by testing them against the way truths concretely improve our lives. The concept of truth as discoverable through testing is an idea I borrowed in my construction of power as self-empowerment, and that is why I spent time with these two towering pragmatic thinkers, from whom I have learned a great deal.

A POWER THAT DOMINATES: THE HOBBESIAN FORMULATION

The most direct and disarmingly honest conceptualization of man as a power-seeking animal was developed at the beginning of the eighteenth century by the famous philosopher, Thomas Hobbes. I will cite this conceptualization in order to transgress it—a transgression that I hope will allow me to originate my own conceptualization of power as a positive quality that human beings can reflectively make their own. My argument will be laid out in the following:

1. Power is not necessarily a negative human quality.

2. Power becomes negative if and only if it is practiced as domination, as I have shown in my long reflective interpretations of power as domination of the self as well as domination of others. I have sought to demonstrate this through my interpretations of the works of Plato, Aristotle, Epictetus, Kant, Plutarch, Aurelius, Dostoyevsky, and Freud.

3. If power is aware of its connection with domination, particularly expressed in the presence of evil as illuminated by Plato and Dostoyevsky, and if human beings, as

power-seeking animals, truly know themselves and willingly control the conversion of power into domination, then power can be practiced as a good quality.

4. I call that new quality of power a good self-empowerment.

5. Self-empowerment is closely associated with self-construction—a construction that is distinctly distinguished from discouraging oneself through (a) imitation of models and (b) habitual doing of things. Self-construction leads to self-empowerment, and self-empowerment is the best solution to the problem of freedom.

To set the stage, I will quote a rather long passage on power from Hobbes:

THE POWER of Man, (to take it Universally), is his present means, to obtain some future apparent Good. And is either Original, or Instrumental.

Natural Power, is the eminence of the Faculties of Body, or Mind: as extraordinary Strength, Forme, Prudence, Arts, Eloquence, Liberality, Nobility. Instrumental are those Powers, which acquired by these, or by fortune, are means and Instruments to acquire more: as Riches, Reputation, Friends, and the secret working of God, which men call Good Luck. For the nature of Power, is in this point, like to Fame, increasing as it proceeds; or like the motion of heavy bodies, which the further they go, make still the more haste.

The Greatest of humane Powers, is that which is compounded of the Powers of most men, united by consent, in one person, Natural, or Civil, that has the use of all their Powers depending on his will; such as is the Power of a Common-wealth; Or depending on the wills of each particular; such as is the Power of a Faction, or of divers factions leagued. Therefore to have servants, is Power; To have friends, is Power: for they are strengths united.

Also Riches joyned with liberality, is Power; because it procureth friends, and servants: Without liberality, not so; because in this case they defend not; but expose men to Envy, as a Prey.

Reputation of power, is Power; because it draweth with it the adherence of those that need protection.

So is Reputation of love of a man's country, (called Popularity,) for the same Reason.[19]

Power, for Hobbes, is a means to an end, not an end in itself. Hobbes's remarkable originality is that his conception of power is empirically useful because it allows us to perceptively and subtly observe what human beings do; more often than not, we see them acting and conducting their lives very much in accordance with Hobbes's conception of man as a power-seeking animal, a thesis that intrigued Foucault. Hobbes believed that human beings used their natural gifts—bodies, minds, physical strength, their forms, prudences, eloquence, liberalities, nobilities—as instruments to acquire more apparent power, such as riches, good reputation, friends, and knowledge of God's works. Powerful were these human beings who mastered the art and science of using natural powers to acquire social and political powers. Power then is a means with an apparent end. Power, in the Hobbesian model, is an instrument aimed at an apparent will to dominate. It is a model that continues to be testable against the way some, if not all, human beings behave on a globally observable level.

The Hobbesian model of power was intended to be a powerful response to the Platonic/Aristotelian conception of man as a being committed to living within a community. This community provides for its own sake the basic necessities of life, such as needs of the body (for example, food, shelter); external needs, such as friends, marriage; and needs of the soul, such as thought and freedom. In the classical tradition, the above needs were not natural powers destined to be used as instruments to acquire more power. Rather, they were human powers that were meant to give us a well-rounded human being—fit to construct a community and equally fit to harmoniously live with other human beings. These human faculties were the tools with which the self could develop selfhood and character. Selfhood and character in turn could, if effectively developed, control the ever present tendency of power to turn into a power that dominates, or in Hobbes's terms, a power that is a means to acquire more power. What we have here are two models of power that seem to be only artificially separated. My claim is that both these models of power are equally true about what human beings do and that neither model alone would give us a complete picture of the self. We need the two models if we are to make some useful statements about human beings. Both models capture the weaknesses and strengths of human character. What we need is to understand ourselves as human beings, capable of ''the will to power,'' as well as capable of the will to overcome ''the will to power.'' When we do the latter—an exceedingly difficult task, we are on our way toward discovering the self—a discovery that may lead us to experience power not as the will to dominate but as the will that could dominate the will to dominate. The latter I call self-empowerment.

THE IDEAL OF SELF-EMPOWERMENT

The notion of self-empowerment is not as famous and as captivating as the notion of the ''will to power.'' The images that the will to power evokes are cruelty, viciousness, aggressiveness, selfishness—each of these images portrayed as a definite dimension of the human condition. The characters of Dostoyevsky, both in *The Possessed* and in *Notes from Underground*, fit quite movingly into the imagistic framework of the will to power on the part of those who possessively and obsessively exercise it—such as Stavrogin. The temptation and hidden desire to drink from the wells of the powerful, found in the underground man's relentless and stubborn quest to be recognized by the powerful and wealthy, is also involved in the will to power. As the powerful joyously practice the instrumental function of power, in the Hobbesian sense, the temporarily powerless dream of one day being able to enjoy the fruit of power. In each case, man has an unquenched thirst for power; in each case, power is a means toward a silent end: the will to dominate, the will not to recognize the humanity of the powerless, the will to subtly oppress the voiceless, the overburdened, the enslaved, the humble, the quiet, the crushed, the depressed, and the helpless. Each of these wills are the effects and manifestations of the "will to power."

The notion of self-empowerment is paradoxical. On the one hand, the self that is to become empowered does so not to exercise power against others since it does not have this need, but because it is aware of the tragic possibility that the self possesses the will to dominate as a disposition. For the self that is deeply aware of its historical nature, the temptation to dominate is an integral part of the human self. That temptation to dominate, or that temptation to will domination, rests in the background in the form of what Plato called *tyranny*, what Aristotle renamed *irrationality*, and what Freud named the *aggressive* instinct. To that list I add my own term, *nonreflective presence*, as an oppressive light. By nonreflective presence, I mean the often tempting human tendency to disengage thought from action, awakening the self's intoxication with power that is the will to dominate. The will to dominate is a permanent possibility that could be revitalized and energized under the guidance of a nonreflective presence. The self that is genuinely empowered (after years of struggle, at least for those human beings who are lucky enough to live a long life directed by the reflective presence) does not have to will the power to dominate. On the other hand though, the self-empowering empirical individual is historically and temporarily situated within an empirical world that is inhabited by human beings whom Hobbes admirably described for us. To these modern individuals, power is a natural gift that is instrumentally used to acquire more power. For the sake of survival, the self that is moving toward self-directed and self-aimed empowerment has the task of fully mastering the wills and desires of Hobbesian man; if the self does not exercise a critical awareness of this phenomenon, that self will be destroyed. Becoming aware of destruction and consciously destroying others are two different things.

Self-empowerment then is a synthesis of the will to transcend the will to power and a critical awareness of the perturbing presence of individuals who are hypnotized and intoxicated with the nonreflective presence of the will to power. Self-empowerment is tragically located among the tasks of understanding a destructive phenomenon that is always ready to burst out—not becoming contaminated by the will to power which is located in the depths of the unconscious and consciously engaging in the control of destructive desires guided by the nonreflective presence. I call this synthesis, following the long tradition of Kant and Kierkegaard, truly paradoxical. The picture of the self that I have here is truly dualistic, but perhaps this is because human beings are marked by duality—the duality of reflection and nonreflection, or more pointedly the duality of goodness and evil.

The self-empowering subject is indeed a paradox but a paradox that is worth having. It is a paradox that gives us a blend of the real and ideal conceptions of the self. It is real because it does not exaggerate the saintliness of human beings—their capacity for compassion, cooperation, selfless devotion to extraordinary causes, sociability, and rationality. A realistic conception of the self seeks to alert us to the permanent possibility of the entrance of evil in the form of thoughtlessness, a repressed aggression, pride, arrogance, and tyrannical self-righteousness. It is idealistic in that human beings are asked to purify their hearts, work on their impulses and desires, and make a lifelong struggle to care for the growth and maturity of the body that is inevitably bound to decay and die. The ideal conception of the self stresses the need to experience life as an open horizon, a historically situated becoming where growth is a permanent possibility accompanied by the dream of a return to an irreversible past—the paradisiacal past. In this sense, self-empowerment is an amalgam of a committed desire to an open future and an equally nostalgic refusal to break with the past, which is seen both as a time of honor and a time of glory.

Power as the Self-mastery of Destructive Desires

As we have discussed, human beings are desiring beings who desire various things such as money, status, power, reputation, and fame. There is nothing wrong with the fact that human beings desire. Life, as we know it, would be boring, meaningless, and painfully intolerable if we human beings did not have objects of desire. The fact that our dreams are replete with fantastic objects of desire attests to the fact that we are desiring beings. These desires are not exhausted by what we expressly want when we are awake. When awake, we desire what society has conveniently called normal desires. We self-consciously desire what others will not find offensive, repulsive, abnormal, or pathological. The desires of the normal subject are precisely those that others have explicitly and implicitly said are good and safe things to desire. It is this insight that Foucault and Freud so perceptively gave us, and which I am putting to use here. The self-conscious moral subject then competently learns the art of adjusting to the dominant reality principle which requires us to make sure we do not offend others or get judged by others. Friends, admirers, and flatterers are our rewards for desiring the acceptable, the nondangerous, the socially safe. We desire all these things because we are ontologically constituted to desire. Note, however, that the objects we desire are not freely chosen. We are desiring what we have been taught to desire, and this type of desiring does not really fulfill us as human beings.

As beings who desire and as beings with desire, our desires hover on two levels. We experience the so-called normal and socially accepted desires, and we thus learn how to repress desire for the unique, eccentric, unacceptable, abnormal, and ''clinically'' pathological. Examples that illustrate the first and second forms of desire are numerous. Thus, normal desires are: marriage, fidelity, honesty, the avoidance of taboo, etc.; unacceptable desires include ''swinging,'' infidelity, etc. Both forms of desiring and their objects are implicitly and explicitly guided by the external judgments of others, such as ordinary individuals, religious leaders, and the professionals and experts of the social sciences.

There is a form of desire, however, first brought to our attention by Freud and neglected by modernity, that I wish to articulate and defend in this book. This is the desire for the fantastic—which is fantastic on two levels: (1) on the level of the forgotten past, and (b) on the level of the "not-yet"—the future. The fantastic truly operates on the continuum of the forgotten past, the inadequate present, and the projected future.

The Level of the Forgotten Past

The past, contrary to public opinion, is not willingly forgotten. In fact, there is a good reason to doubt that the past is ever forgotten. Instead, our ignorance of the past may exist because human beings are not adequately informed about the historical past, writers of history have not always been the most objective reconstructors of the past, or because the historical past has been selectively interpreted by historians. The memory of the historical past on the conscious level has yet to be recorded with an objectivity worthy of its name. Social historians with a deconstructivist bent—such as Michel Foucault, who is one of the modern heroes of this book—as well as many other social historians are taking a long and hard look at the question of the historical origin of modern values. The nostalgic yearning of Rousseau as he sadly looked at the past as well as the dreamy and anarchistic words of Walter Benjamin's historical pen have yet to be interpreted as the powerful weapons that they are, which could bring back the forgotten past.[20] The forgotten past, however, is not only conscious, therefore, retrievable by historical archaeology. The forgotten past is also an unconscious and psychic phenomenon. It is toward this direction that Freud's penetrating eyes gazed, and it is this dimension that has been ever more severely neglected by modernity.

Self-constructing subjects feed on reliving their fantasies—called "unreal" by those who analyze the "denial" functions of dreams. But to those who dream, dreams are not just expressive of behavior. They are attempts to live life the way the dreamer would like to live it. The dreamer sees signs, senses, and even actually lives hitherto untested possibilities for living, in absolute quiet, in the freest solitude, and in the most heroic moments of dream life. During dream time, while enjoying the reflective presence without consciously reflecting, the self is at a juncture in which it could either listen to the voiceless murmur of the forgotten past—the way the world was, once upon a time, the archaic phases of life before it froze into the sedimentations of tradition—or the authoritative directive of the reality principle. The dream world, the world of the forgotten past glows with glimmers of freedom, those days and nights in which the self as self-judge was absent—and this absence compelled the forgotten past to proudly emerge in the quiet of night to intoxicate the bored, dull, and melancholic self. The forgotten past offends, frightens, embarrasses, and even abuses the self of the dream world. The forgotten past abuses the self of the dream world with its honesty, recklessness, childish innocence, and, of course, with its infantile sexuality and barbarity. The forgotten past is replete with the signifiers of decay and death, the so-called "flowers of evil." But the forgotten past is also signified by the language of innocence, the absence of the self that judges, and the presence of the gaze that simply looks. The absence of a judge entails the dispensability of judgment, a necessary condition for the potential emergence of values and norms that are simply livable, enjoyable in their own right. This dimension of the forgotten past calls all values by their names—names not screened by high priests through the voice of God. All values are beyond good and evil. They are values that silently delight the sensibilities of desiring human beings and, equally silently but severely, incite the mind to be wary of the intrinsic limits of the delight of sensibilities gone wild, lacking all sense of control, rocking the deep bottom of our existence. By way of interpreting Baudelaire's interpretation of freedom, Jean-Paul Sartre has written, "He defined the human by its power of creation, not by its power of action. . . . creation is pure freedom; before it there is nothing; it begins by creating its own principles."[21] The forgotten past does not just excite and intoxicate with the seductive promise of a happiness lived in the dream world as absolute transgression; a world of loneliness without standards, without limits of any kind, where everything is fluid, fleeting, and even infantile. The forgotten past, in fact, warns as well as intoxicates. It warns us by showing us in dreams some prophetic and symbolic consequence of the violation of human limits, of the disrespect of worthy standards.

The psychoanalyst with a philosophic bent has a crucial task. His/her task is to help dreamers (whose dreams, when revealed to the meditative psychoanalyst, consist of glimpses of the forgotten past—full of disconnected fragments and images) to recall those fragments, those societally forbidden practices, those apparently nonsensible, problematical, disturbing, "primitive" styles of existence. The psychoanalyst, as a meditative thinker, truly leads the dreamer who, by describing the dream confides and entrusts his/her private life to a fellow friend, to remember, reorganize, recall, and re-articulate the forbidden dream experiences. If this truly admirable human encounter between the dreamer and the interpreter is to acquire an intelligent and humanly speaking moral significance, the psychoanalyst should abandon looking at himself as the normal expert and meet the other as his own other and not as his/her negation.[22] Jean-Paul Sartre has put it well, "According to Baudelaire's conception, man is not a true "state"; he is the clash of two opposing movements which are both centrifugal and of which one is directed upwards and the other downwards"[23] If the encounter is intended to extricate true knowledge about the human condition, the psychoanalyst, as an expert, has to cease looking at dreams as problematical relishes of the past when dreamt by an unadjusted and abnormal individual. Rather, dreams ought to be looked at as deep human desires in which the self-constructing subject lives life as life ought to be lived, except that way of living has been forgotten, closed to imagination. The self-constructing desiring subject seeks to reopen that layer of reality hidden in the abyss. The fact that the forgotten past is dreamt at all must signify to us that the past—the past that emerges within the psychic presence—is still alive and that we must be grateful to the transcendent force that has preserved our hopes and yearnings in the dream forms of the forgotten past. Psychoanalysis's freely chosen task is to cease judging and instead to engage in firm discerning and understanding. To discern and understand under the gentle but firm commitment to the reflective presence—the fusion of the incisive mind and the honest heart—is to control the temptation to judge through language and through the silent critique of the gaze. The psychoanalyst, as a high priest of science, could be held accountable for a judgment that hurts, cripples, and eventually kills. The closed doors to the forgotten past cannot be entered through judgment; the doors may however be opened if we knock, only because we want to see the labyrinths inside, the labyrinths of the incompletely known past, the distorted past, the repressed past, and the disciplined past.

There is a truly remarkable passage in Borges, the dreamer-thinker, the gifted architect of the fantastic, whose insights are indispensable for the creative activity of the construction of human values which empower.

Borges takes a backward look at the remnants and refuse of the great past, and seeks to reconstruct some of them. For Borges, the past cannot be recalled by memory in its totality. One of his characters, a mortal and contingent human being named Funes, the character in ''Funes the Memories,'' can barely remember the outlines of his childhood experiences by the time that he is recalled by the divine. An entire life is not long enough to enable us to remember even the first few years of our childhood. Man, for Borges, is condemned to not remember his past—the past as the totality of lived experience. For Borges, life is not totality; it is infinite. The following passage provides an image of the fantastic, on the level of the forgotten past:

Funes once projected our analogous language, but discarded it because it seemed too general to him, too ambiguous. In fact, Funes remembered not only every leaf of every tree of every wood, but also every one of the times he had perceived or imagined it. He decided to reduce each of his past days to some seventy thousand memories, which would then be defined by means of ciphers. He was dissuaded from this by two considerations: his awareness that the task was interminable, his awareness that it was useless. He thought that by the hour of his death, he would not even have finished classifying all the memories of his childhood.[24]

This insight is wonderfully intelligent as well as disturbing. It is wonderfully intelligent in that it gives us a view of the forgotten past not as repression, the Freudian view, but as the view that the past as past cannot be recalled in its totality. This mode of remembrance, the poet sadly informs us, is not practiced by mortal beings. The infinity that encompasses the world overwhelms humans who are finite beings. Man, within an infinite universe, is like sand on the shores of a sea. The poet wisely advises us, humbles us, subtly teaches us to surrender to the fact of infinity. The insight is disturbing as well. Does the fact of our finitude inexorably preclude us from seeking to piece those fragments and remains of our experience into some kind of working whole, as in the dream world, in which we seem to remember an infinite number of dissociated, disparate images of a way of life, a style of existence, that seems to melt right in our hands when we seek to consciously remember it, through the guidance of reflective memory? Does not the beauty of the futile, vain exercise lay in the act of the exercise and much less in the visibility of the product of the exercise? Should not we, the contingent but curious subjects, be encouraged to look backward into the past—the past of conscious history and the past of the psychic experience—in order to understand who we are and what we can be? Is life, as grounded in the infinite, characterized by the labyrinths: the hopelessly impenetrable, unimaginable? Is not the fact that life is unimaginable itself a human judgment—in this case, the judgment of a sad, humble poet who located his station in the labyrinths. Is not experiencing a world of "forking paths" without a single dominant path leading us to a definite, total destination, to a chaotic world, full of multi-meanings, framed within a totalizing metadiscourse?

The forgotten past, for Borges, is mystical, a synthesis of endless paths, a consummation of heterogeneous experiences, a unity of multiplicities none of which is singularly recallable by the psychoanalyst who attempts to decipher forgotten meanings from dreams. The poet-thinker, who gently and yet firmly awakes us to the fact of our contingent existence, deserves our praise and gratitude. We must appreciate his wonderful intelligence which crafted the chaotic world of art: the novel as the house of the fantastic, the fantastic as memory, and memory's incapacity to recall all that has been lived in the psyche in the form of dreams.

For me, art is homeless. Homeless too are the dreams of the world. The content of art is the fantastic, and the fantastic is backward-looking, as in the level of the forgotten past, and forward-looking as in the level of the future, the not-yet. The present is tortured by images of the past and the future, and yet the present too has its own firm reality. Art is as expression of the unfulfilled wishes of the desires. The desires hope for the possible and wish the impossible. The possible and the impossible are lucidly and courageously represented by images of the fantastic. Courageous are the heroes who have sought—however often they failed—to go behind the curtain of the impenetrable, chaotic labyrinth. These heroes ventured to lucidly commit to language what they saw in crystalline dreams about the archaic past. They worked and struggled ferociously to stumble upon the right words and symbols to express those hopes and yearnings in the language of art: the novel, painting, sculpture, utopian thoughts. Great are the dreamers who dared to flow into the streams of the unconscious. Great too are the dreams that focused their strained and overworked muscles of memory to remember the wish content of the long-forgotten past. The literature that is masterly and splendid is the genre that ventures to explore the underworld of dreams by forcing the imagination, in concert with memory, to relive the forgotten past in the wake of our lonely night full of fantasies. The residuals of the dream night, made up of fragments, inchoate ideas, dissociated and unrelatable symbols, and murmurs of the heart, are all the focus of great literature. Psychoanalytic techniques that seek to help dreamers remember the wish content of their dreams, in collaboration with the sensitive and penetrating imaginations of the poet/writer as thinker, can reconstruct the wish content of the forgotten past. If this hope is realizable, Borges's claim that the labyrinth is infinite and, therefore, unfathomable and ungraspable is indeed questionable. Borges's claim is powerfully humbling precisely because it warns us to guard ourselves against the excessive and arrogant claims of modernity, the arrogance of penetrating everything, including the mysteries of life, through the techniques of science, refusing to let certain things be. For science, everything is knowable, disclosable. The hidden is useless. The hidden becomes useful only when it is open and disclosed.[25] Borges's defense of infinity against the claims of the all-knowing totality makes substantial sense. Infinity humanizes us by gently but firmly warning us against a temptation toward excess, the perennial problem of human beings. Borges is right that the forgotten past, like the whole, which is infinite and includes the forgotten past, may not be revealed to us—no matter how much we try. That fact, however, need not be a stone wall that stubbornly withstands any penetration. From that fact, human beings may come to appreciate their destiny—a destiny of trying to succeed—as a project that gives existence a noble meaning. That nobility is action—an action, however, that is aware of the tragic possibility of failure, catastrophe, or possible surrender to failure.

It is true then that the forgotten past may not function as the source of an inspiring possibility for a way of life. This we have learned from the skeptical mind of Borges. As a warning, the insight is indispensable. As a warning, the insight really sharpens our ability to understand ourselves by opening us up to see our contingent self in the mirror of infinity. The effort is dangerous, vain, and even futile. But, the self, I wish to add, is chosen to try. In this vain hope, Freud, the meditative thinker, freely chose to enter the labyrinth of the dream world and left for us the thesis that all dreams are significant. Dreams, he courageously added, are depositories of wishes, "witnesses of the past," yardsticks by which the present is measured and, if need be, indicted.

The forgotten past is then a witness of the wealth, vastness, and creativity of human beings. The archaic past is witnessed as a source of hope as well as a sign of catastrophe. In the forgotten past, dreams explode with dust, dirt, horror—but not entirely. The past is moody. The same past is also saturated with linguistically undesirable images of the beautiful, the just, the true, and the sublime. In dreams, the Forms appear, but they disappear just as quickly. Memory is frustrated precisely because it cannot linguistically capture the Forms. The Forms are forgotten, broken to pieces. Memory tries to remember them. But what is remembered is a selective piecing together of what is acceptable, tolerable, and harmless to the pride and dignity of the self. The disturbing, insulting, and shocking aspects of the past are not remembered. They become lost to consciousness and to the reflective presence, which mourns over seeing the death of the past. Yet, the past does not really die. It is merely hidden from the dreamy gaze of the present. An intoxicated eye cannot see clearly.

The self, we may say, is tortured by the forgotten past's role as a witness. The self tries to kill this witness. The witness of the past preserves itself as memory. The images of the fantastic that appear in dreams are neither real nor illusory (as idealists such as Berkeley would claim). For example, Borges reports that "Chuang Tzu, some twenty-four centuries ago, dreamt he was a butterfly and did not know, when he awoke, if he was a man who had dreamt he was a butterfly or a butterfly who now dreamt he was a man."

Several points could emerge out of the claims of the dream and its remarkable relevance to the wish content of the forgotten past. For now I will bypass discussion of Borges's questions about time—such as whether or not time exists. What interests me is the remarkable fact that Chuang Tzu dreamt extraordinarily about being a butterfly and a man. A modern person who dreams that he was in "paradise," substituting paradise for butterfly, would equally be a proverbial dreamer. The implications of the dream for our sense of the misery of the present—a present that has given us slavery, colonialism, the Holocaust, world hunger, and unhappiness in the midst of glowing commodities—are quite serious. The image of paradise may be a peaceful ocean; twilight; a calm, cool garden inhabited by human beings from all walks of life: old and wrinkled, young and vital; white with blue, green, hazel, gray eyes; dark and comely with dark, brown, blue eyes; yellow, calm, patient and beautiful; all walking, talking, thinking, dancing, eating, and planning together without tension, with a quiet interaction, without hate and shortsighted conflicts. The images of paradise may also be a flower, the sun, the moon, a fire that caresses without consuming, a deep sea that welcomes and protects. The image of paradise in a dream may also be a sexless, raceless, beautiful form of a being. The image of paradise is the infinite, timeless, spaceless past in the form of what Borges wonderfully called "the half that was always sinking would be the past, that which was always rising would be the future, but the indivisible point at the top, where the tangent touches, would be the extensionless present."[26]

Time, for Borges, is not an empirical reality nor is it precisely divisible into well-defined categories of past, present, and future. Time is a continuum. Borges sings about time: "Time is the substance I am made of. Time is a river which sweeps me along, but I am the river; it is a tiger which destroys me, but I am the tiger; it is a fire which consumes me, but I am the fire. The world, unfortunately, is real; I, unfortunately, am Borges."[27]

I agree with Borges that time is (a) not an empirical reality (b) not a static and divisible absolute thing, nor even (c) a precisely defined substance in itself. If time is neither (a), (b), or (c), neither is the forgotten past either (a), (b), or (c). I wish to add to Borges's conception of time, however, the insight that the forgotten past need not be anything to be useful to human beings. The forgotten past's wonderful use to human beings lies in the fact that it is one of the houses of the surreal, the fantastic, the infinite home of human possibilities, human ventures into different ways of living. It is one of the central pillars of the ethics of life and styles of existence. Human use of the forgotten past is to be located in the depths of the unconscious. Following Borges, I argue that time is an integral part of consciousness. If time is a continuum, and the forgotten past, the inadequate present, and the projected future, as dimensions of time, are integral aspects of time, all that is true about time is also true about the forgotten past. In this sense, Borges's conception of time strengthens even more the usefulness of the forgotten past for human happiness. Splitting time into Freud's schemas of the conscious, preconscious, and unconscious becomes unnecessary. All the hopes and wishes, possibilities and resistances in the depths of the unconscious are realizable by the historical actions and reflections of men and women in their determined struggles to better the world, to make the world an adequate approximation of the way it is in the depths of the unconscious. The unconscious and conscious are the substances of which human beings are made, and the fantastic lucidly and boldly often expresses that substance in the form of dreams. Human beings give us an image of who they are in their dreams. Dreams are divine disclosures of human possibilities. Dreams are the substance of which beings are constituted. The understanding of the fantastic is the key to the nature of the self. In this sense, the usefulness of the forgotten past is beyond dispute. Our challenge is to demystify it. When it is genuinely demystified, we may see images of the beautiful and ugly, just and unjust, joy and suffering, good and evil. The symbol is everything and man is either everything or nothing. But we will never know the difference until we encounter time— time as a witness to the past, present, and future; time as the nefarious home of the dreams of humanity.

All life may be a dream. We never fully know when we are awake and when we are asleep. Again, a passage from Borges would communicate the point powerfully: "Someone said to me: You have not awakened to wakefulness, but to a previous dream. This dream is enclosed within another, and so on to infinity, which is the number of grains of sand. The path you must retrace is interminable and you will die before you even really awake."[28]

The world of dreaming, both the forgotten past and the projected future, is affected by the presence of the "magical" and "symbolic" infinite. Even Freud knew this, and Borges affirms it beautifully in the above passage. I fully concur with Freud's and Borges's conceptions of dreams. However we need to probe further because I think there is more that can be said about the forgotten past both as source of hope and of destruction, two contrasting images of the past that are central to my thinking about the emptiness of modernity. Modernity is increasingly lacking in thinkers of the fantastic, the fantastic that redeems in concert with the classical virtues of self-empowerment and self-control. The self-empowering human being, who has internalized self-generated principles as guidelines of self-control, may be trusted and encouraged to actually construct principles that are worthy of our passions and intelligences—and are manifested in the desires for ways of life and styles of existence.

I have established that the past still lingers in the dream world—the world of the forgotten past. The memory of that past is one of the fantastic. Modernity needs guidance from images of the fantastic as modernity is sadly emptying itself by surrendering to the world of commodities: money, status, drugs, and luring vacations. The materialization of human wishes and hopes is hopelessly emptying the self, the spiritual self. Modernity is itself becoming trivial and self-destructive. Self-impoverishing modernity and spiritual poverty are intersecting. The fact is very sad. A return to the world of dreams is one final attempt to shatter the world of commodities using images of the fantastic to develop a portrait of a rich spiritual self. It is an image of the self that would make a poet cry with a cry caressed by the fire of imagination and thought. The forgotten past is thus one of the contents of the cry of the poet who is a reflective re-memberer and recollector of "successive" experiences.

Invoking the fantastic is not merely an exercise for the mind. It is rather an attempt to take the world of dreams seriously. It is a serious venture into providing the self of modernity with the weapons with which it could refill its empty, trivial, goal-less everyday existence; it is furthermore an attempt at giving life a meaning, a sense, a significance, and a goal. We can learn from human fantasies because fantasies are yearnings for meaning, significance, and purpose. Fantasies are not childish, immature, maladjusted utopias drawn from the unattainable, exaggerated world of fiction. Freud is right that all dreams, therefore the wish contents of dreams, are meaningful and worthy of our deepest respect. What is deeply tragic is that the forgotten past, as a dimension of time, is so fleeting, so momentary that its intoxicating and hope-giving insights into the world of values and the language of possibilities cannot be recollected. Like time itself, fantasies exhibited in the forgotten past, now lived in dreams, cannot be grasped solidly. When the self awakes to the present, it cannot easily remember and recollect all those moments of joy, sadness, horror, victories, and betrayals. True recollection requires the cooperative participation of the reflective presence—the presence of the transcendent. This ultimate privilege, however, is not available to all human beings as dreamers. There are big dreams as well as small ones. On the level of meaning, their significance varies as does their potential to become privileged listeners to the divine discourse of the voiceless transcendent.

The transcendent discloses himself/herself only to those who have devoted themselves to thinking and listening, such as those intelligent beings who are described by Marquez in *One Hundred Years of Solitude* with the following words: "It was in that way that the boys ended up learning that in the southern extremes of Africa, there were men so intelligent and peaceful that their only pastime was to sit and think."[29]

Sitting, thinking, and, if I may add, a sincere desire to know are necessary conditions that make it possible for the transcendent to radiate with those lucid guides to the world of dreams. During those moments, the intoxicating images of the just, beautiful, and truthful strike us and then quickly disappear from the longings and yearnings of memory. Finite humans' self-imposed task is the sustained struggle to solidly capture the images of the dream world. Dreams themselves dazzle us by their seductive charm as they get nearer and nearer the territory of consciousness but never near enough to serve the goal of memory, which is recollecting the forgotten past and thereby generously providing the contingent modern subject with a style of existence and an ethics of living.

The image of the forgotten past was, for example, powerfully and conspicuously present in Baudelaire's poetic songs. Consider the following poem in which the lonely poet, part of the alienated modern age, comes alive, however briefly, through one of his fantasies. The poet, we shall see, burns in the fantasy:

A Passerby

The deafening street roared on. Full, slim, and grand
In mourning and majestic grief, passed down
A woman, lifting with a stately hand
And swaying the black borders of her gown;

Noble and swift, her leg with statues matching;
I drank, convulsed, out of her pensive eye,
A livid sky where hurricanes were hatching,
Sweetness that charms, and joy that makes one die.

A lighting-flash—then darkness! Fleeting chance
Whose look was my rebirth—a single glance!
Through endless time shall I not meet with you?

Far off! too late! or never!—I not knowing
Who you may be, nor you where I am going—
You, whom I might have loved, who know it too![30]

The poet is temporarily emancipated from anguish, from loneliness, through the power of his sensitive eyes—eyes that saw and dug out beauty from the depths of a deafening and uncaring crowd. He genuinely came alive and truly lived during that fleeting moment in which he saw, in which the softness that kills and the pensive eyes that invite were fully disclosed to him. The poet drank from the well of fantasy. He did not care whence the woman came or where she was going. Baudelaire's poem is a towering example of the fantastic—the timeless fantastic that elevates, enervates, and gives rebirth. The poet experienced a rebirth in that deafening street of the modern age.

In another poem, he dreamt eternity. Here is Baudelaire's long description of eternity.

A Former Life

Long since, I lived beneath vast porticoes,
By many ocean-sunsets tinged and fired,

Where mighty pillars, in majestic rows,
Seemed like basaltic caves when day expired.

The rolling surge that mirrored all the skies
Mingles its music, turbulent and rich,
Solemn and mystic, with the colors which
The setting sun reflected in my eyes.

And there I lived amid voluptuous calms,
In splendors of blue sky and wandering wave,
Tended by many a naked, perfumed slave,

Who fanned my languid brow with waving palms,
They were my slaves—the only care they had
To know what secret grief had made me sad.[31]

There might have been a time in human past history in which there existed highly intelligent beings who were unusually trustworthy precisely because of their intelligence, compassion, and discipline. Such an era may be glimpsed in the fleeting exposure of the world of dreams. This optimistic vision of human beings is completely unlike the more common image of human beings that has been "realistically" presented to us. Because of their negative presentation of human beings as vicious, nasty, shortsighted, proud, vain, conceited and vindictive, it has become natural for us to consider positive human qualities as so unacceptable that we relegate them to the suprahuman realm of the fantastic. The infamous Hobbes contributed immensely to historians' refusal to imagine positive possibilities for humanity.

I wish to argue that it is a great mistake to dismiss so-called dreamy, fantastic, and utopian conceptions of the self that are telescopically viewed through silent and reflective dreams. If human beings stand for anything at all, it is for those great possibilities that were once lived by authentic human beings. Those possibilities may still be retrievable with the help of meditative psychoanalysts. May I invite you, my readers, to listen once more to Baudelaire, as the poet of dreams—dreams of the forgotten past. This piece consists of the last three stanzas of a poem called "Weeping and Wandering":

O perfumed paradise, how far removed,
where beneath a clear sky all is love and joy,
Where all we love is worthy to be loved,
And pleasure drowns the heart, but does not cloy,
O Perfumed paradise, so far removed!

But the green paradise of childlike loves,
The walks, the songs, the kisses, and the flowers,
The violins dying behind the hills, the hours
of evening and the wine-flasks in the groves.
But the green paradise of early loves.

The innocent paradise, full of stolen joys,
Is't farther off than eve'n the Indian main?
Can we recall it with our plaintive cries,
Or give it life, with silvery voice, again,
The innocent paradise, full of furtive joys?[32]

I have promised my readers that I will reflect on dreams on two levels: (a) the forgotten past, and (b) the not-yet—the future. I have attempted reflections on (a). Now, let's turn to (b).

The Not-Yet, the Future

Freud was right when he postulated that dreams are expressions of wishes that have not been realized during the wakeful state. I wish to call this state the wish content, the not-yet, or the projection into the future. Fantasies, for me, are projections into the future; fantasies are potential realizations of the not-yet meant to represent concrete realization of human hopes, human possibilities, and human creative activities. The not-yet is not necessarily a wishful, but ultimately unrealizable, utopian cry. There are daring ways of living our tragically short lives, ways that are revealed in the solitude of the dream world, a solitude that is absolutely crucial for human beings to be able to think, to imagine, and that is abundantly provided to them during dream time. Dream time, as nonsensibly and naively understood, is not escape or "fun time." In fact, it is serious time; it is free time. It is the only time in which the unknowable and impenetrable self is revealed to the dreaming self. It is the time that gave us one of the profoundest dreams: the dream that mirrored Chuang Tzu as a butterfly—man as a butterfly, and the butterfly as a symbol of beauty, innocence, freedom, free spirit. There are infinite other meanings. To the psychoanalyst, the dream is a wish content. Perhaps, when the dream is dreamt by an abused person, it is a cry for relief from the wretchedness of being human into the fullness and dignity of the life of a butterfly. To the epistemologist, it is a rather perturbing statement about the fragility of knowledge in that it dogmatically demarcates the illusory and the dreamlike from the real—symbolized by wakefulness. Chuang Tzu hit the bottom of his existence when he questioned whether he was really a man who had been deceived into dogmatically assuming that he was a man or whether he was a butterfly as he dreamt. Chuang Tzu asked himself the profound, perhaps impenetrable, question: Who am I?

The fantastic as the not-yet cannot express itself directly. After the quest for the novel, the active search for a hitherto untested way of life, life remains expressed only as a dream. One may, for example, dream that he/she was in a garden full of people from different walks of life, freely speaking, thinking, and planning about reordering a human society. The dream may have some concretely substantive ways of abolishing hunger and poverty, power and powerlessness, horrible diseases, unnecessary envies and jealousies. In the dream state, the substantive forms of the not-yet could not only be discussed with intelligence, candor, honesty, and spirituality but could also be concretely resolved. After the dream is over and the wakeful state begins, the dreaming subject is confronted with numerous problems. Some of these problems are worth mentioning:

1. The subject who dreamt may not be able to remember the content of the dreams. This problem is, of course, partly solvable by the clinical techniques of Freud's psychoanalytic methods.

2. Not only may the subject who dreamt not remember his/her dreams, but he/she may be convinced that a dream is only a wish. As a wish, it is meant not to be unchained and the dream should not even be remembered. There is nothing in a dream that is actually pragmatically useful to society. Dreams are intended as entertainment for a good-natured and soft soul. As a consequence, from the dream, the dreamer could draw the lesson that only the immature would take the content of a dream seriously.

3. Reality is much harder than the way life is experienced in dreams, and a dreamer may believe a line should be drawn between what is dreamable but not concretely livable and what is concretely livable (however unfulfilled it may be) but not dreamable—precisely because reality is too confining for a dream. A serious person should take the distinction to heart and not muddy the crucial differences. Thus, abolishing hunger may be dreamable but not livable.

4. Given the dogmatic ''facts'' of number 3 above, the dreamer who believes these assertions cannot *dare* to take his/her dreams as realistic expressions of possibilities. Therefore, dreams, to a significant extent, may already be penetrated by societal dogmas. Societal dogmatic penetration may thus affect the psychic structure of the dreamer. The dreamer's capacity to imagine beyond the ''solid'' structure of what is acceptable, of what is factually convincing, is limited. When imagination is penetrated by dogmas, the dreamer's fantasies may not be as free as they should be in order to come up with original dreams—dreams of the authentically not-yet.

5. Finally, certain dreams, dreams about ''evil''—such as Stavrogin's dream in *The Possessed*—may be so horrible, so ugly, so true of the dark side of the self that the dreamer who is morally aware may never tell the truth. The truth may thus be beyond the reach of the most sophisticated techniques of modern psychoanalysis. If this is the case, human beings may never know the true self. We humans may consequently die without knowing this crucial side of the self—the self as tyrannical, permanently dominating, malicious, thoughtless, and even destruction-loving. It is very tragic that human pride and human awareness of the judgment of others stands in the way of truth. The truth that emerges in dreams may thus be inaccessible to us because we do not want to see our true self in dreams containing ugliness. It profoundly hurts in the end to know who we truly are—we, the most pretentious of all beings. For example, Baudelaire, the honest and ''sinful'' poet who laid his heart open to his readers, said: ''There is in every man, at every moment, two simultaneous postulations, one toward

God, the other toward Satan. The invocation of God, or spirituality, is a desire to rise; that of Satan, or bestiality, is a joy of descent."³³

This confession is so true that it ought to be taken as a justification for the validity of certain dream forms—forms of the ugly, the descending that is an unavoidable dimension of the self when it fantasizes about the not-yet. The not-yet, contrary to the wish of the dreamer to ascend to the world of the Forms with its images of paradise, may actually represent a powerful descent to thoughtlessness, irrationality, the love of demolition, and the joy of inflicting pain in his/her apparently innocent dreams. When certain dreams are craftily and judiciously interpreted, they may give us a clue to the total nature of the self. A practical knowledge of the ugly is just as extraordinary as is a knowledge of the beautiful. The dreams of the not-yet are paradoxically a synthesis of ascent and descent, self-empowerment and domination, love and hate, joy and suffering. This is so, I have argued in this book, precisely because the self is potentially capable of the good as well as the bad. It is when we develop a pragmatic conception of power, a conception that I call self-empowerment, that the disposition toward the "bad" may be intelligently controlled by the disposition toward the good. The bad is there but it can be controlled by the reflective presence.

Dreams in the form of the not-yet are powerful in a radical yet truly responsible sense. That sense is the unrealized hope that in dreams, the dreamer sees a novel value, an entirely new way of organizing the world from that actual historical standpoint in which the dreamer stands—a standing that is deeply anchored to the empirical world of tradition, customs, habits, and frozen ways of seeing, hearing, and doing things. The not-yet shatters time, transcends space, offends history. After the shattering, transcending, and offending, new values explode on the empirical world. New values, new norms, new ethics and aesthetics guided by the firm grip of self-control are born. In this sense, fantasies are radical sources of values. It is fantasies that continually reshape our world. It is fantasies that wake us from sleep. It is perhaps through fantasies that the transcendental force speaks to us by reminding us of our duties to renew and examine our character, to reshape our inner world, which would otherwise be asleep, be corrupted by the satanic force of material wealth, or "come to an end" as Baudelaire depicted in one of his prose poems.

The not-yet is a constant challenger, a harbinger of change. It is a gift. It is a gift that can be compared to love and thought. The not-yet loves by challenging, reminding, subtly instructing, waking. Sometimes, it teaches through dreams of horror, disclosure of the ugly. This way, too, is a form of love. It is the type of love that human beings have to face.

However, in human fantasies, given the inconsistencies of human nature, a disposition toward good or evil cannot be completely trusted. Fantasies cannot be completely trusted because we can never assume that the self that is fantasizing has rigorously and detachedly examined its soul and come to the trustworthy conclusion that the content of its fantasies are pure, disinterested, and "right" for it and for those others whom the self is destined to encounter. Fantasies, like the nature that grounds them, are fragile, inconsistent, contaminated, and unsure of the directions they are mapping out for the self. The yearning for the new may be tragically affected in a primordial sense by the fragility, incompleteness, and impurity of fantasies themselves, and fantasies themselves may be fundamentally conditioned by the dualistic nature of the self.

According to the Chinese philosopher Chuang Tzu, during a nonhistorical, paradisiacal time, human beings lived the life of justice, goodness, and happiness. They lived their lives without a historical awareness of their social practices. They lived the good life without consciously thinking of their actions. Their practices disclosed to their eyes, hearts, and minds a sense of who they were, what they must and must not do, what they should and should not hope. They themselves did not consciously, systematically construct rules—rules that produced these great social practices. The Chinese sage said:

They were honest and righteous without realizing that they were "doing their duty." They loved each other and did not know that this was "love of neighbor." They deceived no one yet they did not know that they were "men to be trusted." They were reliable and did not know that this was "good faith." They lived freely together, giving and taking, and did not know that they were generous. For this reason, their deeds have not been marinated. They made no history.[34]

From this remarkable angle, I wish to assert on the behalf of the self's not-yet fantasies that the creative social practices of human beings had a promising start, replete with purity and the quest for the good. This promising start is powerful foundation for what human beings could become since they had once upon a time lived a serene, fantastic life. Given this beginning, it is perfectly appropriate for human beings to reproduce the forgotten past, of which the sage's dream is an intriguing part, in the form of the not-yet, since the past has been completely forgotten. In this sense, the past can be fantastically reproduced in the form of the new, the not-yet as such. The sage's nonhistorical past may as well serve as modernity's not-yet, or modernity's new synthesis of the past, the alienated present, and the not yet, all in one.

Without belaboring the point, but in defense of judiciousness, it is also equally persuasive to imagine the "original position" to consist of the opposite of all the images of Chuang Tzu. Some images would be the presence of self-righteous, all-knowing beings whose social practices were: hatred of one's neighbor, distrust of one's fellow beings, unreliability, bad faith, taking without giving, meanness of spirit. These beings ignorantly enjoyed their social practices. Their image of the not-yet, we may say, was non-existent. The dreams of these human beings were essentially reproductions of their actual social practices. We may further add, they had no conception of the ideal self, or in Chuang Tzu's term, did not follow the Tao (the "divine" and the ordinary human "way"). In oriental thinking, the absence of Tao might be seen as fertile ground for the growth of evil, a synthesis of thoughtlessness and true ignorance in the Socratic sense. The powerless self, when profoundly understood, might as well be powerless when its social practices lack a sense of Tao for the Chinese; the betrayal of Allah for Muslims; and a disturbing absence of what I have called the reflective presence, the presence of the Transcendent, the internally imposed source of principles for the Self-constructing subject.

When the not-yet does not open itself to the transcendent, its wish content is dangerously domination-centered. When the self is centered on domination, its dreams are often one-sided, uncompassionate, and disrespectful of the needs, yearnings, and wishes of others. The fantasies of such a self ought to disturb us. Such a self is spiritually poverty stricken, although it may think and live its life otherwise. Such a self may be materially powerful, but it is spiritually powerless. Its one-sidedness can miserably fail to dig deep into its soul to see if it too has a capacity for the good—a capacity that has become overshadowed by the absence of the reflective presence, or as the Taoist sage would have it, is lacking the divine way. The true self, the self whose vision of the not-yet could be trusted more enduringly, is the one whose discovery of the good was preceded by its awareness of the knowledge of the destructive, the irrational, the pain-giver. For such a balanced self, life itself is a blend of disorder and order, destruction and construction, limitlessness and limits, the real and the ideal. The not-yet is most convincing if it has a hardened—however hurtful—view of its own self as capable of doing the right as well as the wrong. As Chuang Tzu put it rather beautifully:

> Consequently: he who wants to have right without wrong,
> Order without disorder,
> Does not understand the principles
> Of heaven and earth.
> He does not know how
> Things hang together.
> Can a man cling only to heaven
> And know nothing of earth?
> They are correlative: to know one
> is to know the other.
> To refuse one
> Is to refuse both.
> Can a man cling to the positive
> without any negative
> In contrast to which it is seen
> To be positive?
> If he claims to do so,
> He is a rogue or a madman.[35]

I wish to pause here and invite my readers to think about Chuang Tzu's cosmic vision with respect to the way of the not-yet, and the way in which the dream of the conditioned and anguished self may affect the ontology of existence.

In a truly shocking sense, a sense that is foreign to Chuang Tzu, the not-yet is in fact the entirely new. The not-yet, I wish to argue, centers our empirical world in the form of an alien hope, a radical wish of the ostensibly unrealizable. The alien hope disturbs some, offends a substantial number of human beings. The alien hope that is lived in dreams dares to intervene into everyday life. There it frequently encounters very few listeners, and even fewer absolutists. Rather, the not-yet is often dismissed as a dream of the immature, emotionally unstable, and childish libertines. Worse still is the fact that this alien hope, the entirely new transhistorical and transempirical value of the not-yet, is countered by the brutal force of death.

The not-yet of the dream world resembles action. Action and the not-yet share striking similarities. Both are entirely unknowable. Both happen, and we humans do not know how. Both produce shocking values and norms. Some of these values and norms are objectively not good for human beings. Yet, human beings are compelled to choose them. Sometimes, human beings, such as Stavrogin, consciously choose values and norms that destroy them. The great lovers in Tolstoy's novels, such as Anna, chose norms and values in the name of blind love that prepared for the inevitability of a deep sadness followed by tragic death. The not-yet, like action, excites, gives one's life a hope, a reason to live for. The vision of a paradise lived in a dream often compels the dreamer to translate that vision into a practical way of life. From the dream emerges the will to change the frozen empirical world. In this way, an Antigone intoxicated by the idea of fulfilling her own sovereign interpretation of the wishes of the gods dared to challenge the powers-to-be, specifically Creon's dogmatic and self-righteous claim to the legitimacy of his power. She ultimately paid a heavy price for her courageous action—an action that was guided by an alien hope, an expression of the not-yet. Her dream was crushed by her death in the hands of a human power—Creon's power. Antigone is one of the earliest towering examples of the self-constructing subject, albeit a tragic one.

Following Chuang Tzu's claim that there are no new visions that cannot be countered by others and that the only truth beyond dispute is the Tao—a claim that he provocatively advances in "Great Knowledge"[36] as well as the "Pivot"[37]—I wish to assert that the visions implicit in the not-yet of the dream world are as new, as sovereign, and as unknowable as the birth of a baby.[38] Scott Lash has recently observed, "If libido has its basis for Lacan in the symbolic, for Deleuze and Guattari, (for Freud) its grounding is in the Real; its foundations are material, even biological. Freud's libido has its basis in the id and exists in various forms corresponding to biological."[39] I too agree with Deleuze and Guattari's materialistic understanding of desire, based on Freud's arguments, as I attempt to demonstrate in my reading of Freud's works on the levels of the forgotten past, and the not-yet.

The empirical world is enriched, renewed, humbled, and enlightened by the not-yet—the not-yet that may become, may awaken us human beings from our comfortable, indifferent, and frozen present. The Tao provides the appropriate atmosphere for the emergence of the not-yet.

Fantasy then is not entirely useless. It is clearly not useful in the sense that money is. Money has an immediate cash value. Fantasy is useful mediately. The dream content of fantasy on the level of the not-yet provides human beings— as I have repeatedly asserted—with hopes of transforming the miserable present of modernity. The not-yet imperceptibly hides new desires, from which may emerge new pragmatic truths, expressed in such forms of the language of dreams as symbols, metaphors, myths, signs, and colors. In the not-yet, all the fundamentals of power—truth, language, and desires—are lucidly intertwined. The fundamentals of power, however, are used for purposes and goals that are radically different from those of modernity. The fundamentals of power are distressingly abused by the experts of knowledge in modernity. Truth, language, and desires are used to hypnotize and intoxicate the exhausted, overburdened, materially enslaved, calculating, bored, depressed, and alienated subjects and objects of modernity. Truth, language, and the desires, on the level of the not-yet, are used by dreams to imagine possibilities, envision ways of life, recapture lost paradises; to retrieve through the inherent power of memory dimensions of the forgotten past; to concretely struggle to expand and fuse horizons, to unfreeze customs and traditions, and radically create new needs regulated by self-generated principles guided by the inner desires of the heart—such as compassion, care, love, and solidarity. Imagination is not inexorably committed to the will to power as Foucault argued. No. The imaginative self is potentially committed to will truths, in the hands of responsible self-constructing subjects.

In the above concrete sense, the inner laws of the heart and the inner powers of the mind are present in the not-yet. The purer, less self-centered, more reflective and judicious the inner laws of the heart are, the more powerful, more self-controlled, and therefore more reliable is the content of the dreams of the not-yet. Our numerous wishes contained in the dreams of suffering, joy, triumph, betrayals, intrigues, or ''abnormal'' possibilities find temporary refuge in the murmurs, silent cries, complaints, and linguistic protests of dreams. Dreams truly disclose those expressions of thought and emotion much more lucidly and honestly than do the ordinary expressions of conscious everyday language. The symbols, signs, metaphors, and colors of the dream world are profoundly significant and meaningful.

Dreams, on the levels of the forgotten past, the miserable modern present, and the not-yet, challenge us to interpret them—a task that cannot be accomplished by finite human beings alone, certainly not as all-knowing, arrogant, and unmeditative experts of knowledge. The project of interpreting the desires, truths, and language of dreams gently challenges us to empty ourselves of ''useless'' self-awareness, and instead relearn how to sit and think. We have to relearn the exceedingly difficult task of examining ourselves. Fundamental to the possibility of interpreting fantasies expressed in dreams about the not-yet is the need to say to ourselves that we do not yet know how to live, that we have not yet internalized the principles of correct ways of living in our actions. The experience of discovering that we do not know how to live is a humbling one.

I conclude this part of the discussion with the suggestion that dreams can be concretely and pragmatically useful to human beings who hope to empower themselves. It is this theme that concerns me in the following section. The challenge for us, the children of modernity, was put most eloquently by Foucault, when he wrote, "The movement by which, not without effort and uncertainty, dreams and illusions, one detaches oneself from what is accepted as true and seeks other rules—that is philosophy. The displacement and transformation of frameworks of thinking, the changing of received values and all the work that has been done to think otherwise, to do something else, to become other than what one is—that too is philosophy."[40] My humble attempt of developing a vision of a self-construction seeks to rise to Foucault's challenges of engaging in philosophy, aiming at the founding of a new concept of self-legislation of new principles propelled by the activities of desiring subjects. It is toward this end that I chose and affirmed the visions of some of the most compelling writers such as Dostoyevsky, Freud, Mann, Baudelaire, Borges, and Chuang Tzu in my attempts of filling the vessel of self-construction.

The Feminist Perspective Toward Self-Construction

Recently, Allison Jaggar made a powerful argument in defense of the thesis that, contrary to the positivist view that rejects the emotions as sources of knowledge, reason unguided or unstimulated by the emotions in fact is inadequate. Strictly speaking, one reasons only because one is effectively imbued with emotions, the vehicles of desire. Women and oppressed people in general are the most compelling possessors of emotions, precisely because "pain, trauma, compassion and anger," as Susan Griffin paraphrases Jaggar, have deeply conditioned their historical experiences. As Jaggar writes, "This emotional acumen can now be recognized as a skill in political analysis and validated as giving women a special advantage in both understanding the mechanisms of domination and envisioning freer ways to live."[41]

Jaggar's thesis has connections to my project. Self-empowerment, as opposed to domination, is fueled by a compassionate attitude in the human soul. With Jaggar, I agree that where the emotions are absent there is no comprehensive reasoning. *In fact, existential seriousness requires the emotions, in the form of the moral attitude of care.* As Mary Brabeck has thoughtfully argued, "Gilligan's theory enlarges the description of morality offered by Kohlberg. The ethic of care that Gilligan heard reflected in the voices of women and which exists in mythic beliefs about women, expands our notion of morality to include concern for interconnection, harmony, and non-violence."[42] Jaggar is quite right as well when she writes, "We can now see that women's subversive insights owe much to women's outlaw emotions, themselves appropriate responses to the situations of women's subordination."[43] It is my opinion that self-constructing subjects would gain enormous advantages from internalizing the "ethics of care," as brilliantly articulated by Gilligan, in their development as moral subjects.

Out of the several brands of feminism that Jaggar lists, it is radical feminism[44] and the ethics of care that I have fundamental sympathy with, chiefly because radical feminists, as Jaggar presents them, directly address questions of power and domination, as well as care for the self and for others.

Susan Bordo, appropriating Foucauldian insights, argues:

I do not deny the benefits of diet, exercise, and other forms of "body management." Rather, I view our bodies as a site of struggle, where we must work to keep our daily practices in the service of resistance to gender domination, not in the service of "docility" and gender normalization. . . . Popular as we have seen, many speak forcefully through the rhetoric and symbolism of empowerment, personal freedom, "Having it all." Yet female bodies, pursuing these ideals, may find themselves as distracted, depressed and physically ill as female bodies in the nineteenth century, pursuing a feminine ideal of dependency, domesticity, and delicacy.[45]

Bordo is correct that at this time, at the height of modernity and in the name of liberation, women are actually being forced to portray a starved, moody (perhaps because starved) body to men whose own appearance is itself questionable. Domination is not, strictly speaking, merely physical. We have learned from the likes of Fanon (in *The Wretched of the Earth*) and Foucault's powerful work on sexuality[46] that the invisible, psychological dimension of domination is just as pernicious, since it subtly and deeply destroys a person's identity as well as the identities of cultural collectivities, such as the abused cultures of the colonized.

Where I take issue with Bordo is in her offhand dismissal of the precious notion of self-control, so dear to the ethical minds of Socrates, Plato, Aristotle, and Kant, in spite of their numerous masculinist and racist biases. These philosophers were on target when they stressed over and over again that what distinguishes the human being is the fact that she/he struggles sincerely and constantly to regulate the excessive thrust of the irrational wills that lead people to dominate others, such as the very male domination that puts the other's existence, in this sense women's existence, at stake. By raping women, we live life not as pleasure but as violent death that consummates in forced sexual contact.

To begin with, self-control is too precious an ideal to be the exclusive property of "cerebral" males. Women today continue to be taught traditionally "feminine virtues." They must also learn to embody the so-called "masculine" language and values such as self-control, determination, cool emotional discipline, mastery, and so on.[47]

There has been a vulgar commodification of the otherwise rich ethical ideal of self-control, which is precisely intended to help the souls of human beings struggle against the excesses of money, sex, and greed—not on the behalf of upward mobility but on behalf of the preciousness of existence itself. Existentially serious persons do not control themselves in order to gain artificial respect from those whom they falsely impress. Rather they exercise self-control because the will to control a desire for domination seems to be a good that is worth nurturing in a potential member of a comprehensively rational/moral community.

Women, too, are challenged not to morally imitate the vulgar notion of self-control in their upward mobility, but to style themselves after those who exercise self-control as a successful consummation of self-empowerment. Seyla Benhabib is profoundly right when she argues, "The retreat from utopia within feminist theory in the last decade has taken the form of debunking as 'essentialist' any attempt to formulate a feminist ethic, feminist politics, a feminist concept of autonomy and even a feminist aesthetic. . . . Postmodernism can teach us the theoretical and political traps of why utopias and foundational thinking can go wrong, but it should not lead to retreat from utopia altogether. For we, as women, have much to lose by giving up the utopian hope in the wholly other."[48] The notion of self-construction I am developing here is intended to provide a new concept of autonomy guided by self-generated principles of comprehensive reason, along the lines of Benhabib's recent efforts to situate the self in history and temporality.

Self-control and mastery are, in fact, what radical feminists should fervently depend on in their truly worthy attempt to teach males to control their violence so that we will not all die. By self-control, I essentially mean the following. Humans have souls, as Plato and Aristotle concluded, which I demonstrated in chapter 2. Their souls are characterized by three aspects, the rational, the nonrational, and the desires. Running like a red thread through them is reason. According to Plato, even the desires are potentially rational. Thus, when a person is purely dominated by the desires or, to use Jaggar's terminology, by the emotions, he/she is in danger of jeopardizing his/her existence. An interaction between a desiring male and a female could become dangerous to both, if each is seeking to dominate the other. The case of the tyrant whom I discussed earlier is the most perfect example of a person who is willing to destroy the other for the sake of a momentary sexual encounter. It is as a technique of regulating the excesses of desiring beings that Plato introduced the idea of a "self-controlled (*enkrateia*) soul." The tyrant for me can be sexless; at issue, however, is the condition of that person's identity.

For radical feminists, Jaggar argues, sex as practiced in heterosexual relationships denaturalizes women. Genuinely liberated women ought to become lesbians, as lesbianism discloses women's nature in its pure form. Jaggar quotes Barbara Solomon who has written, "We live in a male supremacist shitpile. At its most basic level, this shitpile is upheld by fucking, marriage and breeding.

Straight women serve this system by serving their men. Lesbians reject it by saying we won't fuck, we won't marry, we won't breed and we'll damn well do as we please."[49]

If lesbians participated in sexual practices that were as sadomasochistic as some male's sexuality, what would radical feminists then think of domination? Would they exonerate it? According to Jaggar, there are radical feminists who are fundamentally opposed to sadomasochism even when women practice it: "For women to degrade and hurt each other is to confirm male myths that women are first and foremost sexual objects with all else peripheral, that we are so sex starved and orgasm focused that we will do whatever it takes to make us come—a myth that has steeped out psyches all too often in self-loathing."[50]

Those who defend the practice say, "Both participants agree to engage in a sadomasochistic encounter and that, contrary to appearances, the masochist is actually in control because she can halt the encounter at any time."[51]

This response deserves a detailed analysis. To argue that it is less dangerous for women to practice sadomasochism than men is like saying that a woman who rapes is better than a man who rapes. I am not sure that women's culture would uncritically incorporate this truly moral evil practice. Sadomasochism is by no means—no matter how far we stretch ethical standards—worthy of any culture, any way of life. To succumb to this heinous, culturally determined male practice is to experience sexuality not as pleasure but as "violent death," as Bataille would have it.[52]

Surely men throughout the ages and in almost all known cultures have wrongly identified genuine sexual pleasure with hostility and, in extreme cases, violent death. Hobbesian man has extended the violent nature of men to their very sexuality. Good sex, some men like to think, has to be violent. Dominant hegemonic ideas at schools and on television have not helped men to think otherwise. What may actually be strictly cultural has in some quarters been treated as natural, a view that ultimately justifies men to other men. Sadomasochistic women, in the end, are not helping their cause or the larger cause of human ethical advancement, if they mimic some men's horrible vices in the name of equalizing themselves with men at large. To begin with, "some men" is not "all men," and rapes and sadomasochism are not the only ways in which sex can be enjoyed. There are healthier and deeper ways of enjoying sex. Human nature is not exhausted by sadomasochism, which is another form of the will to dominate.

Jaggar was right when she observed, "Radical feminism indeed has revealed a different reality. It has shown us a world in which men control women into motherhood or sexual slavery. . . . what radical feminism has not yet done is provide an account of the underlying causes of the patriarchal system. To answer these questions would require a comprehensive theory of human nature and human society. Only such a theory can explain why men seek to enslave women."[53]

To deal with this question I wish to advance the following hypothesis.

Domination is a permanent possibility. But it is a possibility that need not be chosen, just because it is there. Humans are equipped with a powerful gift that can help them to struggle against the will to dominate. It is only the morally evil person who would consciously choose to rape another human being. The great ethical writer Aristotle advises us in *Nicomachean Ethics*, "For it is our choice of good or evil that determines our character, not opinion about good or evil. . . . And we choose to take or avoid some good or evil thing."[54] Thus, the morally evil person lacks what Aristotle calls "moral vision" and he/she chooses to act without vision.

I agree, on the other hand, with those feminists whom Harstock interprets to be saying that "rape is not a sexual act but an act of domination and humiliation."[55] It is only those who are morally sick, or lack a moral vision, who would experience women as objects of mastery, control, humiliation, and death. Such persons do not belong to any culture's moral community. Critical moral education would wrongly serve rapists and dominators of all kinds if it justified them in the name of nature. The function of moral education should be to show such individuals how to construct "new souls." I call this particular possibility *education toward empowerment and away from domination.*

The need to humiliate, which is the most complete experience of domination, is not a virtue. It is a disease that must be expunged. Both men and women need to be taught afresh that their bodies should not be violated in order to serve as sources of pleasure, but rather that pleasure can be experienced through firm and gentle treatment. The extremely serious self, critically aware of the permanent presence of moral evil, takes his/her own existence and all others seriously by choosing not to convert the other's existence into an object of thrills, a landscape of meaningless pleasure. The other is allowed dignity, as Kant profoundly argued, only when his body and soul are respected and not violated in the name of frivolous freedom.

Of course, one could argue that it is nobody's business to pry into one's bedroom, and that is a good defense. But just as strongly, one need not abuse one's private style of existence by inflicting it as a model on others. Some radical feminists seem to be doing just that. If they were to remain privately reserved about their practices, nobody would know. In addition, I agree that nobody should be freely entertained by an intimately private act. Radical feminists are advised then to withdraw their argument that the personal is political. In this instance, the defenders of sadomasochism would be better off if they privately enjoyed their sexuality away from the gazes of Aristotelian moral judges.

Radical feminists can always develop such mistaken new ways of being as befits their desires by developing alternative cultures, provided that their followers do not publicly promote domination in the forms of humiliation, wounded scars, etc.

Recently Joan Cocks has observed

A sadistic masculinity and masochistic feminism paraded as truth in "entertainment" movies, in the lyrics of popular music, and album covers, and fashion magazines, in self-confessed pornography, and only somewhat more covertly in a cult of criminality among progressive writers, murderers, and child molesters as liberation heroes flaunting the authoritarianism and puritanism of moral convention and legal right.[56]

These are hardly the noble rebellions against discipline and order, in the Foucauldian sense, that the ''new souls'' of an emancipatory woman's alternative culture would wish for. Disorder, chaos and criminality are not virtues, and Foucault's silence on those perennial themes of modernity does not help much. Sadly those who have dared to challenge Foucault to speak were labeled neo-conservative, homophobic, elitist sentimentalists. This does not advance the query, it merely represses it.

The Sexed Subject: Feminist Interpretations of Foucault

According to Foucault, throughout human history women have been treated not just as persons but as sexed subjects, that is, persons who are sexually distinct. This reproduction of women as sexed subjects, however, is not merely a description of a natural fact.[57] If that were so, sexuality would not be problematized; it would just be another natural property. Exactly like racism, sexuality is a judgment of a person's identity. It connotes a meaning and it represents a style of existence. It determines a person's worth. In this sense, some women as the sexed subjects are different from men. They are fundamentally conceived of as bodies meant for another's pleasure, another's control, another's object of discipline. The state conspires with the males who are in power to define women as sexed subjects. Women are both defined and controlled by masculinist expectations. For Foucault, Biddy Martin contends, ''our subjectivity, our identity and our sexuality are intimately connected.''[58] Sexuality in general, and women's sexed existence in particular, are social constructs or value laden judgments, imbued with power.

As I argued earlier in chapter 1, the experts of knowledge are the ones who define the normal/abnormal, in the process of which, as Sawicki compellingly argued, differences are excluded. A feminist writes, ''Certainly, feminist analysis of the medical, psychiatric, and educational institutions since the nineteenth century would support Foucault's suggestion that the intervention of experts and their knowledge of the female body have everything to do with the constitution of power in our world.''[59]

Our sexuality then is invisibly defined by power. This conception is the Nietzchian dimension of Foucault that I discussed earlier. Our identities are created by language that normalizes and values through judgmental adjectives. Terms used to characterize a person, such as woman's passivity, impulsiveness, emotions, moods, inconstancy, slenderness, etc., are specific products of male discourse. The identity thus gained is an imposed subjectivity, a politically constructed difference that women as persons may or may not choose. They are defined by men in power, through a scientific naturalization of women as sexed subjects.

It is this imposed subjectivity that must be resisted. Woman's novel culture of resistance can be used to dissolve the brutal forces that subdue their bodies, which are the nerve center of their existence. As Martin puts it, "We cannot afford to refuse to take a political stance 'which pins us to our sex' for the sake of a theoretical correctness, but we can refuse to be content with fixed identities or to universalize ourselves as revolutionary subjects."[60]

For me, women then do not have a singular identity, not even a self-imposed one, but multiple identities. Not all women are authentic only if they are lesbians. This style of existence is only one identity among many possible others. To suppose otherwise is to reproduce another "fixed identity" under one dominant category. This would be a form of domination under the misleading name of empowerment. Jana Sawicki is right when she observes, "Perhaps the least dangerous way to discover whether and how specific practices are enslaving or liberating us is not to silence and exclude differences, rather to use them to diversify and renegotiate the arena of radical political struggle."[61]

Furthermore, for Foucault, modernity is a double-edged sword. On the one hand, it gives us unlimited access to liberty; on the other hand, it has enslaved and disciplined our bodies, particularly those of women. Foucault is only half right when he treats all bodies as equally docile. Women's bodies are sexed in a radically different way than men's. Sandra Lee Barky writes, "Women like men are subject to many of the same disciplinary practices Foucault describes. But he is blind to disciplines that produce a modality of embodiment that is peculiarly feminine."[62]

Woman's femininity is defined by the holders of patriarchal power as represented by bodies that are "soft, supple, hairless, and smooth; ideally it [the female body] should betray no sign of wear, experience, age, or deep thought."[63] Jana Sawicki, an esteemed Foucauldian feminist, has aptly observed, "For example, new images of women are created when some women develop strong, muscular bodies. And as female body builders defy the canons of the feminine aesthetic, building their bodies beyond traditional limits, they feminize bodily identity and confuse gender."[64]

Of course some of these feminine properties are not constructed by self-empowering women but rather are "identities" inflicted upon women. Through them women are attributed essences that function peculiarly as social ontologies.

I consider styles of existence that are chosen and nurtured by women themselves as unreserved moments of self-construction leading toward self-empowerment, motivated by desire. Women's struggles, however, need not be restricted to the expression of their otherwise repressed sexuality, as some libertarian feminists insist. The women's movement has also produced powerful articulations of women's rights as part of human rights.[65] Lesbianism is not the only possible reaction to domination by patriarchal power. Indeed, women do not construct values that empower them only in sadomasochism. Rather, "When feminists expand the domain of sexuality to include such issues as abortion and reproduction, they engage in a de-sexualization of their struggles and move away from gender-based identity politics." In contrast, homosexual liberation movements have been (understandably) "caught at the level of demands for their right to their sexuality."[66]

When women assert only their sexuality, for Sawicki, they are constructing universal essences that do not exhaust the meaning of womanhood. Other important issues of women's rights too need the profound recognition that certain women have not been willing to accord them. Hasty essences are as dangerous as hasty differences. The women's movement ought to resist both. Self-construction needs to have a broader view of women's needs and desires as well as the differences that constitute their individuality. As Zamen puts it, "Dialogue between women with different sexual preferences can be opened, not with the aim of eliminating these differences, but rather learning from them and discovering the basis for coalition building."[67]

Sawicki finally credits Foucault, as I do also, when she writes, "Foucault also stressed the specificity and autonomy of the many modes of oppression in modern society. He emphasized the fragmented and open-ended character of the social field."[68] Foucault's theories do not tell us what to do, but rather how some of our ways of thinking and doing are historically linked to particular forms of power and social control.[69]

Diamond and Quinby, however, disagree: "Although Foucault's analytics of power provides an astute revision of how power operates in contemporary societies, he does not particularly illuminate the effects of a society of normalization on the lives of women. We speak here of the routinization of battery, sexual exploitation, harassment, and sexual abuse in contemporary society."[70]

I contended earlier that Foucault's conception of power is not guided by norms that either explicitly or implicitly contain alternatives to power as domination. It is conceivable that Foucault actually lacked an alternative vision, as Habermas argues, or that Foucault descriptively considers such an expectation untenable, as a sort of humanistic prejudice which believes that power is something that comes out of interactions and that it is mutually either shared or controlled by another power that displaces it. Those placements and replacements, presences and absences, are permanent games of power. Strictly speaking then, power is not merely A dominating B but also A and B symmetrically dominating one other. This is one possible interpretation, but I think an inadequate conception of power, to which I have developed an alternative in chapter 2.

So Diamond and Quinby are right when they say that Foucault does not tell us what to do and not do. Particularly lacking in Foucault is an illumination of the effects of power in the forms of sexism and racism. But we continue to learn from Foucault's illumination of the various ways in which we become the sexed and raced subjects of modernity, and that is no easy accomplishment.

Are Power and Domination the Same?

This question is central to the thesis of this book. My answer to the question is that they are not. Power and domination, contrary to the famous Hobbesian answer I discussed earlier (in which Hobbes refuses to distinguish between power and domination), are not the same. I return once again to Hobbes in order to disagree with him.

For Hobbes, power, like pride and fame, is a value. There are human beings who orient their entire existence toward the initial acquisition and eventual excessive accumulation of power. The acquisition of power at the initial stages may be as harmless as the obtaining of money in order to buy the rudimentary necessities of life: food and shelter, for example. Only a fanatic moralist would condemn a person for adjusting to the organizing reality principle of a capitalist society where a person must use money to buy commodities. The mere acquisition of money in order to avoid shameful poverty is the minimum acquisition of power—a healthy form of power. I wish that Hobbes had at least recognized that healthy form of power—power as self-reliance, which helps the modern individual to resist perpetual dependence upon the whims, fantasies, moods, cruelties, arbitrariness, and ultimate domination of those human beings who have gone beyond acquiring a healthy form of power and have excessively accumulated power. There is a major difference between the two forms of power— power as acquisition and power as accumulation. Hobbes failed to distinguish between these two forms of power, so much so that, for him, there is no difference between a power that dominates and a power that does not wish to dominate. I call the first form of power healthy because it desires and values power only because without it an individual would be ontologically dependent upon those for whom, following Hobbes, power is a value with which more power is accumulated. The accumulators of power, consistent with the Hobbesian thesis that power is in itself a value—a value beyond moral criticism— would aggressively and subtly take even that minimum degree of power that otherwise powerless individuals may have.

However painful it may sound, Hobbes is right that there is a form of power that is intertwined with domination. Such is the classical form of power that Stravogrin possesses, and such is the form of excessively self-centered, occasionally brutal, deliberately pain-afflicting, and ultimately insecure and perverse will to power that a considerable portion of modern subjects have made their own. It is perhaps from the latter empirical fact that Hobbes deduced his general theory of human nature—a theory that he dispassionately extended to characterize the human condition.

Hobbes's theory of human nature, as a will to power, is only partially right. His heroic procedure of moving from particular observations of human beings possessed by power, which they manifestly practice as fame, status, vanity, conceit, nastiness, pride, selfishness, distrust, competition, brutality, deceit, etc. to characterize the human condition per se is distressingly inaccurate. Hobbes's dogmatic refusal as a thinker with a scientific temperament, prevented him from dispassionately seeing the limits of observation as well as the limits of his finitude and subjectivity. Hobbes could easily be accused of a scientific arrogance that reduces the complexity of human nature to the observable behavior of morally/rationally weak human beings who have become painfully enslaved by commodities and enslaved by the will to power in a competitively organized economic system. From his observations of human nature, Hobbes drew the refutable conclusion that power per se is domination.

However, this form of power that does not dominate has yet to intervene into the empirical world. As a consequence, Hobbes was not able to observe it. Because Hobbes could not observe it in the actions of human beings, he incorrectly concluded that it could not conceivably exist. Had he chosen to imagine it, Hobbes could have done so. Why he did not, considering his imaginative intellectual power, is a puzzle. Perhaps Hobbes was a firm believer in evil although he did not expressively admit it. If he is a firm believer that human beings are essentially bad and that their evil must be externally controlled by law, then it follows that he believed in evil in the world, including evil that is practiced dominating power, which can be controlled *only* by laws more powerful than the citizens' wills to power. I wish to argue that the most effective way of controlling the hidden and not-so-hidden will to power in human beings to undertake is the difficult task of controlling oneself without the help of externally generated coercive laws.

CONCLUSION

A Pragmatic Conception of Power

''Perfection is the result of struggle.''

This powerful message from the Chinese sage Chuang Tzu may be interpreted in the following way. Perfection is an ideal that is worth striving for in our short stay on earth. Without the ideal of perfection, the self-constructing moral subject could not become a trustworthy individual capable of enjoying the ultimate benefits of self-empowerment. An individual who cannot be trusted with the absolutely delicate value of power could surreptitiously elevate the abuse of power into a dangerous norm. Imperfection is strikingly similar to evil if it is practiced naturally; that is, without examining its pitfalls. Self-empowerment does not come easily. Chuang Tzu was right when he said that the possibility of perfection is a consequence of struggle. I now wish to add to the above insight the idea that imperfection, as the opposite of perfection, is the result of naturalizing evil—evil understood as thoughtlessness, the deliberate decision not to deliberate, the arrogant choice not to think before acting, self-conscious pride in converting ignorance into a virtue. Imperfection is the result of not struggling.

Moreover, imperfection is the result of the decision not to struggle. On the other hand, self-empowerment as a realizable ideal is a decision—a decision that may fail—to learn how to struggle in order to seek the ideal of human perfection. I would like to suggest to my attentive readers that, pragmatically speaking, it is better for our own moral and mental health to have ideals—however difficult it may seem to realize them—than to have no ideals at all. To have ideals gives us a true sense of our humanity, a meaning to our existence, a set of goals for an otherwise goal-less and often cruel everyday life. Ideals make us distinctly and usefully intelligent and self-respecting beings. The goal of perfection, in particular, is a noble goal that seems to have been carved out for human beings, given human imperfection.

The ideal of perfection, though, is a heavy burden to carry. Heavier and more painful still is the fact that perfection comes as a struggle—a struggle that may easily last one's whole lifetime. Considering that human beings in general are too lazy to be voluntarily challenged by the demands of powerful and exacting ideals (such as the ideal of perfection) and that human beings are often indifferent to the plight of others, the burdensome weight of perfection uncomfortably rests on the shoulders of those infinitely few human beings who truly care. It is that minute number of individuals with genuine moral/intellectual courage and a solid emotional constitution who willfully strive to perfect themselves, that the project of self-construction depends.

Self-constructing moral subjects who wish to empower themselves are the ones who consciously struggle to perfect themselves. The conscious process of self-growth—toward a perfectibility that aims at healthily giving moral/intellectual and emotional power to the genuinely needy subjects of modernity—begins at a very early stage.

The ideal of perfection, like the sublime tower of knowledge, is the highest privilege that human beings could ever be given. Human beings are so weak, so inconsistent, so arrogant that it is hard for us to believe that we could ever, ever change, let alone become perfect.

It is with a clear awareness of what we really are—nasty, cruel, inconsistent, hypocritical, vain, selfish, weak, brutish, in short, power seekers—that we experience the ideal of perfection as an unbearable weight. A substantial number of human beings are crushed by this weight. Others find sophisticated means of escaping from the painful awareness of who they truly are by saying to themselves that imperfection is natural. Since they feel imperfection is as natural as drinking water, they do not even worry about it. Others still are conscious of the fact that imperfection is a vice—a vice that they sometimes try to reform or radically eradicate. For some individuals, the consciousness of a vice comes so easily, that they do not even feel the pain of the weight. It is easy for them to eradicate a vice. They pay very heavily for the ease of their consciousness. They really do not change. They remain the same: easygoing, light, naive, forgetful, and unreflective. They do not and cannot experience anything, either joy or sadness, profoundly. Such individuals do not experience despair or anguish. In their already constructed world, they experience life lightly. There, everything is provided for; even imperfection is a way of life that they simply and without tension acknowledge as present.

Power as domination, for example, is natural in their world. The imperfection of human beings is its ultimate justification. Wherever imperfection resides, there is power. In that world, power as self-empowerment is neither a need that can be satisfied nor an imperative that commands, nor even a value that can be cultivated through the gentle participation of the forgotten past and the future. However, both these powers can be remembered during the quest for self-empowerment. It is through remembrance that our inherent imperfection may perhaps be controlled for our own sake, for our individuality as well as our communality.

The ideal of perfection resides outside the world of imperfection. As such, it has its own language, signs, symbols, ethics, and aesthetics. Perfection, or the will to bring it forth, as the highest act of self-empowerment, seeks to make full use of the images of the forgotten past in concert with the not-yet. To make the dream a reality, memory is invited along with remembrance.

Memory has an inherent power to extract from the deeply concealed forgotten past ways of redeeming us from the unbearable burden of misery that modernity has created. For those who are in tune with themselves, who as a consequence are aware of their habitual imperfections and who genuinely want to reform themselves, memory and remembrance are capable of providing them with re-demptive power. Redemption, in a deep sense, is a purifier of the willing self. Through redemption, habitually ingrained imperfections can be gradually but effectively removed from the psychic structure of the self. One of the ways in which such purification of the self can be effected is through the radical eradi-cation of a reality principle that naturalizes historically chosen social imperfec-tions, such as selfishness, unhealthy competitiveness, cruelty, shortsightedness, and the will to power. These social imperfections can be uprooted by revolu-tionary critical activities in which genuinely change-seeking individuals are the main participants. The will to be freed from imperfection is a condition neces-sary to the development of the self-empowering itself. The self that wants to be self-empowered is the self that says: ''I want to be freed from imperfections that dominate and enslave me—freed from a domination and enslavement that habitually compels me to will power that dominates. I want to dominate my own imperfections and relearn how to lead my life as a reasonable and ethical being who can peacefully and socially live with other human beings and external nature.'' Pragmatically speaking, an empowered self finds peace, cooperation, and sociability powerful social tools with which it can fulfill its own life am-bitions: excellence, extraordinariness, and even finite happiness. I have called this particular orientation toward everyday living with other human beings and external nature—for example, stones, minerals, land, and trees, a pragmatic con-ception of power—power as self-empowerment.[71]

To acquire power as self-empowerment makes good sense as well as eventually providing practically useful and very much needed restfulness. Such restfulness makes it possible for human beings to sit and think with the minimal intervention of commodities and the endless quests for power, money, status, reputation, flattering friends, contacts, etc., and to desire self-empowerment as a value and a norm. As William James brilliantly but simply said, the value of the pragmatic conception of life is that, without giving us an absolute standard, life provides us with numerous values and norms, which lead us eventually to be at peace with ourselves, others, and the world. The social consequence of the pragmatic orientation to the world, such as peacefulness, cooperation, and sociability, can be effectively guided only by the societal presence of individuals who are so self-empowered that they genuinely desire to get rid of all impediments that make it difficult for them to be healthy human beings. The self-empowered human being, I wish to argue, does not voluntarily choose power as domination in the Hobbesian sense. That individuals continue to desire more power even after they have gained power is a fact that gives human beings no peace, no time to profoundly sit and think, but rather compels them to continuously experience anguish, dread, and, what is even worse, fear of what powerless, thus resentful, individuals could do against them. This last fact alone is enough to explain why modernity is infested with anxious, nervous, overstressed, exhausted, forgetful, neurotic, narcissistic subjects. These modern subjects spend a substantial amount of their time at psychiatric offices, and not, as they otherwise could, in sitting and thinking before acting. I think that such a mode of living does not have practically useful consequences unless we choose to reason perversely, so perversely that (a) we elevate psychoses and neuroses, exhaustion and anguish into natural vices that are pleasurable in themselves, or (b) decide that, as perversities, there is nothing we can do to change them, apart from surrendering to them as fates. My argument against both choices, which are developed by human beings as definitive reality principles, is that if the consequences of emotional problems are so detrimental to the psychic structure of the self, they ought to be changed. Critical education and reflective thinking can play an indispensable redemptive and awareness-raising role in changing the useless reality principles to which we have unnecessarily surrendered. Promising redemption and raising awareness may not uproot the tyrannical tendency of human beings to enjoy social imperfections. Indeed, some individuals may actually be hopelessly possessed by evil in the Dostoyevskian sense. But some individuals are not all individuals. Those who inherently take pleasure in willing power that inflicts evil on others should be intelligently identified and given no empirical power. Rather, we must be vigilant against becoming contaminated by their imperfections. It is, however, a sad fact that there are differences among human beings and that these differences matter philosophically and politically.

Human Differences That Matter

It is commonplace to assert that, in a fundamental sense, human beings are the same in several senses:

1. If one is a Judeo-Christian, one thinks and believes that all human beings are born in the image of God, as His/Her children. If God is intelligent, just, forgiving, loving, tolerant, all knowing, etc., it would follow that His/Her children may also possess all those qualities to some extent.

2. Human beings are factually equal with respect to intelligence, rationality, compassion, etc. This equality could be empirically tested in a climate in which all individuals were to be raised with identical opportunities, such that their virtues could be tested. A solid and just educational formation may bring out these hidden virtues in the course of time.

Similarly, one could also assert that human beings are different. They are different because as the children of God, their various capacities for intelligence, justice, forgiveness, tolerance, knowledge, etc. are only potentialities. This is a rather crucial modification of the first condition of sameness. It is crucial because unlike number 1 above this statement of difference does not naively assume that the children of God partake of the qualities of their Father/Mother. Rather, it subtly asserts that just because God-like qualities are there in the form of potentialities, it does not follow that they are actualities. As potentialities, these qualities require an enormous amount of struggle under the guidance of the reflective presence and self-control before they can become actual human powers with which the self becomes authentically self-empowered.

Self-empowerment then, as naively understood, is not a given. It may not even be a given for the most gifted saint. The saint too might have struggled, without our knowledge, to earn the noble virtue of pure self-empowerment. We simply do not empirically know how the virtue was earned. Leaving saints aside, though, I wish to assert that ordinary individuals do not partake of God-like qualities to the extent that they could, simply by saying that they are images of God. That is not enough, except as an assertion of truth in the form of faith. I deeply appreciate it as a statement of faith, but I also would want to extract pragmatically usable insights from that faith to guide concrete existence or concrete social practices. When I demand the latter, I also demand that the potentialities become actualities that guide life. These actualities would provide the self with practical answers to perplexing questions: Should I be just to my fellow human being? Should I belittle and ridicule those individuals who disagree with me? Individuals can, if they so wish, develop answers to these questions with the guide of those potential powers, those God-like qualities. The extent to which these powers are developed is not determined by faith. It is not enough to believe. One must also struggle, and the struggle influences the kind of human beings we become. Those who work on their potentialities, in a sense, become different from those who do not, from those who miss real opportunities. In this sense, there are differences that truly matter among human beings, and one way in which these differences can be established is by making the distinction between potentialities and actualities. Given these distinctions, we can effectively argue that there are important differences among human beings and that these differences are generated not by genetics as much as they are by the demanding challenge of the self-imposed task of improving our characters toward the possibility of moral/rational progress, or toward autonomy—an autonomy that is readily and heroically visible in self-empowerment.

Human beings, contrary to arguments about sameness, are factually unequal, or have become so with respect to intelligence, rationality, and compassion. This reflects the unequal availability of positive resources: money, genuinely supportive educators, counselors, friends, caring parents, a non-prejudicial societal and political climate, adequate nutritional necessities for the body—and an encouraging environment that allows maximum freedom to think, create, and act without the disapproving gaze of others. Such an attitude can contribute to the gradual cultivation of citizens—citizens who have not actively exercised their intelligence and passions to the extent that is required to produce intelligent, rational, and compassionate human beings.

Visible inequalities among human beings, when we courageously assert their existence, should not come as a surprise to us. What is really surprising to some, shocking to others and even alarming to quite a few is the belief that human beings are the same in the senses that I have articulated as generally accepted, but also fundamentally different due to historical genealogy, as we learned from Foucault in chapter 1. Our surprises should reveal to us the depth of our ignorance. It should instruct us to harshly expose ourselves to the facts of inequalities and the ways that some power-holders deliberately and systematically engender this by exposing some to positive resources and denying a considerable number of others those crucial positive resources. Instead, those in power socialize the disadvantaged to become dependent, insecure, cowardly, self-doubting, helpless, abusable, materially and spiritually bankrupt, and slavish. All the above negative conditions encourage not the virtue of autonomy or self-empowerment but rather the truly crippling opposites: heteronomy coupled with slavishness.

Human qualities that demonstrate sameness and differences could easily be learned. Depending on the motives of human beings toward one another, sameness and differences could actually be manufactured. Sameness and differences are significantly conditioned by the historical process of socialization, a socialization to what I called hegemonic ideas[72] in my book on the nature of political action. Sameness and differences, I argue below, are also effected in subtle and explicit ways by the powers of judgment, the blessings of the experts of knowledge, as well as by the detrimental and determining roles of education at the most formative stages: the earlier phases of ''bourgeois'' formal schools, beginning with preschools (for the lucky ones) and ending in the so-called visible universities (the bastions of superior schooling of the upper class). The section below is devoted to the above themes.

Is Power a Fact or a Possibility?

My initial answer to the question is this. Power is a fact if the one who exercises it does so in the form of a power that dominates, and if the power-holder believes and thinks that this form of power is constitutive of human nature. When the power-holder orients his/her entire existence toward the practice of power as domination, the practice gradually takes the form of a static and nature-like structure. In this particular sense, power is a practice—a practice that is a fact. As a fact, the power-holder believes power as domination cannot be changed by education but can be deterred from becoming intolerably dominating, repressive, and pain-inflicting by another power in the form of the law. The will to power as a fact resists change through the power of ideas—ideas that impose change through the force of inquiry, dialogue, critical discourse, and reflective rhetoric that appeal to the mind by passionately stirring the heart or by putting the heart in a serene, relaxing, trusting psychological state so that it can listen, think, see, meditate, and examine the bases of the will to power. When one believes power is a fact, one also believes that it cannot be gently penetrated by thought and thus cannot be changed for the better.

But power is also a possibility. Possibility at a foundational level means that power is the product of both a conscious and perhaps even unconscious historical process—the process that it took to develop values, norms, tastes, interests and ways of living. From this angle, a particular value, norm, taste, or interest did not just come into being out of nowhere. Rather, the value, norm, taste, or interest may have been the product of dialogue among our original cultural ancestors; or particularly fierce, vicious, and nasty wars of ideas—ideas diffused from the thinkers of a particular age, down to such salespersons of ideas as priests, teachers, bureaucrats, merchants, poets, concrete and powerful political leaders; or authentic debates among the opinion framers of the age in collaboration with those who held power and thus handed down the ultimate judgments, which were backed by the powers embodied in the state. Values, norms, tastes, and interests could also prevail in the world of the powerless in the form of habits and social practices, sanctioned by the emotional bonds of solidarity, brotherhood, and sisterhood. Possibility then is traceable to origin, and origin is itself a product of the historical actions of men and women.

Possibility is also an act of becoming. As an act of becoming, it is a transcendence of possibility as a fact. Becoming is itself a historical act. It is the concrete transcendence of facticity. Let's say a value, norm, taste, or interest which exists in history at a given point A was a fact. At point B, the fact gives way as a possibility to another fact. The first fact is transcended by the second. The infinite transcendence of facts shows that facts are not static, but rather dynamic possibilities. Becoming is itself stimulated by human experiences such as experiences of joy, or the need for them; the intensity of suffering, and the revolutionary task of overcoming some kinds of suffering through the critical power of transcendence aided by the reflective presence. Each of these experiences, which over a long stretch of time have been experienced as realities, therefore as resisting change, were once only possibilities. But the leading powers of the age and anguished, often fatalistic powerless, subjects have experienced and continue to experience values, norms, tastes, and interests not as factors open to change by thought and action but simply as immutable facts. As such, facts are lived as mysterious powers to which we must surrender. Socialization, I now wish to argue, plays a decisive role here, in leading the self to internalize power as domination. In what follows I explicate how the mechanism works.

Socialization, Hegemonic Ideas, and Power That Disciplines

From the traceable beginning to the end of time, we humans are subjected to the subtle process of education, and this leads education toward hegemonic ideas that imprison self-empowering thought and liberating imagination by disciplining and domesticating our capacity to determine our thoughts and actions.

Education is itself a mode of socialization. In education, as a formative experience, ideas, power, and discipline work in a subtle concert. Unless the person who is undergoing the formative process of education is critically aware of the power of ideas, he/she could easily lose the precious freedom of will and find himself/herself internalizing ideas that imprison and subjugate one's freedom of thought. A given person might have never made much of the fact that he/she has white skin, hazel eyes, blonde hair, and much else, but he/she could be trained to impute powerful significance to biological facts. These biological facts could be translated into dangerously politicized values, norms, tastes, and interests. As biological facts that mark differences, the facts are not intrinsically dangerous. It is when judgmental meanings are systematically appended to them that the facts become politicized. They become facts that stir the emotions. These stirred emotions in turn produce modes of thinking that cold-bloodedly distinguish cultural symbols. Cultural symbols are further deliberately distorted. The distortions take on a life of power that privileges certain values as intrinsically superior when compared to others. It is ultimately when otherwise intrinsically harmless differences—such as skin color, eye color, etc.—are made symbols of superiority and inferiority, and they become integral aspects of formative education that the danger begins. Innocent differences are changed into deeply divisive tools of language, desire, and truth. A generation of children, adults, educators, and experts grow up by internalizing these differences in the depths of the unconscious. By the time that children become adults, adults become opinion-framers, and both are subjected to the indiscriminate invitation of aging, the years have often dulled the senses and solidified long-held prejudices. At that point, the possibility of autonomous thinking, aided by intelligent values of tradition and custom, becomes exceedingly difficult to achieve.

The great and truly sensitive writer, Thomas Mann, was intelligently aware of the formative power of values, norms, and tastes that shape the growing self. Mann captured the essence of how children are exposed to values that give them a sense of identity, a sense that either strengthens their character or damages it. The process is observed by the keen eyes of the narrator in ''Tonio Kroger.''

Tonio, like many other "sensitive" human beings, is an enigmatic figure who doubts the merits of his own identity, a doubting that is increased by the judgments of the other who looks and behaves very differently from himself. Tonio is both proud and ashamed of his identity. He did not seem to have had a great respect for his Italian name. Thus, he laments with the "ironic" words: "Yes, it is a silly name—Lord knows I'd rather be called Heinrich or Wilhelm. It's all because I'm named after my mother's brother Antonio. She comes from down there."[73] Tonio may not have wanted to assimilate the other "low" values of Hans, such as the latter's rather embarrassing interest in riding horses and dislike of thinking and literature. There are more "ironic" passages that communicate the politicized values of judgment. For example: "Tonio Kroger looked at them both, these two for whom he had in time past suffered love—at Hans and Ingeborg. They were Hans and Ingeborg not so much by virtue of individual traits and similarity of costume as by similarity of race and type. This was the blond, fair-haired breed of the steel blue eyes, which stood to him for the pure, the blithe, the untroubled in life; for a virginal aloofness that was at once both simple and full of pride."[74]

Tonio Kroger's mother was a negative representation of Hans—Tonio's ideal self—the ideal to which he had undoubtedly become socialized through the disciplinary power of ideas that had subtly instructed him in the form of ideals. Thus, his mother, who came from the nameless "down there," was dark, fiery, passionate, undisciplined, irregular, and careless.[75] Kroger, however, was enormously proud of his "northern" father's ancestry. The name itself, Kroger, his father's name, radiated brilliance, dignity, light, and even beauty. Tonio Kroger himself describes it almost perfectly. Here are his words: "My father, you know, had the temperament of the north: solid, reflective, puritanically correct, with a tendency to melancholia."[76]

If we grouped together the dominant values and norms by whose presence Tonio is enlivened and given a self-image, here are the values we get. Noble are the blondes with their steel-blue eyes. Their bodies disclose sublime beauty. So do their souls. Their souls communicate the presence of a mind that produces the power of reflection grounded upon solidity, puritanical firmness of intent and resolve, and a deep appreciation for the tragic dimension of life. Inferior are the types whose bodies fervently move toward the fleshy, the sensuous, the festive, the sexual, the irregular, the self-determining. It is toward such values, and many others besides, that human beings have been getting socialized since the dawn of history. This assertion could become compelling if it is backed up by empirical documentation, which has to be done. Foucault's archeological and genealogical studies are convincing good starts.

Socialization is not an abstract concept as I have used it above. It is a concrete mode of education. It becomes even more concrete when we analyze how it works in the context of the functional roles of hegemonic ideology, education, and power as domination.

Ideology, Education, and Power As Domination

Education in the abstract, like many ideas in this world, is harmless. Receiving an education and gaining a distorted sense of how life should be lived are not necessarily simultaneous. Education, very much like food and shelter, is an intrinsic good. Again, like food and shelter, education benefits the body and the mind. The effects of education on the body may not be as transparent as those of food and shelter. It is empirically much easier to see a body revived by food and shelter. Harder to notice is a body that is revived, enlivened, and even beautified by the educational effects of powerful ideas. Nevertheless, there should not be any doubt in our minds that ideas, in concert with food and shelter, revive, enliven, form, transform, depress, and radiate the self's body and mind. Just because we cannot readily see the effects of ideas upon the self as easily as we can see the effects of food and shelter, we should not become sloppy empiricists and dismiss effects that cannot be seen as nonexistent. That would reflect a mode of socializing human beings, rampant in certain circles of modernity to conceive of thinking in a hopelessly limiting way only through demonstrable concepts. From this we get simple propositions such as ''I can see a healthy body, but I cannot see a healthy soul.'' These propositions are depressingly simplistic. They educate us by miseducating us. They miseducate us by severely limiting our concept of the act of seeing to the merely observable.

One cannot see a healthy soul in the same way that one can see a healthy body. At work are two radically different conceptions of seeing. There are apparently legitimate signifiers of health in a healthy body: radiance of the face, for instance. The signifiers of a healthy soul have yet to be recognized. At the bare minimum, I wish to argue, one must be intelligently sensitive to intuit a soul, a character, that is hungry for ideas that revive, challenge, reduce anxiety, strengthen, and enrich morally, that give a tragic and yet fulfilling justification of human existence, that even dare to give images of perfection and horror, paradise and hell, finitude and infinity, goals and labyrinths.

Let us recall once again the dominant values that I gleaned from Thomas Mann's ''Tonio Kroger.'' These values are: skin color and corresponding intellectual, moral, emotional and aesthetic virtues: reflective ability, moral solidity, emotional stability, the color of the eyes and the aesthetic beauty therein. Note that these dominant values are values that are mediated by ideas—ideas that become ideologies, which then become integral aspects of school systems. These ideologies infest the very language that young students incorporate into their everyday linguistic interaction. The words that are thusly used are not merely facilitators of innocent ''locutionary'' communication as much as they are (1) tools of power—the power that compares, say, one's skin color with another's. Through the comparison of skin colors, a definite hierarchy of virtues is systematically established. And not merely that, they are (2) the conveyors of certain privileges. Rights are also granted to those who are inherently perceived to be virtuous, and certain rights and privileges are denied to those who are inherently nonvirtuous. And these words are (3) the most sophisticated tools with which minds and hearts are disciplined. It is, in fact, on this dimension that ideologies, schools, and power conspire to produce the modern highly disciplined and frequently mindless individual. This is an important claim that I wish to elaborate.

The modern individual is really disciplined by a highly distorting educational experience. The educational experience is distorted by ideas that become ideologies. As ideologies, ideas systematically divert the otherwise potentially creative individual from his/her imaginative creative powers. When creative powers are undermined, what we have as a result is a disciplined individual who cannot think autonomously, freshly, and responsibly. Rather, such an individual could easily become intoxicated by ideologies and hypnotized by the ideas of ''magical'' demagogues and rhetorical politicians.

The disciplined individual is not distinctly modern. Disciplined individuals have always existed. It is the depth of the disciplining power of intoxicating and hypnotizing hegemonic ideas that is peculiar to modernity. It is unfortunate that education has become a form of intoxication and hypnosis, as opposed to a forum for inquiry and meditative thought.

I argued earlier that education is an intrinsically good experience. In the abstract, I further added, education is harmless. It is a neutral power. When education's role is examined within the context of ideologies, socialization, and power, however, we clearly see its truly harmful effects on the body and character of the individual, particularly the modern individual who is a consummation of the history of all individuals of the past.

An individual, whose conception of himself/herself and all those ''others'' is seriously based on skin color, color of the eyes, size of the head, or structure of the bones, is a depressing example of the subtle destruction of the creative powers of the self. When we are reduced to inconsequential outside appearances, we do damage to our ultimate sense of ourselves as beings who are capable of deep reasoning power. This is a power which, when fully and wholeheartedly exercised, may even show us the severe limitations of making judgments based on appearance, the angle through which evil in the cloak of thoughtlessness, tyranny, arrogance, and dogma may enter the empirical world of everyday life.

An educational experience that does not foster clear thinking or the need to mistrust the claims that outside appearances have on us (as frail, weak, lazy, proud, forgetful, nasty, and selfishly self-interested human beings) is not an authentic education worthy of us. That this severely crippling mode of education has worked and continues to work is not a justification for not criticizing it. We can, however, wage a merciless attack on modern education by criticizing those very effects that we can directly see: the ''sick,'' ''illiterate,'' ''selfish,'' mindless consumers of modern society. These modern individuals are the bearers of a tradition of faulty education. They are concrete living witnesses of the past. The faults can be corrected only if we create schools that encourage individuals to think and act freely through a direct experience of constructing human values that genuinely empower.

Recognition and Power

Self-empowerment or the pragmatic conception of power, a construct I am still in the process of articulating and developing, has several components. Values, norms, and tastes are its integral parts. To say that human beings are self-constructing and self-empowering raises the questions: What and how do individuals construct, and given the construction, how do they become powerful, in the sense that they use values, norms, and tastes to judge, classify, categorize, recognize, and fail to recognize others, particularly those others who are different from them? To illustrate the claim, I used Tonio Kroger's values and norms and strove to show how values and norms were used as justifications for racial, gender, and cultural claims, have given us slavery, colonialism, the Holocaust, and the permanently dependent and poor members of the non-Western world. I further claimed that socialization, in concert with formal education, plays a central role in producing the modern "educated" individual—the individual as intoxicated and hypnotized by hegemonic ideas.

I now wish to add a new claim. On a formal level, power as domination and power as self-empowerment can both be systematically cultivated by formal education—education toward ideas that intoxicate, hypnotize, and discipline or imprison the mind and body. But that is not all. Power as domination, in particular, could also be effected through the subtle role of recognition. The thinker who provided us with the concept of recognition is Hegel, in his *The Phenomenology of Spirit*. I will now provide a brief discussion of the concept of recognition in that text.

In a general sense, we become powerful as well as powerless through the affective ways in which others do and do not recognize what we do, what we wish to do, how we actually do it, and how we wished to do it. That sense of recognition, so crucial for the development of personality or character is selectively extended to human beings. Unfortunately, across the vast and turbulent stretch of empirical history, recognition has been used as one of the most effective tools of power by the dominators against the dominated. It is one of the greatest merits of Hegel that he unfolded the function of recognition in any human interaction within the family, the workplace, and society at large.

The nature of power as domination and of self-empowerment can be deeply understood on the level of recognition—the recognition of (a) self as self on the level of self-empowerment, (b) self and others, (c) the recognizer and the recognized. Long before recognition is deployed within the formal institutions of education, where we have rigid roles such as the educator and the educated, dominant ideas and peripheral ideas, it is firmly embedded in human interaction outside of these educational structures.

When we speak a language at all, we are using words to recognize the meanings and nonmeanings of what we intend to say. Those with whom we are speaking play a key role in this basic interaction. It is they who may or may not be able to recognize our meaning. It is they as well who decide to extend or not extend recognition to the act of speaking, as we learned from Habermas and the speech act theorists. The capacities, decisions, intentions, motives, and goals of those with whom we speak affect the kinds of characters (dominated, susceptible to domination, or self-empowered) we develop.

Speaking then is not a lonely activity. Surely, the self can speak to itself. In fact, one of the deepest forms of speaking does take place in solitude. However, the form of speaking that interests me here is the form that allows human beings to interact with the sincere intention of understanding each other. My sense of understanding here does not aim at a crystal clear, transparent, and perfect communication of thoughts and feelings. Rather, understanding, for me, could never result in perfect, transparent understanding. Understanding is always an approximation of transparency, and seeking this transparency is a goal. The joy of the quest for understanding lies not in the result, which may never be attained, but rather in the sincere struggle for transparent meaning. In the quest for understanding each other, the place of recognition looms large.

The phenomenon of recognition, for Hegel, is explicitly present in one particular interactive space of domination. That space is the one that is occupied by a bondsman and a master in the feudalistic stages of European history. To begin with, bondage and lordship, on the level of the formative genealogy of concepts, are really nothing more than two linguistic labels. Immediately speaking, they are simply words. These linguistic labels, however, very much like the color concepts—white, blonde, blue-eyed, etc.—do become politically mediated and are thus given particular meanings. These meanings are invested with power. The meanings themselves carry relationships of power. Thus bondage connotes a structurally mediated meaning of inferiority, slavishness, being born to be dominated. Lordship, on the other hand, bears the ultimate virtue of nobility. Thus, the feudal landlord bears the name of the all-mighty, all-knowing, awesome lord of lords. Lordship is a symbol of the power born to command, authorize, and dominate. It is a symbol of superiority.

The two linguistic labels, however, do not become actual, concrete languages of power until after they are recognized by those human beings whose spatial habitat they so effectively define. Without recognition, in the form of the internalization of linguistic labels, words, therefore relationships, are meaningless.

For Hegel, the relationship between the bondsperson and the master are founded on the integral dependence of one upon the other. The bondsman is taught to think and live as if he is inherently dependent upon the master. Inherent dependence, like bondage itself, is recognized by the bondsman as a natural relationship created by the lord of lords himself. Similarly, inherent independence—the independence that is thought and lived by the master or the lord—is recognized by the lord as well by the bondsman as a natural relationship authorized by the lord of lords. The bondsman and the master both recognize the power of words. Both transform words into ways of life effectively translated into the relationship of a natural will to power, the will to dominate and be dominated.

In order for the bondsman and the lord to naturally participate in the inter-active experience of domination, language must first lay the groundwork, or else the relationship will not work. It works effectively only after language confers definitive meanings to the relationship of two human beings (with inalienable needs and rights of equality)—a relationship of inequality, in which one is to be the dominator and the other the dominated. The inherent dignity of two human beings is violated by language and transformed into a relationship of servitude and mastery. Servitude and mastery are subtly but effectively inter-nalized and recognized by human beings as natural relationships, founded upon the wishes and desires of the lord himself. The structure of a relationship of inequality is thus treated as if it were natural and unchangeable. A historical relationship is thus translated into a natural relationship that cannot be chal-lenged by the wills, passions, and intelligence of those human beings who cannot endure a relationship of misery and mistreatment in the hands of the beastly bearers of the so-called ''civilization.''

The historical relationship of domination, which is systematically rooted in language, is experienced both by the lord and the bondsman as a definite aspect of natural consciousness. Consciousness, Hegel argues, duplicates itself to form a dual consciousness made up of independence symbolized by the lord and dependence symbolized by the bondsman. Consciousness itself requires the du-plication. Without the necessary duplication, consciousness cannot exist. In for-mal language, one can assert that this duplication is an ontological ground of consciousness. Initially, and for a long stretch of human history, the duplication of consciousness is experienced by the bearers of tradition as natural, as an experience that must be endured both by those who enjoy it (for example, the lord) and those who suffered silently (for example, the bondsman). For the bondsmen, suffering, endurance, anguish, and sadness are the necessary tests of the lord before he can be considered worthy of eventual redemption are thus recognized by the lord of lords.[77]

The lord experiences his privileged position of nobility, independence, ma-terial abundance, arrogance and pride, all of which confer definite material power on his character as intrinsically good. The intrinsic goodness is lived as a gift from God. The lord considers himself as uniquely gifted, deliberately privileged. The lord ultimately considers himself, I wish to add, as born to be happy, chosen to enjoy. The other side of the coin, where we encounter the bondsman, is a position of dirt and dust, anguish and desolation, self-humiliation and deep sadness, self-doubt and severe self-judgment. Some bondsmen toler-ated servitude as the lord's way of testing their capacity to endure. Some of the bondsmen, however, actually considered themselves members of the race of Cain, cursed to perpetually suffer. Other bondsmen were consistently stoical, silent sufferers who never stopped dreaming about the not-yet, as a fantasy made possible through eventual redemption. Clearly, responses to bondage are ex-tremely varied, and Hegel fully recognized the human diversity of responses to servitude. Hegel himself stipulates his own response in the following passage:

In the master, the bondsman feels self-existence to be something external an objective fact; in fear. Self-existence is present within himself; in fashioning the thing, self-existence comes to be felt explicitly as his own proper being, and he attains the consciousness that he himself exists in its own right and on its own account (an und fur sich). By the fact that the form is objectified, it does not become something other than the consciousness molding the thing through work; for just that form is his pure self-existence, which therein becomes truly realized. Thus precisely in labor where there seemed to be merely some outsider's mind and ideas involved, the bondsman becomes aware, through his re-discovery of himself by himself, of having and being a "mind of his own."[78]

Previously, I argued, recognition played a rather passive role. Language was used to mystify, mask, and render a human relationship that was anchored upon a blind acceptance of the world as an empirical given, a rendering of the lord into a power that cannot be unmasked or criticized. The lord was ignorantly under the guidance of fear and dread, reified into an alien will to power beyond and above empirical history. In certain religious corners of the world, the lord was accepted and recognized as the appointee, the great Leviathan sent by God. In the above sense, recognition played a passive role. The natural duplication of consciousness was the last act of recognition as a pacifier, as the force of language that imposed fate and surrender upon the world of the sufferers, such as the bondsmen.

Eventually though, recognition began to play a rather astonishing role. Recognition has stimulated the bondsman to rediscover his existence. Existence was rediscovered not as an act of God outside history, time, and space, but rather as an act of self-construction and self-empowerment—an act that is inspired by the God-given will, passion, and intelligence. This is, I think, the hidden message of Hegel's words in the last passage that I quoted, upon which I would like to elaborate further.

Labor and work are the new self-empowering insights that the bondsman discovered to reaffirm the novel awareness of existence as an act of self-determining freedom. The bondsman has now reawakened from his passive existence: the existence of words that domesticated, enslaved, and impoverished him; words that made dependence natural and servitude a necessary result of dependence. This was a dependence of man upon man, dependence of powerless upon the whims and wills of the powerful, and the ultimate dependence of the dominated upon the dominators, the vanquished upon the victors. All these relationships that were once solidified and stabilized by language have now been reopened and destroyed, to be reconstructed anew.

Recognition in its active form produces in order to destroy the permanently harmful, the traditionally effective understanding that the empirical world is an act of God. Tradition, custom, blind obedience to authority are exploded. In their stead, new forms of life are in the process of discovery. The bondsman's newly found sense of being as a laborer—a worker who, by his sweat, his mixing of physical labor and the direct involvement of his will, intelligence and passion—allows him to see the inner architectonic of the things upon which he works from beginning to end, as a result of which he develops an aesthetic and ethical orientation toward minerals and stones—the external consciousness of humankind. Out of the interaction with the "things" of the world, the bonds-man, in contrast to the lord, emerges as the true master of labor. Through labor, the world is created. Through the aesthetic and ethical appreciation of the things of the world and the hard labor that is invested, the laborer profoundly under-stands the ordeal of laboring—an ordeal that was beautifully and sensitively captured by Van Gogh, the painter of the miners' world—a world characterized by dignity, authentic pride, anguish, a deep sense of mission, a yearning for redemption.

This passage, upon a repeated reading, strikes me as deeply tragic. It is a pity that human beings learn about each other's indispensable importance not through reflection, care, and compassion but rather through the direct use of violence or the threat to use it. The freedom that those who are free enjoy, for some inex-plicable reason, is not regarded (by the free) as crucially important for those who are not free. Thus, the lord, born to freedom, cannot and is not willing to recognize the burning desire of the bondsman, who is born to servitude. The lord mindlessly or perhaps deliberately considers the bondsman to be unfit for freedom, material comfort, and an existence freed from anguish, fear, and per-petual dependence. The stubborn refusal of the lord to recognize the bondsman as a person with needs and rights that are similar to the lord's, produces a tense condition, which as Hobbes puts it, is the war of all against all, power against power, ego against ego, desire against desire, bestiality against bestiality. In this tense, hateful and explosive condition, there may never arise victors and losers. The only result is timeless death—the death of precious human lives, the death of those human beings who reluctantly participated in the ultimately meaningless project: war, a condition that fulfills the pathological dreams and sick aesthetic desires of warmongers, killers—the rapists of nations and nationalities.

I have just summarized Hegel's conception of recognition in a highly specific interactive process: the lord-and-bondsman relationship. I now wish to add my own thoughts and observations about the role of recognition within the family, a context in which individuals spend a considerable amount of their formative years, learning the internalization of power as domination. This learning, how-ever, can be unlearned, and children can and must be taught how to empower themselves without domination.

Summary: Is It Possible to Be Freed from Power Per Se?

This question is a forbiddingly difficult one. I cannot imagine any other ques-tion that is as amorphous and ultimate as this one. It is a question that digs deep into the "nature" of what human beings have become. It is really about the nature of the questioner, one who is asking about his/her own deep inner being. The question is about the nature of Dasein as Heidegger would have put it.

Throughout this book, in more than one way, beginning with Plato, Aristotle, Epictetus, Aurelius, and then down to the terrain of Hobbes, Kant, Dostoyevsky, and Freud, followed by Dewey and James, ending up with Hegel, I have been struggling to develop an answer to the question. What I learned from the quest is that this question is really not singularly answerable. None of the disarmingly deep thinkers that I studied was resolutely sure of having the answer. Rather, each one of them had his own answers, which I could sum up as follows.

For Plato, the power that feeds on tyranny, in which tyranny is understood as excessive, an almost obsessive reliance on unreason is a permanent presence. Insofar as unreason guides the self, the self will always be a will to power—a will that does not only dream evil but actively and consciously seeks to realize it in everyday life.

Aristotle builds on Plato. Power as the will to tyranny could easily become habitual. The habituality of power as the will to tyranny gradually develops into a self with a definite intellectual, moral, and emotional constitution that is character. Character, though, is not static. It is dynamic, so dynamic that the self embodies growth, change, and maturity. The authentically mature self can, with consistent and constant work on its inner life, transcend the power that is a will to tyranny or domination. For Aristotle, upon whom I build my own conception of power as self-empowerment, there is a power that is a will to tyranny or domination—the Platonic insight—and a power that originates from principles that can transcend the will that dominates. For Aristotle then one can be freed from power—power as domination.

Epictetus, following Plato and Aristotle, originates his highly uplifting conception of the self as moral progress. As moral progress, the self can emancipate itself from any element that blocks the possibility of growth. The self has the invisible moral faculty with which it can struggle against inner desires to dominate others, quest for wealth and all the attendant vices. The self is capable of morally and emotionally taking care of itself. Like Aristotle, as well as Christ, for Epictetus moral progress is the result of a resolute decision to control everything that is within the sphere of the controllable. The will to dominate is within the sphere of the controllable. Given the resolute decision to rid oneself of all the corrupting elements of character, and given God's help, one can be freed from power as the will to dominate. Marcus Aurelius essentially follows Epictetus and blends the Epictetean message with some rigid Christian tenets, such as a more explicit stress on prayer and meditation—as avenues toward transcendental freedom.

Stimulated by the classical thinkers but above all stirred by the metaphysical firmament, the restless mind of Emmanuel Kant joined the discussion of the enigmatic question of power—power as freedom from the will to dominate and power as authentic autonomy—the ultimate ground of self-determination. In many dazzling respects, Kant is really a synthesis of the noble aspects of Plato,

Aristotle, and Epictetus. It is Kant who pushed forward to a far-reaching horizon the Platonic ideal of the invisible world of Forms; Forms, in the hands of Kant, become morally pure regulative ideals—ideals that command categorically. Plato's Forms, which Aristotle called Principles, are renamed by Kant as Noumena. If the self is to ever determine the way it should lead its life, it must strive to do the seemingly impossible: the self must struggle against its corrupting impulses by controlling them. Moral life is a struggle for Kant. It is a struggle between good and evil. The self must resolutely choose. There is no alternative to choosing. The self can choose to be dominated by its impulses. When this happens, the result is the construction of unfreedom. When the self chooses to struggle against its impulses, there is the *possibility* that there will germinate a self that is freed from power that dominates. For Kant, freedom from power and domination is a possibility but one that must be earned. There is no guarantee. There are none in the moral sphere. One can and must try, if authentic freedom means anything at all.

I need not spend much time on Hobbes for whom man is a will to power and who believes that nothing can change this definite fact. All that can be done is to control man, the killer, by stringent and uncompromising laws of the state. We cannot expect any *moral progress* in the sense that Epictetus viewed man. Man, for Hobbes, is in fact *moral regress*, an impersonation of primitivity and savagery. Man is born alone, dreams alone, and dies alone. He/she must be watched, disciplined, controlled, and intimidated by formal laws.

This powerful, albeit pessimistic, thesis is rethought on fresh ground by one of the greatest novelists of modernity—Fyodor Dostoyevsky. I think that Dostoyevsky will not strongly resist the Hobbesian characterization of man; in fact, he deepens it.

Dostoyevsky's man has a dualistic nature. Human beings are disposed, given certain circumstances, toward the good as well as toward evil. Good and evil are powerful possibilities, but not—as is popularly assumed—rigid actualities. Thus, the will to power is a manifestation of the disposition toward evil, which cannot be eliminated but can become effectively controlled. Like Hobbes before him, Dostoyevsky believed that evil behavior could be controlled by such stern laws. Saintly or morally heroic actions—to the extent that they occur, which they do not frequently do in Dostoyevsky's moralistic novels—are examples of the disposition toward the good. In this sense, I think a Dostoyevskian response to the question, Is it possible to overcome power as a will to dominate? would be both yes and no. It depends on the force of the choices that human beings make. It depends as well on God's generosity to help those who want to be good, but do not know how.

When the same question is put to Freud, he, in a remarkably original way, takes us to Borges's Labyrinth—the world of the unconscious. It is within the abyss of the unconscious that the choices human beings make are fought for. The forces of evil and good inform human dreams. Dreams themselves are revelations of the nature of truth. Dreams are (a) symbolic, (b) prophetic, and

(c) expressions of unfulfilled wishes. Dreams have three dimensions—the archaic, the inadequate present, and the not-yet. On these three levels, dreams tell us about ourselves. They are particularly powerful ways of examining the nature of power. The dreams that are propelled by the aggressive death instinct as well as those that are propelled by the pleasure and reality principles are revelations of human yearning for the good and the demonic. Dreams show who we are, where we have been, and what we wish to become in one sweep. They show us visions of paradise and hell, visions of human goodness buried in the abyss, and visions of the horror and cruelty that we are capable of delivering. With a shocking honesty, Freud compels us to see ourselves through the mirrors of our dream world. In the hands of Freud, the question of power is answered through a complex synthesis of hope and despair, affirmation and negation, optimism and pessimism. Freud is an analyst of power and not a visionary of how power as the will to dominate can be overcome.

Resolutely deciding to choose either the good or evil is not a purely conscious, that is, controllable, act. Human actions are, in a disturbing sense, layers of habits that have become part of the unconscious mental apparatus. Sometimes, when human beings truly desire to control the impulses toward evil, they can and do miserably fail. Overcome by the sheer robust force of the death instinct, human beings have actually acted contrary to their best interest—the interests of reason and morality. It is when an individual feels a strong need to critically analyze destructive interests, for example, joy in inflicting pain, in order to become free, that Freud's psychoanalysis is an indispensable tool. If we follow Freud's method, we will understand ourselves and this understanding may enable us to struggle with the question; Is it possible to be freed from power per se? The time has now come for me to struggle with the question myself and share it with my patient readers.

Freeing ourselves from the subjectively perceived and consequently highly desired benefits of power—such as riches, respect, reputation, the ability to acquire and accumulate anything that one desires—is not easy. It must therefore be admitted—however painful the admission may be—that power both as the will to dominate and as the will to transcend the will to dominate is tempting. I must therefore emphasize the primordial fact that power intrinsically (power as self-empowerment) and extrinsically (power as domination) is neither easy to transcend nor to be freed from. Power enslaves when it is mindlessly but joyfully practiced as domination. Power can be transcended when one ceases to be enslaved by power as domination. I have called this particular form of transcending power self-empowerment. One can be freed from power as domination via the self-willed struggle (which is guided by the reflective presence) to overcome the ever present temptation to desiring power as the will to dominate.

Throughout history, nearly in all known cultures, including the cultures of the animal kingdom, power as domination has served as a value. Rarely have individuals questioned their conscious internalization of this value as a problem. Rather, the contrary has been the case. Individuals have actually enjoyed visibly practicing this value. Newborns had to be systematically educated to assimilate the so-called "natural value" as a virtue. Virtuous became those who could exercise power upon others mercilessly but invisibly. They were trained not so much to dispense with this value, but to avoid being caught as they maliciously mistreated others. The value or norm of power as a healthy form of self-empowerment, which I am introducing here, would have to become part of a new educational experience that modernity can incorporate into both formal and informal educational settings. Parents as teachers and educators may reflect on ways to consistently and devotedly introduce the young and old to read, think, discuss, converse about, and debate issues, themes, and topics from this human angle. In this concrete way, the generations to come may benefit from the groundwork that could be done by the present generation. We human beings have done an extraordinary job of training human beings in the values of calculation, coldness, mistrust, cruelty, and the will to dominate. Our job has been so successful that the young, the middle-aged, as well as the old, have assimilated values that took centuries to establish. These values have become second nature to them.

If we so wish, however impossible my proposal may sound, we can (a) through authentically critical education, and (b) through critical even revolutionary activity, succeed in at least establishing a groundwork for a radically new ethics and aesthetics. Self-empowerment may after all become a new norm toward which we can move. We can at least start now before it is really too late.

NOTES

1. One of the best treatments of pragmatism and philosophy is *Pragmatic Philosophy*, ed. Amelie Rorty (New York: Anchor Books, 1966). See also R. M. Martin, *Toward a Systematic Pragmatics* (Amsterdam: North Holland Publishing Company, 1959).

2. William James, *Pragmatism* (New York: Meridian Books, 1907), p. 250.

3. Ibid., p. 229.

4. Ibid. See chapter 7.

5. I have discussed this in detail in Teodros Kiros, "Self-determination and the Crisis in the Horn in Africa," *Quest: Philosophical Discussions*, vol. 2 (Spring 1987), pp. 72–85.

6. James, *Pragmatism*, p. 230.

7. Ibid. This is a further extension of pragmatism.

8. Ibid., pp. 249–250.

9. Ibid., pp. 255–256. See G. E. Moore, "William James' Pragmatism," in *Pragmatic Philosophy*, ed. Amelie Rorty, pp. 328–339.

10. For an illuminating interpretation of James's and Dewey's pragmatism, see Bertrand Russell, "Pragmatism," in *Pragmatic Philosophy*, ed. Amelie Rorty.

11. John Dewey, *Theory of the Moral Life* (New York: Holt, Rinehart and Winston, 1960), p. 148.

12. Ibid. For a lively introduction to the politics of John Dewey see Gary Bullert, *The Politics of John Dewey* (New York: Prometheus Books, 1983). In *Nichomachean Ethics*,

Aristotle framed the nature of choice in a similar language. See my interpretations of Aristotle in chapter 3 above.

13. Ibid., p. 150. Hannah Arendt in *The Human Condition* (Chicago: University of Chicago Press, 1958) interprets action in a similar way. For her, who we are is disclosed through what we do. The Aristotelian influence on her thinking has been acknowledged by many of her students.

14. Ibid., p. 154.

15. Alfonso J. Damico, *Individuality and Community: The Social and Political Thought of John Dewey* (Gainesville: University Press of Florida, 1978), p. 30.

16. Dewey, *Theory of the Moral Life*, p. 158.

17. Ibid., p. 171.

18. Ibid., p. 172.

19. See Thomas Hobbes, *Leviathan* (New York: Penguin, 1968), p. 150.

20. The work of Baudelaire, *The Flowers of Evil*, could also be read in this light. For a fresh interpretation, see Teodros Kiros, "Toward the Construction of a Theory of Alienation in Aesthetics" (master's thesis, Kent State University, 1982).

21. Jean-Paul Sartre, *Baudelaire* (Norfolk: Directions 17, 1950), pp. 43–44.

22. For a truly original interrogation of these themes see Joel Whitebook, *Perversion and Utopia* (Cambridge: MIT Press, 1995).

23. Sartre, *Baudelaire*, p. 39.

24. Jorge Luis Borges, *Labyrinths* (New York: New Directions Books, 1964), p. 65.

25. Heidegger's much misunderstood attack of technology is very much grounded in the exposure of the limits of transparency. See Martin Heidegger, "The Question Concerning Technology," in *The Question Concerning Technology and Other Essays*, trans. and intro. William Lovitt (New York: Harper and Row, 1977).

26. Ibid., p. 233. This theme is beautifully discussed in Borges, "Literature as Pleasure," in *Conversations with Jorge Luis Borges*, ed. Richard Burgin (New York: Holt, Rinehart and Winston, 1969).

27. Ibid., p. 234.

28. Ibid., p. 235.

29. Gabriel Garcia Marquez, *One Hundred Years of Solitude* (New York: Avon Books, 1971), p. 24.

30. Charles Baudelaire, *Flowers of Evil*, ed. Jackson and Marthiel Mathews (New York: New Directions, 1955), p. 118.

31. T. R. Smith, ed., *Baudelaire: His Prose and Poetry* (New York: Modern Library, 1925), p. 147.

32. Ibid., pp. 203–204. The two poems seem to harbor two conflicting conceptions of human nature. For a compelling existential interpretation of Baudelaire, see Sartre's masterful portrait, *Baudelaire*.

33. Ibid., p. 229. This theme is masterfully analyzed in Pierre Emmanuel, *Baudelaire* (Tuscaloosa: University of Alabama Press, 1967), pp. 105–127.

34. "When Life Was Full, There Was No History," in Thomas Merton, *The Way of Chuang Tzu* (New York: New Directions, 1969), p. 76.

35. Ibid., p. 88.

36. Ibid., pp. 40–41.

37. Ibid., pp. 42–43.

38. Hannah Arendt's notion of natality brilliantly captures the idea that every birth

implies the emergence of a new human value. See *The Human Condition*. I stumbled upon a similar idea as I was thinking through the radical meaning of originality here.

39. Scott Lash, "Genealogy and the Body," in *Michel Foucault: Critical Assessments*, ed. Barry Smart, vol. 3, p. 22.

40. Michel Foucault, "The Masked Philosopher" (1980).

41. Allison M. Jaggar and Susan R. Bordo, *Gender/Body/Knowledge* (London: Rutgers University Press, 1986), p. 165. Seyla Benhabib makes similar observations in *Situating the Self* (New York: Routledge, 1992). See pp. 178–204. There she rigorously examines the moral status of feminism as a moral theory.

42. Mary Brabeck, "Moral Judgment," in *An Ethic of Care*, ed. Mary Jeanne Larrabee (New York, London: Routledge, 1993), p. 48.

43. Jaggar and Bordo, *Gender/Body/Knowledge*, p. 164.

44. For a very recent reconstruction of the history of radical feminism, see Nancy Whittier's *Feminist Generations: The Persistence of the Radical Women's Movement* (Philadelphia: Temple University Press, 1995), pp. 248–258. For Whittier, radical feminism constitutes a social movement in search of a collective identity. There are radical feminists who are engaged across the gender divide and are actively working with gay men. For a "new style" of feminist politics that claims to be unhostile to men's agendas see Naomi Wolf, *Fire with Fire* (New York: Random House, 1993).

45. Jaggar and Bordo, *Gender/Body/Knowledge*, pp. 22–28.

46. I am presently developing a book on the politics and ethics of sexuality in the later Foucault.

47. Jaggar and Bordo, *Gender/Body/Knowledge*, p. 19.

48. Seyla Benhabib, *Situating the Self* (New York: Routledge, 1992), p. 230.

49. Alison M. Jaggar, *Feminist Politics and Human Nature* (Sussex: Harvester Press, 1983), pp. 273–274.

50. Ibid., p. 275.

51. Ibid.

52. Nancy C. M. Harstock, *Money, Sex and Power* (New York, London: Longman, 1983), pp. 164–166.

53. Jaggar, *Feminist Politics*, p. 287.

54. See Aristotle, *Nicomachean Ethics* (Indianapolis: Bobbs-Merrill, 1962), p. 133.

55. Hartsock, *Money, Sex*, p. 165.

56. Joan Cocks, *The Oppositional Imagination: Feminism, Critique, and Political Theory* (London, New York: Routledge, 1989), p. 127.

57. Irene Diamond and Lee Quinby, *Feminism and Foucault: Reflection on Resistance* (Boston: Northeastern University Press, 1988), p. 9.

58. Ibid., p. 9.

59. Ibid., p. 10.

60. Ibid., p. 16.

61. Jana Sawicki, *Disciplining Foucault: Feminism, Power and the Body* (New York: Routledge, 1991), p. 48.

62. Diamond and Quinby, *Feminism and Foucault*, p. 64.

63. Ibid., p. 68.

64. Jana Sawicki, *Disciplining Foucault*, p. 64. See also her remarkable discussions of libertarian and radical feminisms as explored in p. 48.

65. Whittier, *Feminist Generations*.

66. Diamond and Quinby, *Feminism and Foucault*, p. 183.

67. Ibid., p. 187.

68. Ibid., p. 188.

69. Ibid., p. 189.

70. Ibid., p. 197.

71. I have developed this theme in Teodros Kiros, ''Alienation and Aesthetics in Marx and Tolstoy: A Comparative Analysis,'' *Man and World* 2, no. 18 (1985).

72. Teodros Kiros, *Toward the Construction of a Theory of Political Action* (New York, Lanham, London: University Press of America), see particularly pp. 200–233.

73. Thomas Mann, ''Tonio Kroger,'' in *Death in Venice and Seven Other Stories* (New York: Vintage Books, 1959), p. 83.

74. Ibid., p. 128.

75. Ibid., pp. 78, 133.

76. Ibid., p. 133.

77. G. W. F. Hegel, *The Phenomenology of Mind* (New York: Harper and Row, 1967), pp. 128–134.

78. Ibid., p. 239.

5

Conclusion

It is my thesis that in the human world, there are so many ways that may eventually lead to the world of a singular, comprehensive, luminous, eternal truth. But this truth is so far away, so illusive, and so deep, and as a consequence so overwhelming that it is considerably more relaxing to assume that there is no such thing as truth. Rather, there are truths. These truths, we may, if we so choose, choose reflectively. Assume that one is moving toward that eternal truth. At any rate, one can safely but responsibly argue that we can speak of truth in at least six ways.

1. There is a singular, absolute truth. This truth is so infinite that it could never be known by finite human beings. One single human being, given the singularity of his/her faculty, cannot possibly know this truth.

2. This singular truth cannot be known, in the sense that this knowledge can be precisely communicated from one human being to another. Knowledge, in this sense, cannot be (an object for language), although knowledge about this truth is an object for language. This truth can only be imagined through intuition—an intuition that varies from one person to another. Thus individuals can be said to know this truth to the extent that they feel it, that they imagine it. Their images, however, can be similar as well as dissimilar.

3. There are truths. These truths are acts of self-construction. The selves that construct them do so through the indispensable help of passion, feeling, desires, and principles. Each act of self-construction is a disclosure of the moment of truth to the person who is engaged in the creative act.

4. It is conceivable, although very hard to demonstrate, that each act of self-construction, which is a disclosure of the moment of truth, may itself be an aspect of the singular truth—the truth that is an object of feeling and intuition.

In this sense, the singular truth may itself be a consummation of the infinite moments of truth that are the acts of self-construction.

5. Truth, in a manner that profoundly and mystically reminds us of the Transcendent God, is strictly an object of faith, as Kant taught us. Thus, those who say they definitely know are actually saying that they believe. Truth, for them, is an object of faith and not merely an object of demonstrable knowledge or an object of feeling and intuition, nor even the distillation of the moments of truth as disclosed in acts of self-construction, but peculiarly and emphatically an object of an unfathomable, nondiscursive mode of faith.

6. Truth is also a standard against which we test the validity, coherence, usefulness, and purposefulness of the infinite values, norms, interests, and tastes by which we guide ourselves. A given mode of existence passes the acid tests of coherence, usefulness, and purposefulness if and only if the way of life, the style of existence, the ethics and aesthetics that we favor are such that (a) they do not jeopardize our health and ultimately our minds, and (b) they do not unnecessarily put other selves at jeopardy as well.

The various propositions through which we communicate our feelings, intentions, wants, and desires are disclosing or communicative of truth if and only if they are categorically useful to me and others.

SELF-CONSTRUCTION AND DESIRES THAT ENRICH THE SELF AS A CONSTRUCTION OF TRUTH

Construction as such is a very complicated activity. It can be said that construction is probably one of the most demanding activities that human beings can perform. In contrast to a habitual performance of activities as well as to the slightly difficult task of patterning activity by following models, the activity of construction is quite challenging, stimulating, and in the end very rewarding. The lessons learned by those who have constructed anything at all—a thought, chair, painting, poem—are quite unforgettable. They are lessons that are committed to remembrance and memory.

The construction of a form of life, which is quite unlike the construction of chair and tables, is what specifically concerns me here. The construction of a way of life, a style of existence, an orientation toward others, or the act of learning in a community is not easy. That we take it for granted is not a substitute for the assumption that it is easy to do. When we dig deeply into the world of construction, moral/intellectual construction, we begin to realize how complex and burdensome self-construction is. The self that constructs a way of life has one striking feature. That feature may be called *existential seriousness.* By existential seriousness, I understand the following.

A given self is existentially serious if it takes the fact that it exists as a gift—a peculiar kind of gift. The body that it possesses and the mind that grounds the body are both so delicate and indispensable that they require an exceptional mode of attentiveness and care, recognition and love, admiration and nurturing.

When existence is itself understood as a synthesis of the self's body and mind, one can then begin to realize that a healthy body and a healthy mind are the indispensable cements of existence—existence profoundly understood as a moral gift. The existentially serious self then does not take existence for granted. For the existentially serious self, existence is such a rare gift that just as we unconditionally extend respect to any gift that we value highly, we should also value the fact that we empirically exist.

When existence is thus understood, one can take a risk with individual human beings by granting them the freedom that is needed to take care of their very selves, to attend to the nurturing of their individual existence. When individuals are thus trusted, they can be said to be self-constructing the values, norms, and interests that are crucial to a form of life that can be lived excellently. Such individuals do eventually become self-empowered as well.

The self-constructing subject does not merely live. Living is not enough. The self-constructing moral/rational subject is existentially serious in the sense that I characterized existential seriousness.

One of the concrete tests of an existentially serious self-constructing moral/rational subject is his/her comportment and attitude toward the desires—the very sources of tragedy and happiness, alienation and fulfillment, chaos and stability, responsibility and morbidity, freedom and unfreedom, domination and self-empowerment.

A rather long tradition in human thought had upheld the conception that human beings can be characterized as pleasure seeking. I agree with this realistic and honest characterization of humans. Such a characterization could be morally and intellectually uplifting of human character if the desires were always good—good in a specifically pragmatic sense. Desires can be said to be good if they lead human beings along the turbulent road of existence toward a manifest destiny—the destiny of living our lives as extraordinary human beings. Extraordinariness as such is an ideal. We may achieve it or we may not. But we must at least be aware that we should strive for it when we realize that we are living too ordinarily. Ordinariness is not a virtue. In fact, ordinariness can lead to chaos and alienation in many ways. One such way, I suggest, is the case where the ordinary is blended with directionless, goal-less desires. In the second sense, desires can be quite harmful. I will discuss this point below. Let me now return to the notion of extraordinariness blended with good desires as one of the activities of the existentially serious self-constructing moral/rational subject.

Existentially speaking, peace is a virtue, although many human beings (we have had two major world wars and numerous regional conflicts in the formation of our "civilized" planet) do not seem to know this existential fact. By existential fact, I simply mean that the perpetuation of the body and mind is directly dependent upon the availability of peace-respecting human beings. Peace, therefore, is a necessary condition for the perpetual existence of human life. The existentially serious individual is painfully aware of the existential fact and comports his/her entire desire toward the realization of their self-imposed goal. It is crucial that we realize—since many of us do not know or seem to know, but do not care to know more solidly—that it is our desires that make it either possible or impossible for us to concretely become peace respecting and peace loving. I want to contend that it is via the help of good desires that we may come to respect and love peace. This self-imposed good is one of the acts of self-construction.

Peace, as a value and norm, can be practiced only by a person whom we may describe as peaceful, or whose character is respectful of the value of peace. It would be highly unlikely for a war, conflict, and tension-admiring person to appreciate the value of peace because such a character is distinctly and abundantly infested by desires that inevitably produce hate, indifference, callousness, and the general atmosphere of war.

The desire for peace is itself an exceptionally powerful example of a good desire. The desire itself, to a marked extent, is good because it is governed by the judicious and yet stern, decisive and yet meditative faculty of comprehensive reason. Reason becomes comprehensive not when it is disengaged from the equally powerful guides of the faculties of compassion and feeling, but when it is harmoniously blended with them. A reason that is lacking in compassion and feeling is no reason at all; it is simply a machinelike device that brutally calculates, divides, fragments, and endlessly pontificates. This mode of reason is so limited that it cannot be of any use to the existentially serious self-constructing moral/rational subject. If self-construction is to be performed meaningfully and enduringly, it must be benefited by the presence of comprehensive reason. I have already identified this mode of reason by the name, *reflective presence*. The reflective presence is chiefly occupied by a reason that is comprehensive precisely because it is an amalgamation of the mind and the heart, thought and feeling, coolness and affection, restraint and warmth, and the ability to forgive without forgetting.

A self whose goal is to become peaceful decides to ceaselessly control the ever-present turmoil of the tyrannical disposition from becoming excessively present in its character. Such a self is the most humble and severe judge of its own character. This self, just because it is disposed toward peace, does not preposterously assume that each and every time it desires something this desire successfully consummates in the desire for peace. To assume this will not only be arrogant but rather silly. It is only saints who are gifted with this particular consistency of desire and realization, where A consistently desires B and C is the ever present realization. Ordinary human beings sometimes aim at extraordinary goals. Saints are the exemplary figures who consistently realize extraordinary goals.

Ordinary human beings rarely realize extraordinary goals. At this point, something important deserves a mention. Between an extraordinary goal that is propelled by the good desire for peace is the ever present possibility that evil in the form of bad pleasures hinders the activity of self-construction.

I think that hideous bad desires, such as the desires to deliberately subvert the movement of thought in the form of activity away from the cultivation of a peaceful character, are bad both for the doer A and the recipient B. The bad desire, in the long run, destroys both A and B, although A experiences the bad desire as if it is good. A does not even know the difference between good and bad at that crucial phase in which A is amorously engaged with a bad desire. Person A who consciously inflicts pain upon B is, of course, a normal person of sorts. But, profoundly speaking, A is really not a complete person. Person A lives only for the moment as a successful banker, a famous professor, etc. However, none of these labels produce intrinsic respect. A complete character realizes that although he/she would like to desire peace and inconsistently does so, he/she has no control over what he/she would really like to be. A does not choose the desired goal. Rather, A is controlled by bad desires. There is a difference, though, between A who wishes to do B but is controlled by C to do D, and B who neither wishes to do X nor desires to control Y that compels him/her not to do Z. There is hope for A to truly change but no hope at all for B. A would like to become self-empowered by getting rid of those ever present bad desires that stand in the way. B, on the other hand, simply enjoys power as domination. It is toward a further discussion of person A that I now turn.

Person A knows that, just like B, when one is guided by bad desires, one inevitably faces the possibility of surrendering to the realization of certain bad goals. The desire for power as a domination is an ever present bad goal that we, contingent human beings, are conditioned by. The most severe decision to repress the will to power is not entirely successful. Bad desires are just as permanently characteristic of the self as good desires. Character is essentially composed of both. Precisely because character is composed of both, the self is conceived as pleasure seeking. For some human beings, however diseased they may seem to us, a bad desire expressed by a need for pain is one expression of pleasure; the pleasure of inflicting pain on others as well as willingly receiving it is natural to these human beings. Pleasure seeking then, as we may hope, is not always to aim at only the intrinsically good. The desire and respect for peace is only an aspect of pleasure seeking. It does not exhaustively empty what we mean by pleasure seeking. Insofar as individuals, such as A, are peace-desiring beings, however often they may fail, and individuals, such as B, are pain-desiring beings (desires for which there may be numerous causal explanations), we must be honest and conceive of human beings as pleasure seeking. The pleasures they seek, however, are both good and bad; the good is grounded on good desires and the bad on bad ones.

The self-empowering A wants to be self-emancipated from the bad desires because he/she is existentially serious. For A, as an existentially serious person, self-empowerment means freeing oneself from power as domination. For A, power and domination are not the same. To be emancipated from power as domination is freedom for A. It is self-empowerment itself. For C, against whom

I contrast A, power is simply domination, and that may as well be B's conception of freedom—the freedom to do as one pleases, up to and including intensely disliking, hating, and even killing some human beings.

A is existentially aware that disliking and intense hate are feelings that he/she might have experienced in dreams. When A remembered these feelings in a wakeful state, he/she was authentically ashamed of the dream content. A did not experience the feelings shamelessly. A did not conclude that these are natural feelings that need not be sources of worry. A silently suffered and worried and this led him through deep thought to the slow realization that the desires of the unconscious abyss are not always good. It is through the mirror of dreams that are unconsciously lived and are disturbingly bad that the self can know a completely developed character.

The possibility of emancipation from the disturbingly bad desires that A vicariously lives in dreams, and that B performs consciously without remorse and shame, does not happen just because A does not do bad things consciously. The fact that he had bad dreams is living proof of the possibility that if A chooses, he/she too, like B, can practice power as domination. Whereas B chose to live power as domination, or mildly put, B did not show any genuine sign of wishing to practice power differently, A is critically aware that he/she can be controlled by the will to power and, as a consequence, wants to struggle against that possibility.

Self-empowerment, as a value, emerges precisely at that crucial encounter of the self with power as domination. A's profound inner struggle of A against A, of comprehensive reason against the brutal instincts begins. The beginning of that tension, that inner struggle, introduces the will to develop a new value, a new norm, that I have called self-empowerment. In a way, self-empowerment is a sincere effort by the existentially serious person to control the overwhelming negative power of bad desires. The resolute choice to be free and to existentially orient one's short life toward that possibility is one of the acts of self-construction—the construction of self-empowerment as a value.

In an ideal setting, which is probably not immediately or perhaps not ever realizable, a true community—as opposed to the numerous pseudo-communities that human beings have had—is possible if and only if persons are (a) primordially trusted, (b) seriously educated, (c) respected, (d) encouraged, and, of course, (e) loved. Trust, education, respect, encouragement, and love are the glues of an authentic community. A community can be said to exist if it is firmly embedded in the above five pillars.

Given the above noble pillars, a community could then proceed to actively and willingly—without the fear of its natural inhabitants, its citizens—encourage real, as opposed to pseudo-participation. Participation, contrary to some myths advanced by paranoid philosophers, is, in fact, very much like peace, which, I argue, is a good desire, another fundamental good. One could justly and persuasively argue that participation itself is another example of a good desire.

Participation is a solid cement of a well-ordered community. A community without the value of participation is like a stomach that is hungry for food.

The need for an authentic community that is bound by those fundamental pillars of trust, education, encouragement, respect, and love—pillars that firmly support the spirit of participation—is enormously appealing to human beings who (a) are existentially serious, (b) are fed up with a commonplace, ordinary existence, and as a consequence, (c) seriously aspire to transcend the inherently limited horizon of the commonplace by moving toward (d) becoming extraordinary human beings—an extraordinariness that is exemplified in morally/rationally courageous stances and activities they seek to practice. For example, such individuals would go as far as cutting all ties from their families, loved ones, traditional groups, cultural tastes, or professional membership for the sake of consistently and constantly adhering to a well-thought-out, carefully examined standard of truth, or principles guiding one's existential/moral conduct.

For such individuals, the participatory spirit that binds a community is a high privilege; a privilege that they fully use. This use concretely provides them with a free forum, in which, as John Stuart Mill would say, they grow like a tree. Participation in a community for the existentially serious person is a spiritual food. It is through consistent and constant participation that the truly sublime activities of thought, meditation, inquiry, wondering, dreaming, and crafting utopias are learned. These sublime virtues are developed only by serious action in a manner that is also consistent and constant. Of course, these virtues are not easy to practice. All sublime virtues are noble and difficult. It is perhaps easier to imagine than possess them. Precisely because they can easily be imagined—indeed imagination is free—they may after all be exceedingly difficult to achieve. They are so difficult that we human beings are notorious for our dismissal of these virtues as utopias, figments of imagination, the practice of lazy dreamers and immature children of darkness. But this claim should not be taken seriously. Pitiful, however, is the fact that those who squander their lives by practicing the commonplace and the ordinary take these weak claims seriously. They take these shots so seriously that the good desire of participation has been dismissed by them as unpractical, undesirable, and what is even more as too utopian! This easy dismissal saddens me deeply. In modernity, the cynical attitude toward life, to a significant extent, is based upon the rejection of the possibility of participatory community. In its stead, pseudo-representatives, such as the self-proclaimed experts of knowledge, have displaced the participatory spirit. The citizens at large have been left to pursue the commodity as mindless consumers. In the end, the citizens are not trusted, educated, respected, encouraged, or loved.

The ideal of the actual construction of partcipatory community is worth struggling for in spite of the serious obstacles that the ordinary person faces in his effort to profoundly trust himself as capable of participatory acts of self-construction that gradually aim at equipping the self with power (power that is generative of principles of moral/rational conduct on the one hand, and power capable of controlling the impulses of domination on the other). If there is anything that is worth struggling for, I would like to humbly suggest to my patient readers, it is the ideal of a participatory community. Indeed, as I have repeatedly emphasized in this book, taking charge of one's existence, consistently and constantly struggling to discover, originate, and rediscover principles of moral/rational conduct, learning how to courageously and responsibly think, freely provoking one's mind and sensibilities to dream new dreams and practicing the exceedingly difficult task of effacing the proud, evil, egotistical, and conceited self during genuine acts of communication that aim at the genuine quest for truth seem to be so prohibitively grandiose that one is tempted to doubt their practical application.

There is, however, a paradox that I have observed in human beings that is worth thinking through. Some thoughtful and yet cynical persons resist the idea of participatory community, claiming it is utopian and impossible to attain. And yet, and in this lies the paradox, the same individuals relish and excessively glorify the virtues of inquiry and imagination. These individuals want to freely inquire as well as spontaneously imagine. The practices of inquiry and imagination, they say, are the marks, the conspicuous features of a free society. They are, beyond any dispute, correct. Now I want to put the following questions to them.

1. To argue that inquiry and imagination are the marks of a free society is to presuppose an environment in which one can inquire and imagine without threat from power holders. What kind of an environment, and what kind of society is capable of fostering inquiry and imagination?

2. Can a society that, as Marx effectively argues, advances the superiority of the commodity at the same time foster inquiry and imagination for all members of humankind—the poor and the rich, enslaved workers and leisurely aristocrats, the insensitive and yet wealthy, the sensitive and marginalized?

3. Character, we have learned from Plato, Aristotle, and Epictetus, to just name three, is an indispensable component of any society. The formation of character, however, did not historically develop to the advantage of all human beings. The character of a self that is deliberately enslaved by another human being is radically different from a character that is enslaved to money. Both are forms of slavishness. Although we have become hopelessly socialized into associating slavery with poverty and freedom with the commodity, a mindless consumer is just as slavish as the slave who depends on the mercy of his/her master. How is it possible for a free society to generate inquiring and imaginative citizens if both types of citizens live their lives fighting poverty (the case of the poor slave, or even a poor modern worker) and pursuing the commodity—the avenue of material greatness? In both instances, are not inquiry and imagination being displaced by other pursuits?

4. Finally, how can the human powers of inquiry and imagination flourish in the absence of human beings with the free time to think, read, or learn how to

love, when some of them squander their days washing dishes, picking fruit, and others sail away on big yachts?

The glorification of inquiry and imagination cannot prosper without a community that is devoted to the spiritual/transcendental ideal of participatory community.

In spite of the arrogance and pride that tell us that we are modern precisely because we know, that we are highly civilized because we have conquered space, that we are intelligent because we have engineered computers that may one day directly think and write for us, we human beings, particular we children of modernity, have not even learned the art of living together. The toil of those whom we have exploited by making them work day and night to develop empires and whom we have called incapable of thinking and imagining apart from working, under the threat of the whip and the gaze of factory masters, to lay the material foundation of civilization, may be reduced to the ashes of history. Unless we learn how to live together, that is to say, unless we relearn how to think via the reflective presence—a mode of thinking that silently shows us why we should not to do to others what we are not willing to do against ourselves we are not very far from destroying what took centuries to build. These thoughts and conclusions are part of a pragmatic way of empowering human beings—a way of thinking that may redeem us from our deep, deep sleep.

Living together, like many other things in this world, can be learned. As human beings, we came to this world not because of choice. Being part of this world is not located in what Epictetus rather accurately called our sphere of control. We are simply born to this cruel world; no matter how hard we tried, we could not have possibly terminated the primordial fact of our birth. Given this fundamental characteristic of our highly finite existence, there are still limited areas that we can, if we so choose, effectively control. The manners of our existence and the art of learning to live together within a community are such areas.

We must learn how to live together. The resolute decision to struggle, to genuinely try to respect and love our fellow human beings is itself a project—a project for the existentially serious individual. True, the wealthy and powerful person may think that the poor, unimportant, and powerless person is of no material use to him/her, and therefore it makes no sense, not even a pragmatic one, to learn how to respect and love that kind of person. This type of person is not only existentially nonserious and therefore profoundly speaking, not a spiritually complete human being, but, pragmatically speaking, he/she is embarking on a dangerous road that will destroy him/her as well as the community in which he/she is located.

The deliberate disregard of the intrinsic dignity of one person by another is ultimately destructive. Examples of destruction of human dignity as in the cases of slavery, colonialism, the Holocaust, and the simultaneous perpetuation of enormous wealth and poverty illustrate the use of power as domination. Just because the dominator, like Plato's tyrant, thinks that he/she is free and therefore powerful, it does not follow that he/she is actually free and powerful. When dominators deliberately violate the humanity of those who live at their mercy by thinking that this is a natural course of things that can never be changed, they are really taking a risk that their children will one day blame them for.

Human dignity can be violated over and over again. Each time it is violated, history is being written in memory. Anguish, pain, misery, humiliation, betrayal, and deep sorrow are silently passed from the generation that suffers to the one that is not yet born. It is as if the not yet born are destined to enter a world where living memory has already decided that the newly born must revitalize the old wounds. In this way, hate, resentment, and war displace the project of learning how to live together by learning how to forgive without forgetting, or how to attempt to forget by learning how to forgive. Forgiving and forgetting are integral parts of being profoundly human. The successful learning of these two powerful human emotions might one day pave the path of learning how to live together within a community. A genuinely self-empowering being, for the sake of his/her own existence, makes a sincere effort to take care of his/her own self by consistently and constantly teaching and learning from others the mystical powers of forgiving and forgetting.

It is a serious mistake to relate ourselves to others because (a) they give us pleasure, (b) they are materially useful to us, or (c) we temporarily need them for psychological reasons. This orientation, which we have been globally practicing for centuries during the wake of modernity, has given us empty human beings. Modernity continues to give us citizens who love no one except themselves; citizens without a sense of the past, or an acute understanding of the present, and without a fertile imagination that can originate human possibilities; citizens who quickly forget because they have never seriously absorbed the bitterness and joy of life. Worst of all, during the modern age, the capacity for love, which is conspicuously absent, is increasingly producing individuals who can never forgive.

Where the capacities to respect, love, forgive, and even forget (when it is appropriate) are not present, it makes no sense to talk about community, with or without the disappearance of a capitalism that has gone wild. The cultivation of existentially serious citizens within the context of an "ethical community" is worth struggling for.

If I have accomplished anything at all in this book, it is not that I have laid the groundwork of an ethical community—a task for the future—but that I have attempted to argue for the importance of the project and point out how modernity has neglected and continues to neglect the project as the dream of naive utopians. I have sought to argue here that the project is one that an existentially serious thinker cannot neglect. The neglect of this theme is equivalent to the neglect of one's humanity. This is a truly irresponsible neglect that may demolish our world. Even reasonable and moral beings may honestly think and act as if nothing that happens in this world matters. This attitude is exemplified by the indifference, cruelties, and arrogance of the power that judges, massive poverty, mindless consumers, a hypnotized and permanently drugged citizenry, purposeless children, infighting among self-proclaimed radicals, the cynicism of self-proclaimed conservatives, and the puritanically correct moralists' selective harassment of those who disagree with them. To counter such misery, the world must change.

Central to the possibility of that change and the decisions that we contingent human beings must make is the need to will self-change. Perhaps the time has come to revitalize what Plato, Aristotle, and Epictetus never failed to emphasize when they repeatedly said that true change must come from within—from the contexts of the presence of the unconscious (Freud) and the eternal return of the irrational (Dostoyevsky). It is the individual as an individual who must will change; it is the individual who must say to himself/herself: I want to take care of my self; I want to become existentially serious; I want to intelligently construct values and norms that enrich me as a human being; I want to be freed from domination and thus become healthily powerful by submitting all my acts to guidance by the reflective presence. Above all, I desire to become an extraordinary human being. Perhaps, an authentic community might one day emerge as a concrete totality of changed human beings—human beings who can then begin to enjoy the art of living together. As authentically changing human beings, they can then proceed to participate in the actual construction of an "ethical community."

Bibliography

Anderson, Roger B. *Dostoevsky: Myth of Duality*. Gainesville: University Press of Florida, 1986.

Arendt, Hannah. *The Human Condition*. Chicago: University of Chicago Press, 1958.

Aristotle. *Nichomachean Ethics*. Indianapolis: Bobbs-Merrill, 1962.

Aronowitz, Stanley. "History as Disruption: On Benjamin and Foucault." In *Michel Foucault*, ed. Smart. London and New York: Routledge, 1994.

Baudelaire, Charles. *Flowers of Evil*, edited by Jackson and Marthiel Mathews. New York: New Directions Books, 1955.

Benhabib, Seyla. *Situating the Self*. New York: Routledge, 1992.

Bernstein, R. J., ed. *Habermas and Modernity*. Cambridge: Polity Press, 1985.

Best, Steven. *The Politics of Historical Vision: Marx, Foucault, Habermas*. London: The Guilford Press, 1997.

Bloom, Alan. *The Republic of Plato*. New York: Basic Books, 1968.

Borges, Jorge Luis. *Labyrinths*. New York: New Directions Books, 1964.

Bove, Paul. "The End of Humanism: Michel Foucault and the Power of Disciplines." In *Michel Foucault*, ed. Smart. London and New York: Routledge, 1994.

Brabeck, Mary. "Moral Judgment." In *An Ethic of Care: Feminist and Interdisciplinary Perspectives*, edited by Mary Jeanne Larrabee. New York, London: Routledge, 1993.

Bullert, Gary. *The Politics of John Dewey*. New York: Prometheus Books, 1983.

Burgin, Richard. ed. *Conversations with Jorge Luis Borges*. New York: Holt, Rinehart, Winston, 1969.

Certeau, Michel de. "The Black Sun of Language." In *Michel Foucault*, ed. Smart. London and New York: Routledge, 1994.

Cherness, Harold. "The Sources of Evil According to Plato." In *Plato: A Collection of Critical Essays*, edited by Gregory Vlastos. Notre Dame: University of Notre Dame, 1978.

Cocks, Joan. *The Oppositional Imagination: Feminism, Critique, and Political Theory.* London and New York: Routledge, 1989.

Comay, Rebecca. "Excavating the Repressive Hypothesis." In *Michel Foucault: Critical Assessments*, edited by Barry Smart. *3 vol.* London and New York: 1994.

Damico, Alfonso J. *Individuality and Community: The Social and Political Thought of John Dewey.* Gainesville: University Press of Florida, 1978.

Deleuze, Gilles. "A New Archivist." In *Michel Foucault*, ed. Smart. London and New York: Routledge, 1994.

Dewey, John. *Freedom and Culture.* New York: Capricorn Books, 1939.

———. *Theory of the Moral Life.* New York: Holt, Rinehart and Winston, 1960.

Diamond, Irene, and Lee Quinby. *Feminism and Foucault: Reflection on Resistance.* Boston: Northeastern University Press, 1988.

Dostoevsky, Fyodor. *Notes from Underground and the Grand Inquisitor.* New York: A. Dutton Paperback, 1960.

———. *The Possessed.* New York: Signet Classics, 1962.

Dreyfus, H. L., and P. Rabinow. *Michel Foucault: Beyond Structuralism and Hermeneutics.* Chicago: University of Chicago Press, 1982.

Epictetus, *The Discourses I.* Cambridge: Harvard University Press, 1979.

Farrell, Brian, ed. *Philosophy and Psychoanalysis.* Toronto: Macmillan College Publishing Company, 1994.

Foucault, Michel. *The Archeology of Knowledge.* New York: Pantheon Books, 1972.

———. *The Care of the Self.* New York: Pantheon Books, 1986.

———. *Discipline and Punish.* New York: Vintage Books, 1979.

———. *The Order of Things.* New York: Vintage Books, 1973.

———. *Power/Knowledge.* New York: Pantheon Books, 1980.

———. "The Subject and Power." In *Michel Foucault: Beyond Structuralism and Hermeneutics*, ed. Hubert L. Dreyfus and Paul Rabinow. Chicago: University of Chicago Press, 1982.

———. *The Use of Pleasure.* New York: Vintage Books, 1986.

Frank, Joseph. *Dostoevsky: The Stir of Liberation 1860–1865.* Princeton: Princeton University Press, 1986.

Freud, Sigmund. *Beyond the Pleasure Principle.* New York: W. W. Norton, 1961.

———. *Civilization and Its Discontents.* New York: W. W. Norton, 1962.

———. *The Interpretation of Dreams.* New York: Avon Books, 1965.

———. *An Outline of Psychoanalysis.* New York: W. W. Norton, 1969.

Fromm, Erich. *The Anatomy of Human Destructiveness.* New York: Holt, Rinehart and Winston, 1973.

Gutman, Amy, ed. *Multiculturalism.* Princeton: Princeton University Press, 1994.

Habermas, Jürgen. *Autonomy and Solidarity.* London and New York, 1992.

———. *Knowledge and Human Interests.* London: Heinemann, 1972.

———. *The Philosophical Discourses of Modernity. Twelve Lectures.* Translated by Frederick Lawrence. Cambridge: Massachusetts Institute of Technology Press, 1987.

———. *Postmetaphysical Thinking. Philosophical Essays.* Translated by W. M. Hohengarten. Cambridge: MIT Press, 1992.

———. *The Theory of Communicative Action.* Vol. 2. Boston: Beacon Press, 1987.

Harrigan, John J. *Empty Pockets, Empty Dreams.* New York: Macmillan, 1993.

Harstock, N. C. M. *Money, Sex and Power.* New York, London: Longman, 1983.

Hegel, G.W.F. *The Phenomenology of Mind*. New York: Harper and Row, 1967.

Heidegger, Martin. "The Question Concerning Technology." In *The Question Concerning Technology and Other Essays*. Translation and introduction by William Lovitt. New York: Harper and Row, 1977.

Hobbes, Thomas. *Leviathan*. New York: Penguin, 1968.

Hollinger, David A. *Postethnic America*. New York: Basic Books, 1995.

Honneth, Axel. *The Critique of Power: Reflective Stages in a Critical Social Theory*. Translated by Kenneth Baynes. Cambridge: MIT Press, 1991.

Hoy, David Couzens. "Two Conflicting Conceptions of How to Naturalize Philosophy: Foucault versus Habermas." In *Michel Foucault*. ed. Smart, vol. 3. London and New York: Routledge, 1994.

Hutchinson, D. S. *The Virtues of Aristotle*. London, New York: Routledge and Keagan Paul, 1986.

Ivanov, Vyacheslav. *Freedom and the Tragic Life*. New York: Noonday Press, 1960.

Jaggar, Alison M. *Feminist Politics and Human Nature*. Sussex: Harvester Press, 1983.

Jaggar, Allison M., and Susan R. Bordo. *Gender/Body/Knowledge*. London: Rutgers University Press, 1986.

James, William. *Pragmatism*. New York: Meridian Books, 1907.

Jay, Martin. "Limit and Transgression in Contemporary European Thought." *Constellations* 2, no. 2 (1995).

Kant, Immanuel. *Essays on History*. New York: Bobbs-Merrill, 1956.

———. *Foundations of the Metaphysics of Morals*. Indianapolis: Bobbs-Merrill, 1959.

———. "What Is Enlightenment." In *On History*. New York: Bobbs-Merrill, 1963.

Kelly, Michael, ed. *Critique and Power*. Cambridge: MIT Press, 1994.

Kermode, Frank. "Crisis Critic." In *Michel Foucault*. ed. Smart. London and New York: Routledge, 1994.

Kiros, Teodros. "Doing African Philosophy." *New Political Science* 2, no. 32 (Summer 1995), pp. 95–117.

———. "Self-construction." *Journal of Social Philosophy* 25, no. 1 (1994).

———. "Self-determination and the Crisis in the Horn in Africa." *Quest: Philosophical Discussions* 2 (spring 1987).

———. *Toward the Construction of a Theory of Political Action*. New York, Lanham, London: University Press of America, 1985.

———. *Moral Philosophy and Development*. Athens, Ohio: Ohio University Press, 1992.

———. *The Promise of Multiculturalism*. New York: Routledge, 1998.

Kundera, Milan. *The Book of Laughter and Forgetting*. New York: Penguin, 1980.

Lash, Scott. "Genealogy and the Body." In *Michel Foucault*. ed. Barry Smart, vol. 3. London and New York: Routledge, 1994.

Lyotard, Jean-François. *The Postmodern Condition: A Report on Knowledge*. Minneapolis: University of Minnesota Press, 1979.

Mann, Thomas. *Death in Venice and Seven Other Stories*. New York: Vintage Books, 1959.

Marcuse, Herbert. *Eros and Civilization*. Boston: Beacon Press, 1955.

———. *Five Lectures*. Boston: Beacon Press, 1970.

Marquez, Gabriel Garcia. *One Hundred Years of Solitude*. New York: Avon Books, 1971.

Martin, R. M. *Toward a Systematic Pragmatics*. Amsterdam: North Holland Publishing Company, 1959.

Matlaw, Ralph E. trans., introduction to *Notes from Underground and The Grand In-quisitor*. New York: Dutton Press, 1960.

McCarthy, Thomas. *The Critical Theory of Jürgen Habermas*. Cambridge: MIT Press, 1978.

———. "The Critique of Impure Reason." In *Critique and Power*. Cambridge: MIT Press, 1994.

Merton, Thomas. *The Way of Chuang Tzu*. New York: New Directions, 1969.

Miller, James. *The Passion of Michel Foucault*. New York: Simon and Schuster, 1993.

Moore, G. E. "William James' Pragmatism." In *Pragmatic Philosophy*, ed. Amelie Rorty. New York: Anchor Books, 1966.

Mure, G.R.G. *Aristotle*. New York: Oxford Press, 1964.

Nietzsche, Friedrich. *On the Genealogy of Morals and Ecce Homo*. Edited by Walter Kaufmann. New York: Vintage Books, 1969.

Plato. *The Collected Dialogues of Plato*. ed. Edith Hamilton. New Jersey: Princeton University Press, 1973.

Rajchman, John. "Ethics after Foucault." In *Michel Foucault: Critical Assessments*, edited by Barry Smart. London and New York: Routledge, 1994.

Rawls, John. *Political Liberalism*. New York: Columbia University Press, 1993.

Richters, Annemick. "Modernity-Postmodernity Controversies: Habermas and Fou-cault." In *Michel Foucault*, ed. Smart. London and New York: Routledge, 1994.

Ricouer, Paul. *Freud and Philosophy*. New Haven: Yale University Press, 1970.

Rorty, Amelie, ed. *Pragmatic Philosophy*. New York: Anchor Books, 1966.

Rorty, Richard. "Foucault and Epistemology." In *Michel Foucault*, ed. Smart. London and New York: Routledge, 1994.

———. *Pragmatic Philosophy*. New York: Anchor Books, 1966.

Rutherford, R. B. *The Meditations of Marcus Aurelius*. Oxford: Clarendon Press, 1989.

Said, Edward. "An Ethics of Language." In *Michel Foucault*, ed. Smart, vol. 2. London and New York: Routledge, 1994.

Sartre, Jean-Paul. *Baudelaire*. Norfolk: Directions 17, 1950.

Sawicki, Jana. *Disciplining Foucault: Feminism, Power and the Body*. New York: Rout-ledge, 1991.

Smart, Barry, ed. *Michel Foucault (1): Critical Assessments*. 3 vols. London and New York: Routledge, 1994.

Smith, T. R., ed. *Baudelaire: His Prose and Poetry*. New York: Modern Library, 1925.

Taylor, Charles. *Multiculturalism*. New Jersey: Princeton University Press, 1995.

———. *Sources of the Self*. Cambridge: Harvard University Press, 1989.

Tugendhat, Ernst. *Self-Consciousness and Self-Determination*. Cambridge: Massachusetts Institute of Technology Press, 1986.

Vlastos, Gregory, ed. *Plato: A Collection of Critical Essays*. Notre Dame: University of Notre Dame Press, 1971.

Whitebook, Joel. *Perversion and Utopia*. Cambridge: MIT Press, 1995.

Whittier, Nancy. *Feminist Generations: The Persistence of the Radical Women's Move-ment*. Philadelphia: Temple University Press, 1995.

Wittgenstein, Ludwig. *Philosophical Investigations*. New York: Macmillan, 1945.

———. "Remarks on Freud." In *Philosophy and Psychoanalysis*, ed. Brian Farrell. Toronto: Macmillan College Publishing Company, 1994.

Wolf, Naomi. *Fire with Fire*. New York: Random House, 1993.

Index

About the Author

TEODROS KIROS is Master Lecturer in Philosophy at Suffolk University and Associate-in-Residence in the Department of Afro-American Studies, Harvard University. He is the author of *Toward the Construction of a Theory of Political Action*: *Antonio Gramsci* (1985), *Moral Philosophy and Development*: *The Human Condition in Africa* (1992), and numerous journal articles.

ISBN 0-313-30808-X

90000>

HARDCOVER BAR CODE